How Come I'm Always Luigi?

Bill Amend

Other FoxTrot Books by Bill Amend

FoxTrot • Pass the Loot • Black Bart Says Draw • Eight Yards, Down and Out
Bury My Heart at Fun-Fun Mountain • Say Hello to Cactus Flats • May the Force Be with Us, Please
Take Us to Your Mall • The Return of the Lone Iguana • At Least This Place Sells T-shirts
Come Closer, Roger, There's a Mosquito on Your Nose • Welcome to Jasorassic Park
I'm Flying, Jack . . . I Mean, Roger • Think iFruity • Death by Field Trip
Encyclopedias Brown and White • His Code Name Was The Fox
Your Momma Thinks Square Roots Are Vegetables • Who's Up for Some Bonding?
Am I a Mutant or What! • Orlando Bloom Has Ruined Everything
My Hot Dog Went Out, Can I Have Another?

Anthologies

FoxTrot: The Works • FoxTrot *en masse* • Enormously FoxTrot • Wildly FoxTrot
FoxTrot Beyond a Doubt • Camp FoxTrot • Assorted FoxTrot • FoxTrot: Assembled with Care
FoxTrotius Maximus

How Come I'm Always Luigi?

A FoxTrot Collection by Bill Amend

**Andrews McMeel
Publishing, LLC**

Kansas City

FoxTrot is distributed internationally by Universal Press Syndicate.

06 07 08 09 10 BBG 10 9 8 7 6 5 4 3 2 1

ISBN-13: 978-0-7407-5683-2
ISBN-10: 0-7407-5683-4

Library of Congress Control Number: 2005936211

───── **ATTENTION: SCHOOLS AND BUSINESSES** ─────

Andrews McMeel books are available at quantity discounts with bulk purchase for educational, business, or sales promotional use. For information, please write to: Special Sales Department, Andrews McMeel Publishing, LLC, 4520 Main Street, Kansas City, Missouri 64111.

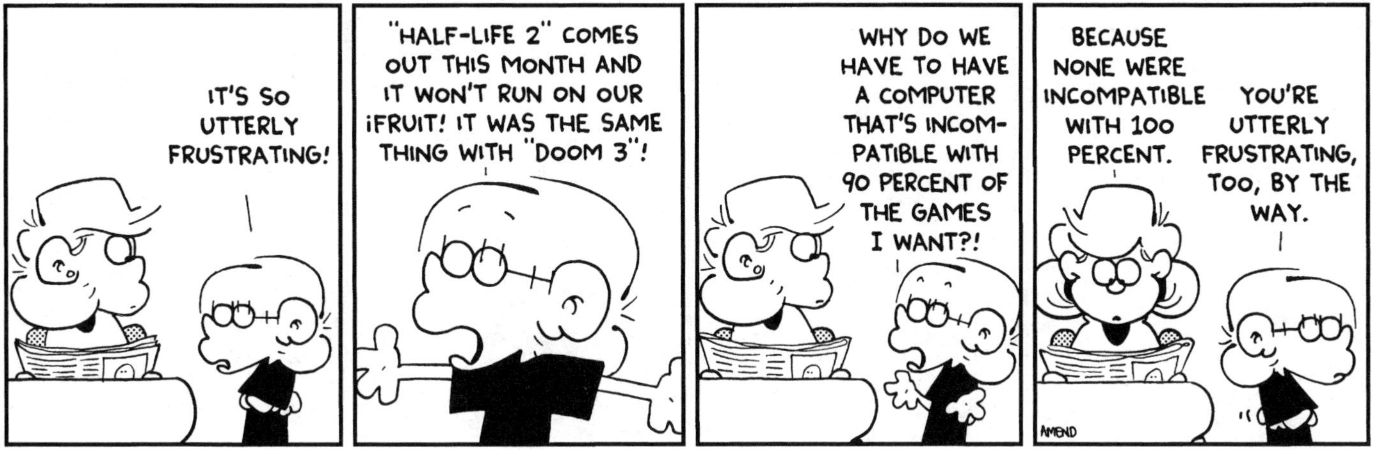
IT'S SO UTTERLY FRUSTRATING!
"HALF-LIFE 2" COMES OUT THIS MONTH AND IT WON'T RUN ON OUR iFRUIT! IT WAS THE SAME THING WITH "DOOM 3"!
WHY DO WE HAVE TO HAVE A COMPUTER THAT'S INCOMPATIBLE WITH 90 PERCENT OF THE GAMES I WANT?!
BECAUSE NONE WERE INCOMPATIBLE WITH 100 PERCENT.
YOU'RE UTTERLY FRUSTRATING, TOO, BY THE WAY.
AMEND

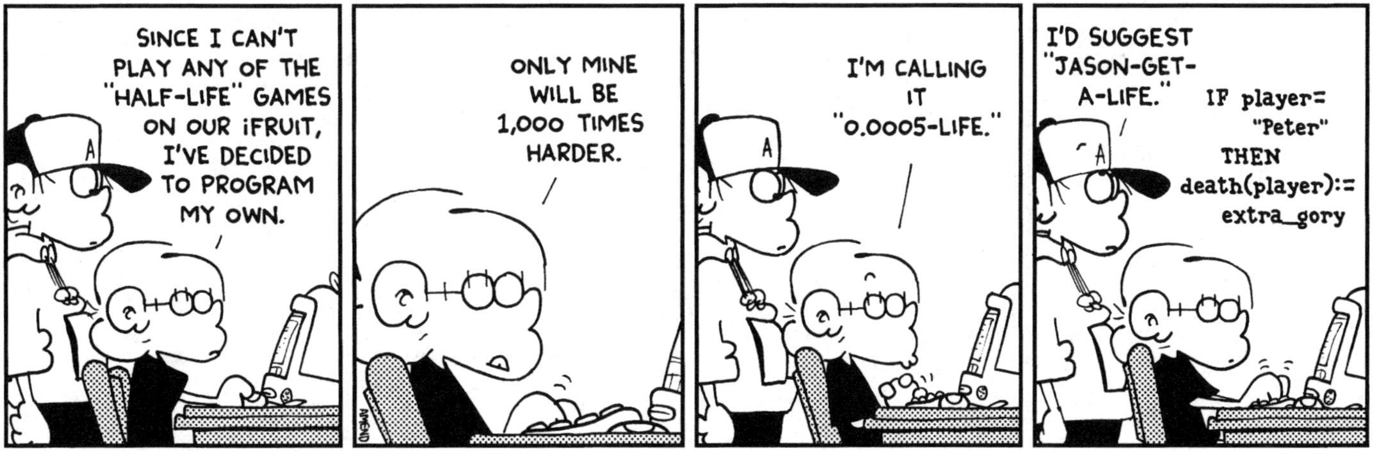
SINCE I CAN'T PLAY ANY OF THE "HALF-LIFE" GAMES ON OUR iFRUIT, I'VE DECIDED TO PROGRAM MY OWN.
ONLY MINE WILL BE 1,000 TIMES HARDER.
AMEND
I'M CALLING IT "0.0005-LIFE."
I'D SUGGEST "JASON-GET-A-LIFE."
IF player= "Peter" THEN death(player):= extra_gory

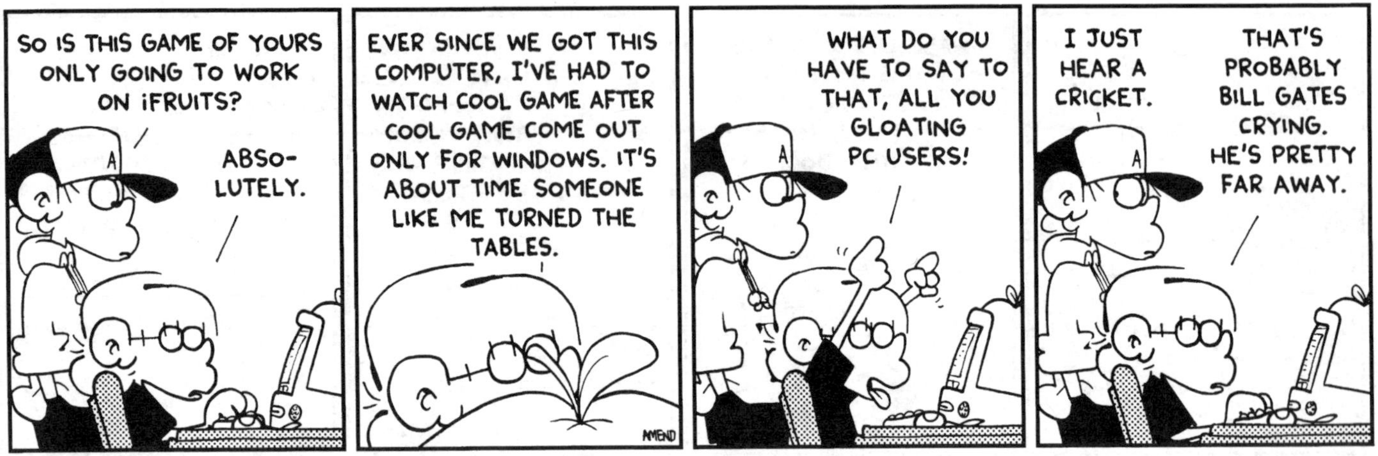
SO IS THIS GAME OF YOURS ONLY GOING TO WORK ON iFRUITS?
ABSO-LUTELY.
EVER SINCE WE GOT THIS COMPUTER, I'VE HAD TO WATCH COOL GAME AFTER COOL GAME COME OUT ONLY FOR WINDOWS. IT'S ABOUT TIME SOMEONE LIKE ME TURNED THE TABLES.
WHAT DO YOU HAVE TO SAY TO THAT, ALL YOU GLOATING PC USERS!
I JUST HEAR A CRICKET.
THAT'S PROBABLY BILL GATES CRYING. HE'S PRETTY FAR AWAY.
AMEND

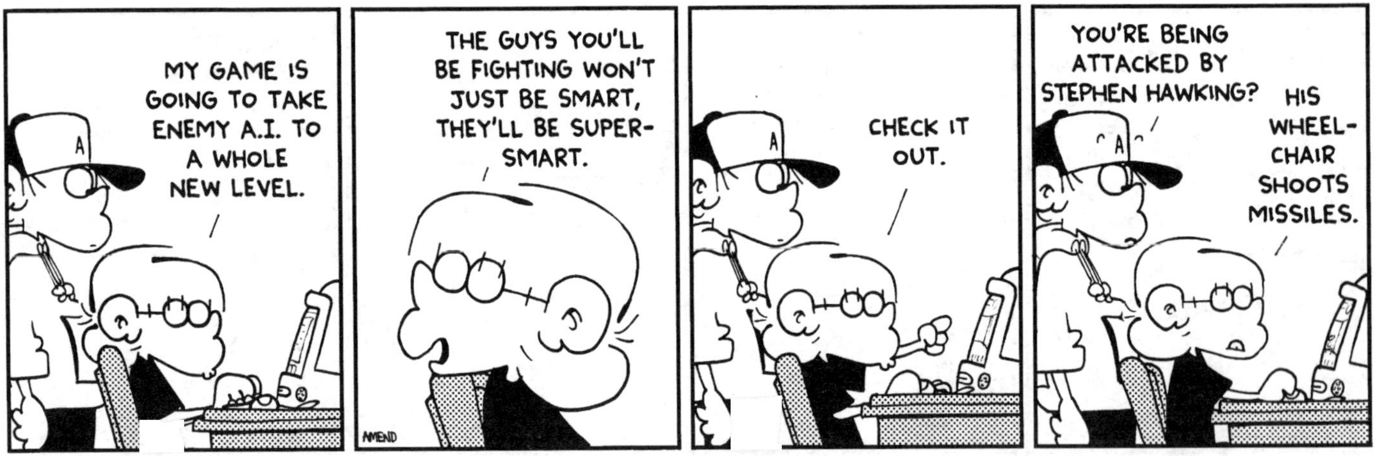
MY GAME IS GOING TO TAKE ENEMY A.I. TO A WHOLE NEW LEVEL.
THE GUYS YOU'LL BE FIGHTING WON'T JUST BE SMART, THEY'LL BE SUPER-SMART.
AMEND
CHECK IT OUT.
YOU'RE BEING ATTACKED BY STEPHEN HAWKING?
HIS WHEEL-CHAIR SHOOTS MISSILES.

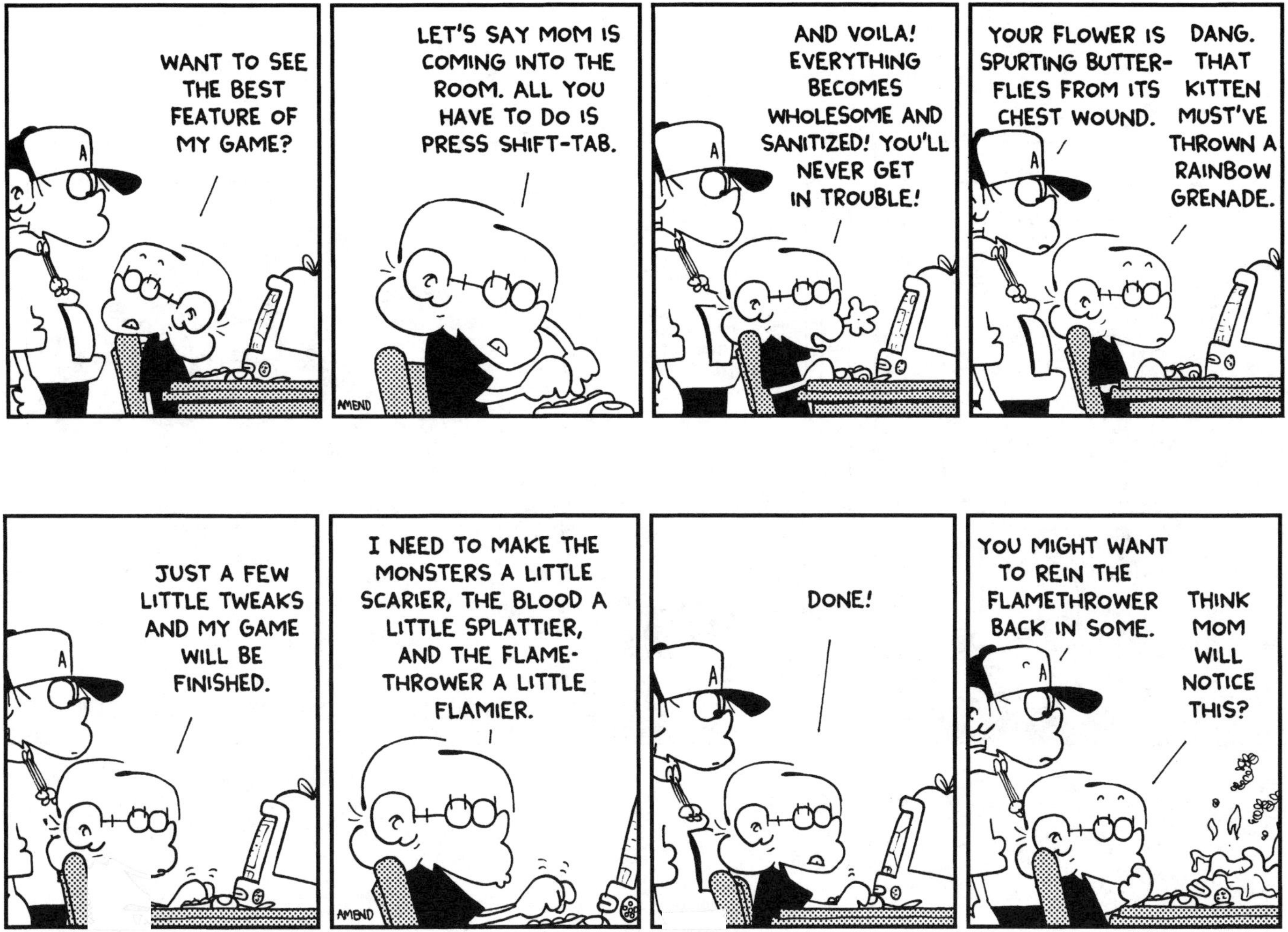
WANT TO SEE THE BEST FEATURE OF MY GAME?
LET'S SAY MOM IS COMING INTO THE ROOM. ALL YOU HAVE TO DO IS PRESS SHIFT-TAB.
AMEND
AND VOILA! EVERYTHING BECOMES WHOLESOME AND SANITIZED! YOU'LL NEVER GET IN TROUBLE!
YOUR FLOWER IS SPURTING BUTTER-FLIES FROM ITS CHEST WOUND.
DANG. THAT KITTEN MUST'VE THROWN A RAINBOW GRENADE.
JUST A FEW LITTLE TWEAKS AND MY GAME WILL BE FINISHED.
I NEED TO MAKE THE MONSTERS A LITTLE SCARIER, THE BLOOD A LITTLE SPLATTIER, AND THE FLAME-THROWER A LITTLE FLAMIER.
AMEND
DONE!
YOU MIGHT WANT TO REIN THE FLAMETHROWER BACK IN SOME.
THINK MOM WILL NOTICE THIS?

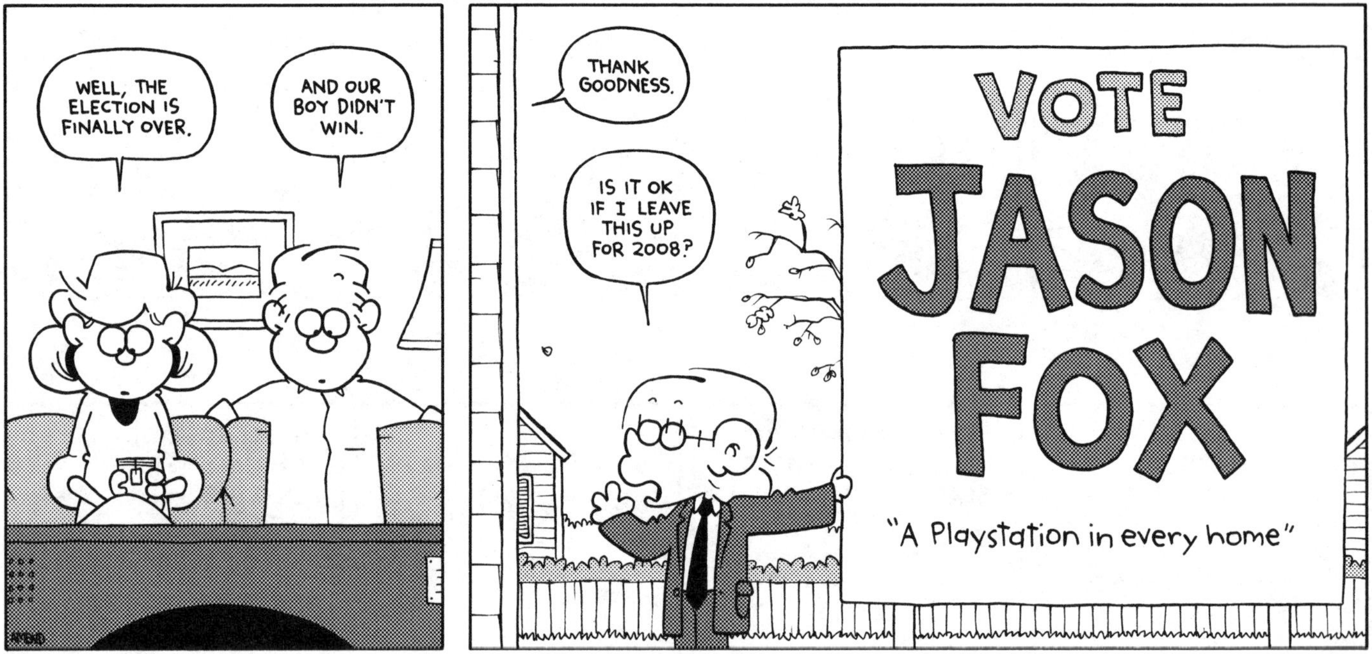
WELL, THE ELECTION IS FINALLY OVER.
AND OUR BOY DIDN'T WIN.
THANK GOODNESS.
IS IT OK IF I LEAVE THIS UP FOR 2008?
VOTE
JASON
FOX
"A Playstation in every home"

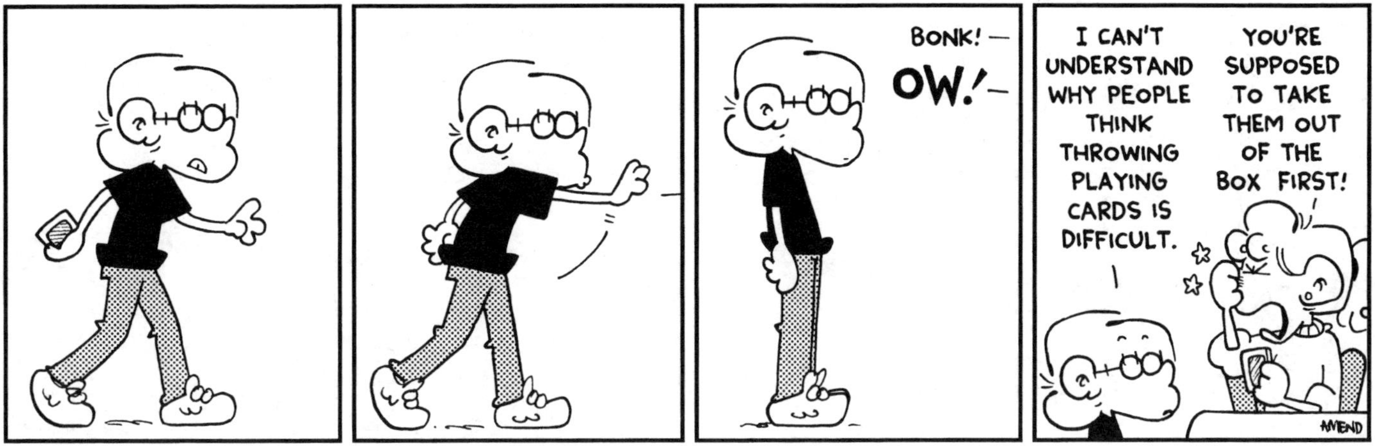
BONK!
OW!
I CAN'T UNDERSTAND WHY PEOPLE THINK THROWING PLAYING CARDS IS DIFFICULT.
YOU'RE SUPPOSED TO TAKE THEM OUT OF THE BOX FIRST!
AMEND

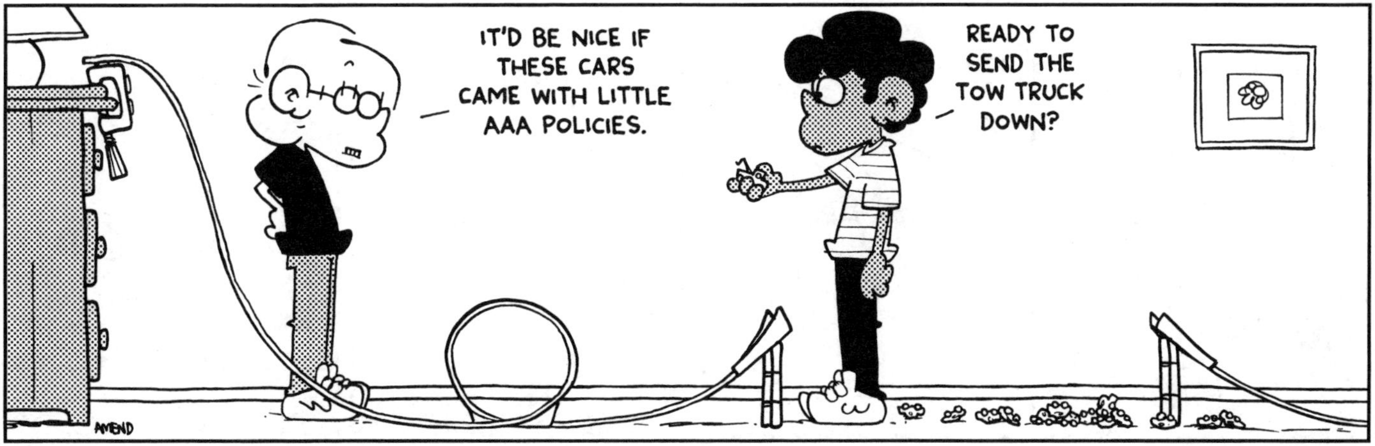
IT'D BE NICE IF THESE CARS CAME WITH LITTLE AAA POLICIES.
READY TO SEND THE TOW TRUCK DOWN?
AMEND

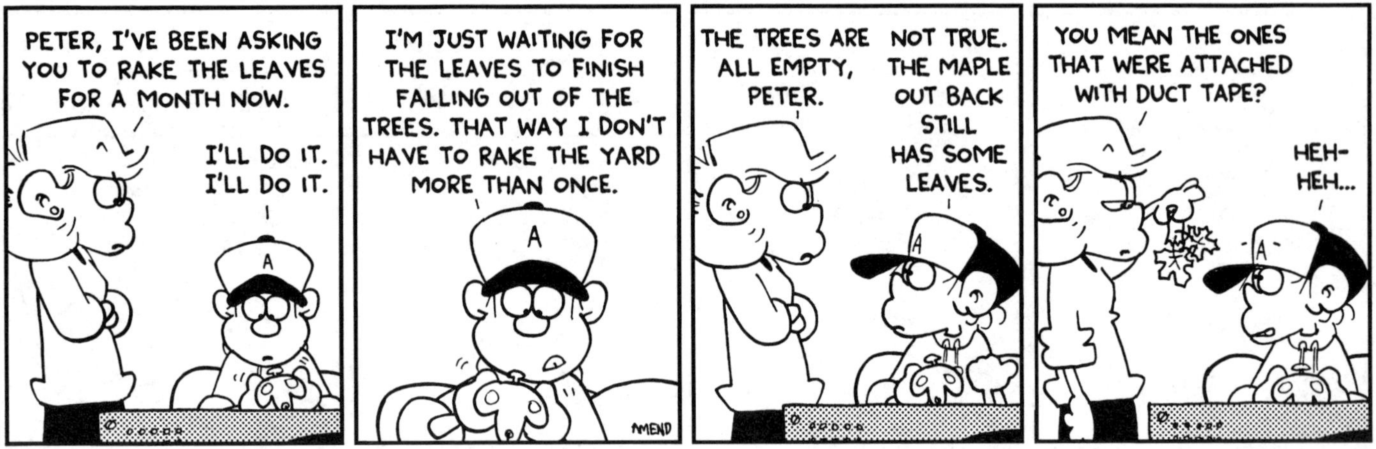
PETER, I'VE BEEN ASKING YOU TO RAKE THE LEAVES FOR A MONTH NOW.
I'LL DO IT. I'LL DO IT.
I'M JUST WAITING FOR THE LEAVES TO FINISH FALLING OUT OF THE TREES. THAT WAY I DON'T HAVE TO RAKE THE YARD MORE THAN ONCE.
AMEND
THE TREES ARE ALL EMPTY, PETER.
NOT TRUE. THE MAPLE OUT BACK STILL HAS SOME LEAVES.
YOU MEAN THE ONES THAT WERE ATTACHED WITH DUCT TAPE?
HEH-HEH...

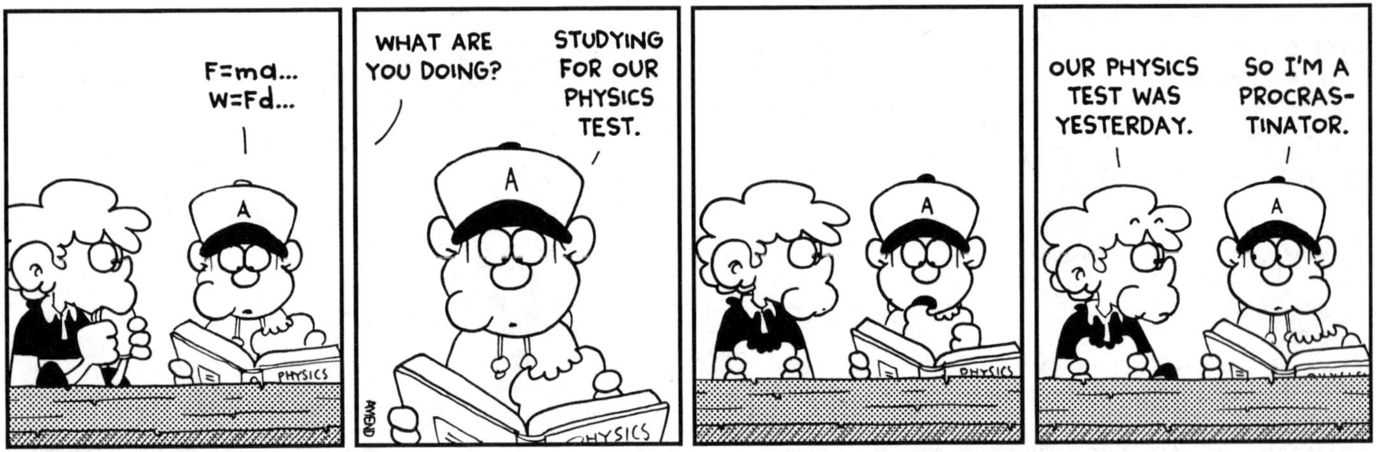
F=ma... W=Fd...
PHYSICS
WHAT ARE YOU DOING?
STUDYING FOR OUR PHYSICS TEST.
AMEND
PHYSICS
PHYSICS
OUR PHYSICS TEST WAS YESTERDAY.
SO I'M A PROCRAS-TINATOR.

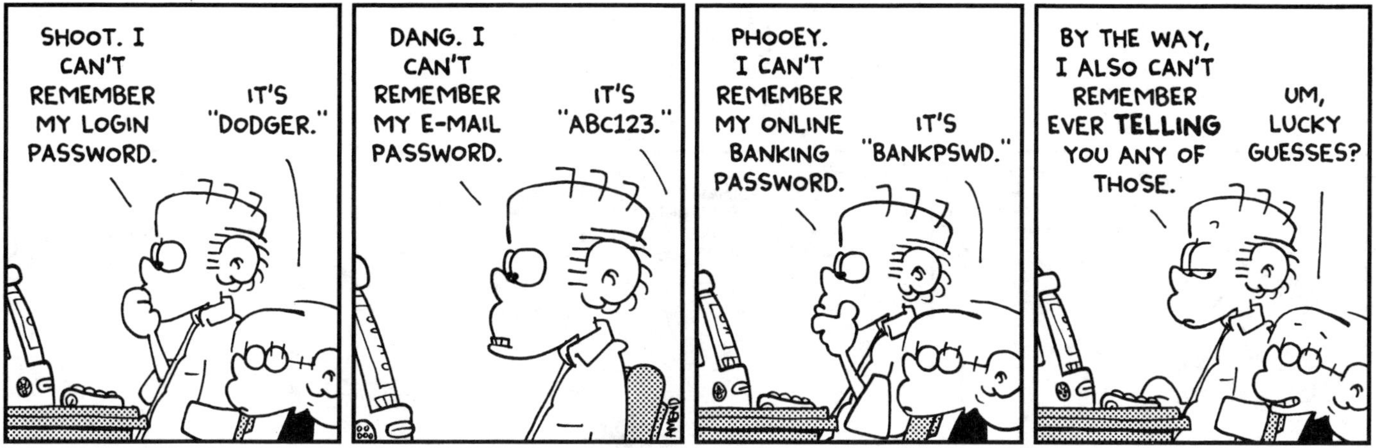
SHOOT. I CAN'T REMEMBER MY LOGIN PASSWORD.
IT'S "DODGER."
DANG. I CAN'T REMEMBER MY E-MAIL PASSWORD.
IT'S "ABC123."
PHOOEY. I CAN'T REMEMBER MY ONLINE BANKING PASSWORD.
IT'S "BANKPSWD."
BY THE WAY, I ALSO CAN'T REMEMBER EVER TELLING YOU ANY OF THOSE.
UM, LUCKY GUESSES?
AMEND

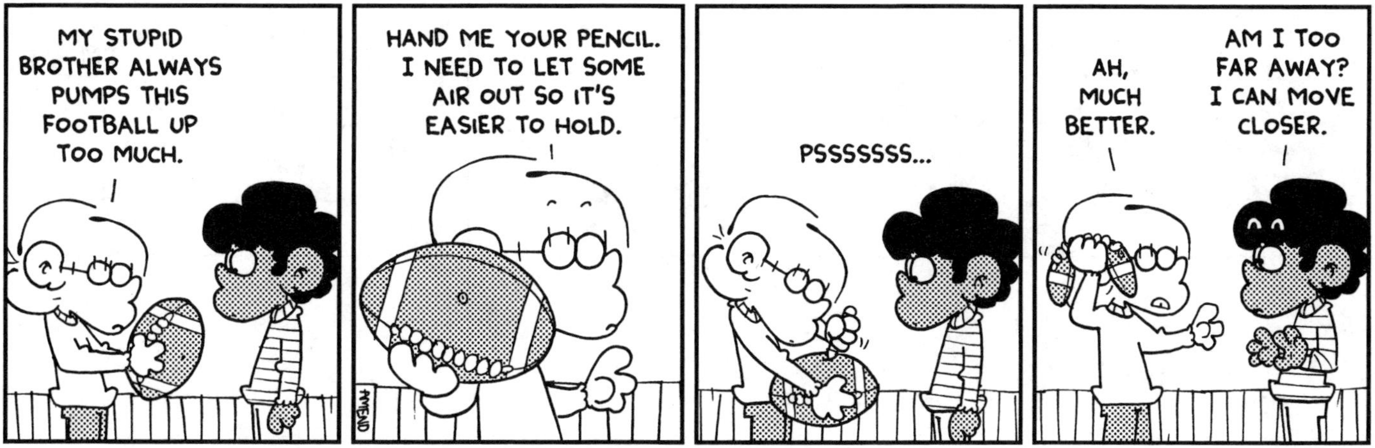
MY STUPID BROTHER ALWAYS PUMPS THIS FOOTBALL UP TOO MUCH.
HAND ME YOUR PENCIL. I NEED TO LET SOME AIR OUT SO IT'S EASIER TO HOLD.
AMEND
PSSSSSSS...
AH, MUCH BETTER.
AM I TOO FAR AWAY? I CAN MOVE CLOSER.

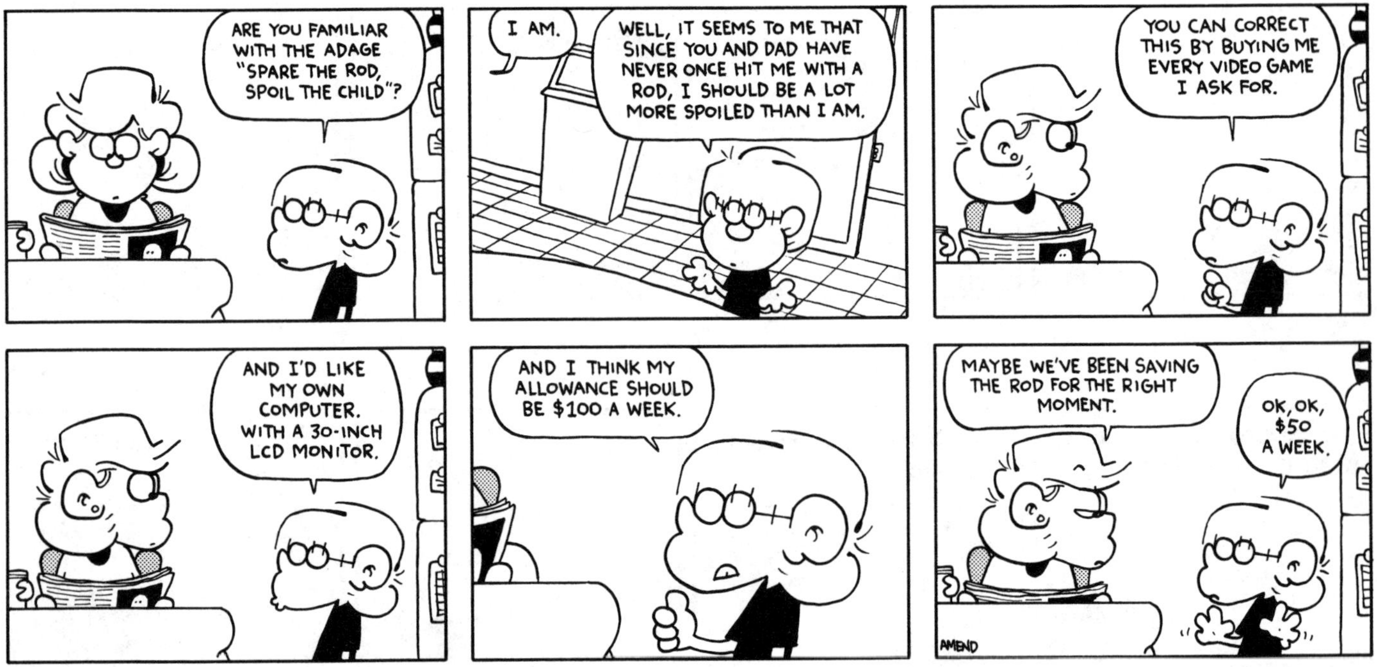
ARE YOU FAMILIAR WITH THE ADAGE "SPARE THE ROD, SPOIL THE CHILD"?
I AM.
WELL, IT SEEMS TO ME THAT SINCE YOU AND DAD HAVE NEVER ONCE HIT ME WITH A ROD, I SHOULD BE A LOT MORE SPOILED THAN I AM.
YOU CAN CORRECT THIS BY BUYING ME EVERY VIDEO GAME I ASK FOR.
AND I'D LIKE MY OWN COMPUTER. WITH A 30-INCH LCD MONITOR.
AND I THINK MY ALLOWANCE SHOULD BE $100 A WEEK.
MAYBE WE'VE BEEN SAVING THE ROD FOR THE RIGHT MOMENT.
OK, OK, $50 A WEEK.
AMEND

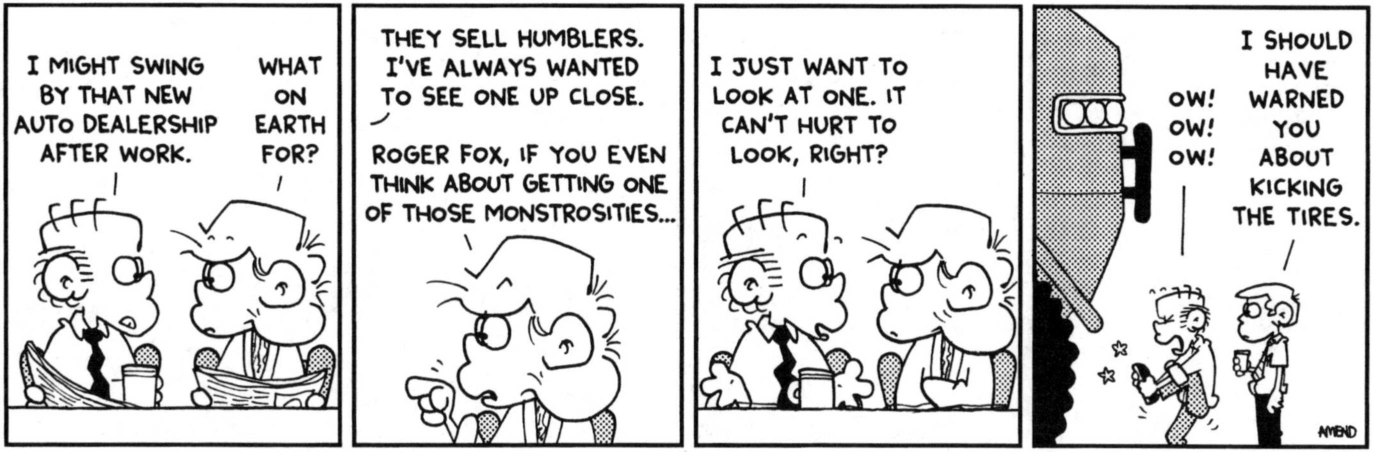
I MIGHT SWING BY THAT NEW AUTO DEALERSHIP AFTER WORK.
WHAT ON EARTH FOR?
THEY SELL HUMBLERS. I'VE ALWAYS WANTED TO SEE ONE UP CLOSE.
ROGER FOX, IF YOU EVEN THINK ABOUT GETTING ONE OF THOSE MONSTROSITIES...
I JUST WANT TO LOOK AT ONE. IT CAN'T HURT TO LOOK, RIGHT?
OW! OW! OW!
I SHOULD HAVE WARNED YOU ABOUT KICKING THE TIRES.
AMEND

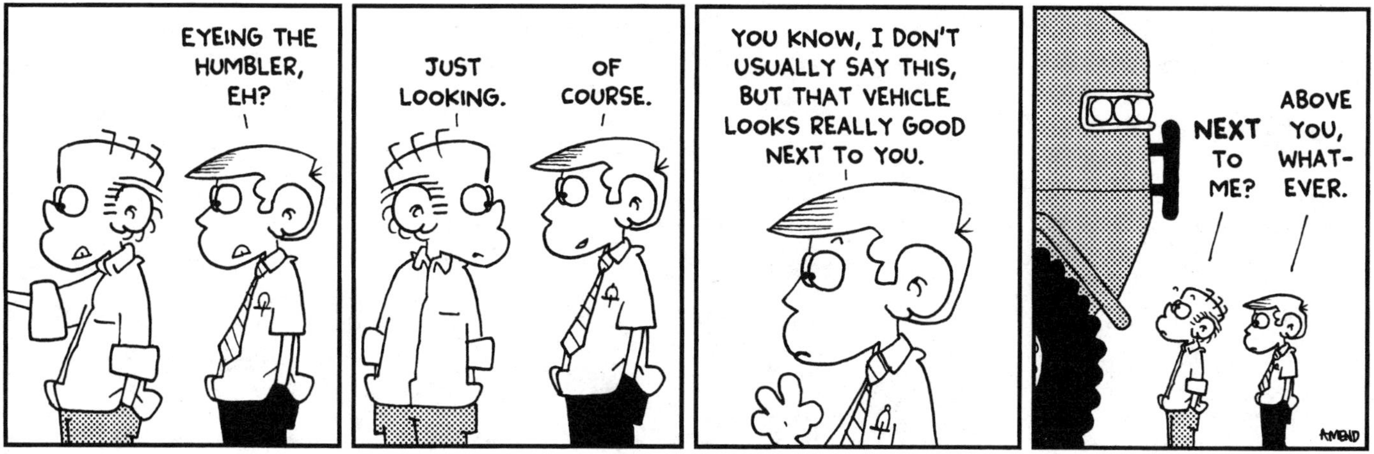
EYEING THE HUMBLER, EH?
JUST LOOKING.
OF COURSE.
YOU KNOW, I DON'T USUALLY SAY THIS, BUT THAT VEHICLE LOOKS REALLY GOOD NEXT TO YOU.
NEXT TO ME?
ABOVE YOU, WHATEVER.
AMEND

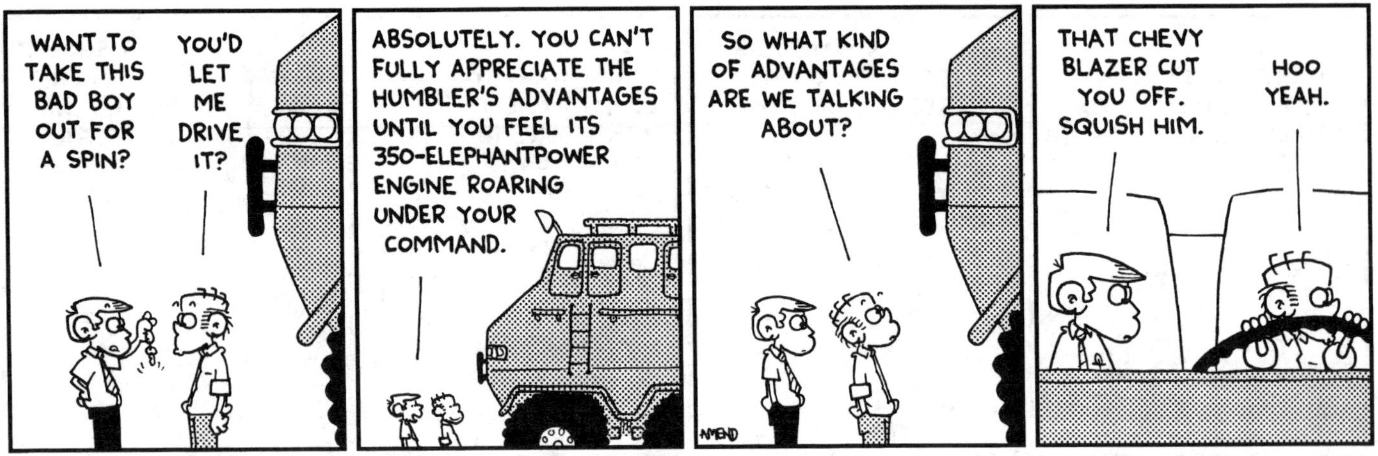
WANT TO TAKE THIS BAD BOY OUT FOR A SPIN?
YOU'D LET ME DRIVE IT?
ABSOLUTELY. YOU CAN'T FULLY APPRECIATE THE HUMBLER'S ADVANTAGES UNTIL YOU FEEL ITS 350-ELEPHANTPOWER ENGINE ROARING UNDER YOUR COMMAND.
SO WHAT KIND OF ADVANTAGES ARE WE TALKING ABOUT?
AMEND
THAT CHEVY BLAZER CUT YOU OFF. SQUISH HIM.
HOO YEAH.

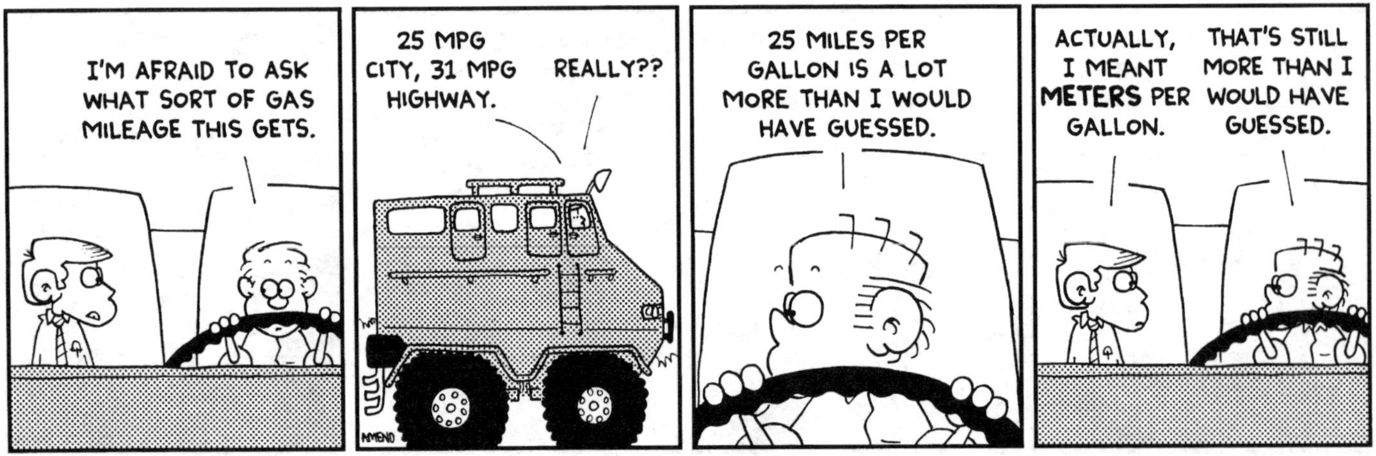
I'M AFRAID TO ASK WHAT SORT OF GAS MILEAGE THIS GETS.
25 MPG CITY, 31 MPG HIGHWAY.
REALLY??
AMEND
25 MILES PER GALLON IS A LOT MORE THAN I WOULD HAVE GUESSED.
ACTUALLY, I MEANT **METERS** PER GALLON.
THAT'S STILL MORE THAN I WOULD HAVE GUESSED.

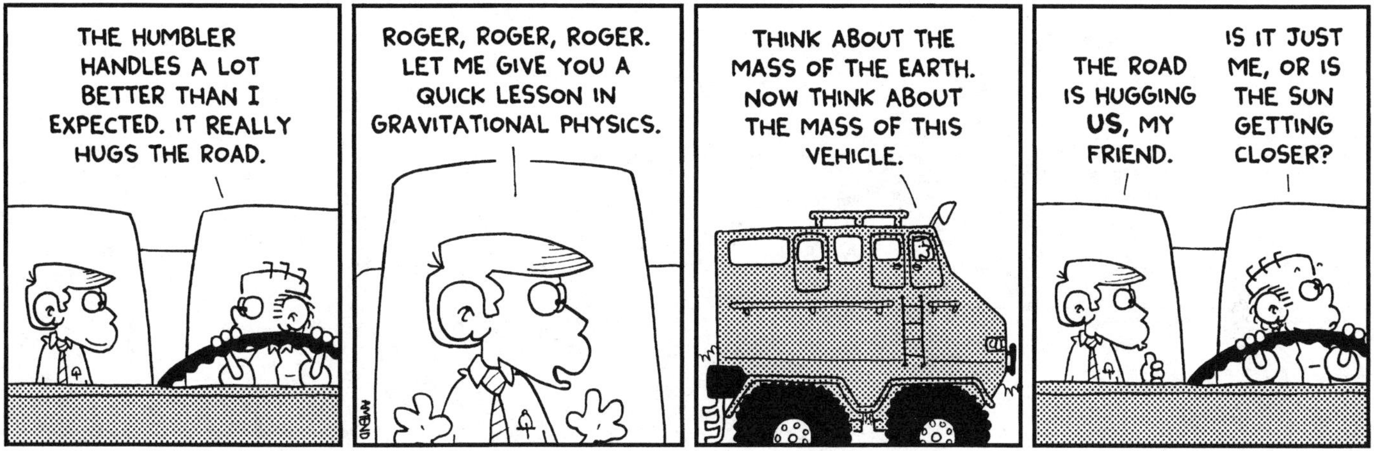
THE HUMBLER HANDLES A LOT BETTER THAN I EXPECTED. IT REALLY HUGS THE ROAD.
ROGER, ROGER, ROGER. LET ME GIVE YOU A QUICK LESSON IN GRAVITATIONAL PHYSICS.
THINK ABOUT THE MASS OF THE EARTH. NOW THINK ABOUT THE MASS OF THIS VEHICLE.
THE ROAD IS HUGGING **US**, MY FRIEND.
IS IT JUST ME, OR IS THE SUN GETTING CLOSER?

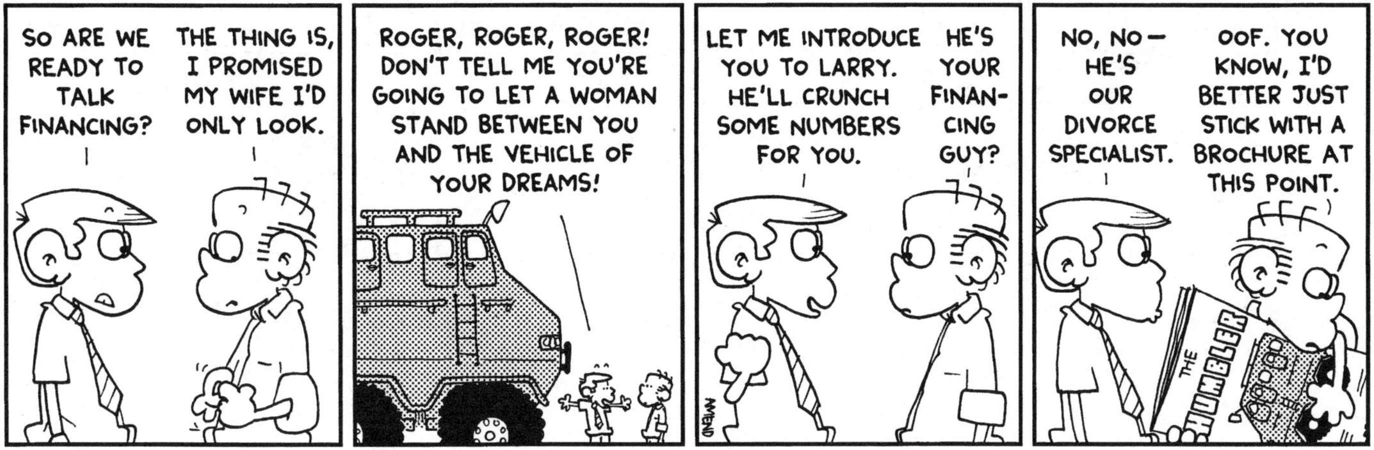
SO ARE WE READY TO TALK FINANCING?
THE THING IS, I PROMISED MY WIFE I'D ONLY LOOK.
ROGER, ROGER, ROGER! DON'T TELL ME YOU'RE GOING TO LET A WOMAN STAND BETWEEN YOU AND THE VEHICLE OF YOUR DREAMS!
LET ME INTRODUCE YOU TO LARRY. HE'LL CRUNCH SOME NUMBERS FOR YOU.
HE'S YOUR FINANCING GUY?
NO, NO— HE'S OUR DIVORCE SPECIALIST.
OOF. YOU KNOW, I'D BETTER JUST STICK WITH A BROCHURE AT THIS POINT.
THE HUMBLER

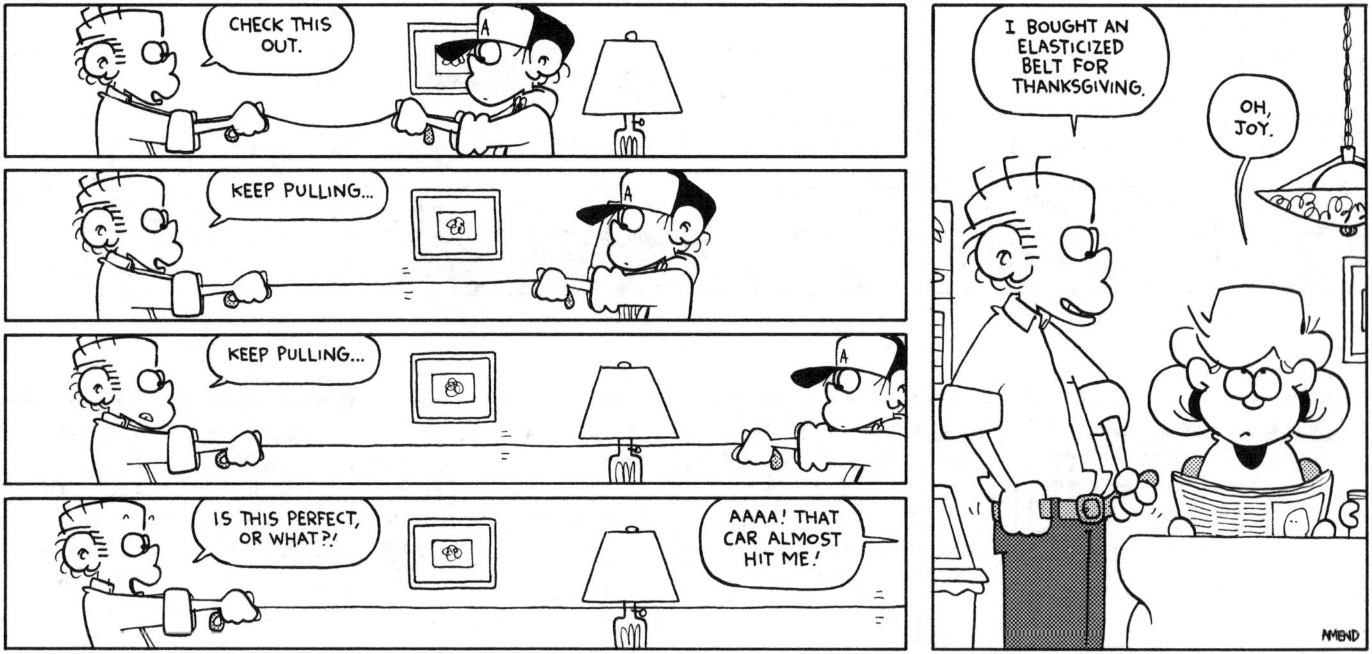
CHECK THIS OUT.
KEEP PULLING...
KEEP PULLING...
IS THIS PERFECT, OR WHAT?!
AAAA! THAT CAR ALMOST HIT ME!
I BOUGHT AN ELASTICIZED BELT FOR THANKSGIVING.
OH, JOY.
AMEND

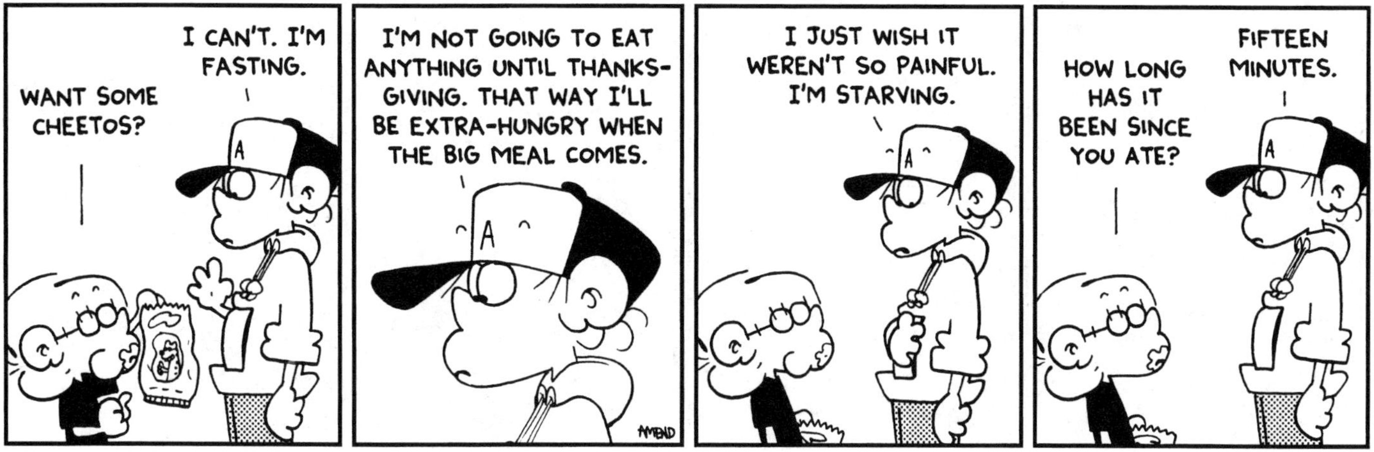
WANT SOME CHEETOS?
I CAN'T. I'M FASTING.
I'M NOT GOING TO EAT ANYTHING UNTIL THANKSGIVING. THAT WAY I'LL BE EXTRA-HUNGRY WHEN THE BIG MEAL COMES.
AMEND
I JUST WISH IT WEREN'T SO PAINFUL. I'M STARVING.
HOW LONG HAS IT BEEN SINCE YOU ATE?
FIFTEEN MINUTES.

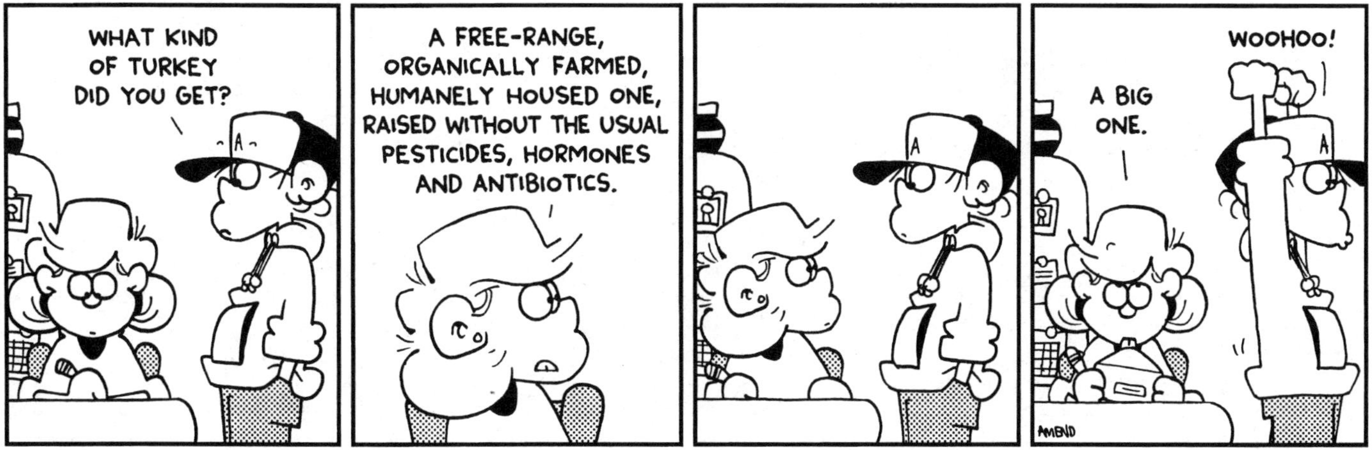
WHAT KIND OF TURKEY DID YOU GET?
A FREE-RANGE, ORGANICALLY FARMED, HUMANELY HOUSED ONE, RAISED WITHOUT THE USUAL PESTICIDES, HORMONES AND ANTIBIOTICS.
A BIG ONE.
WOOHOO!
AMEND

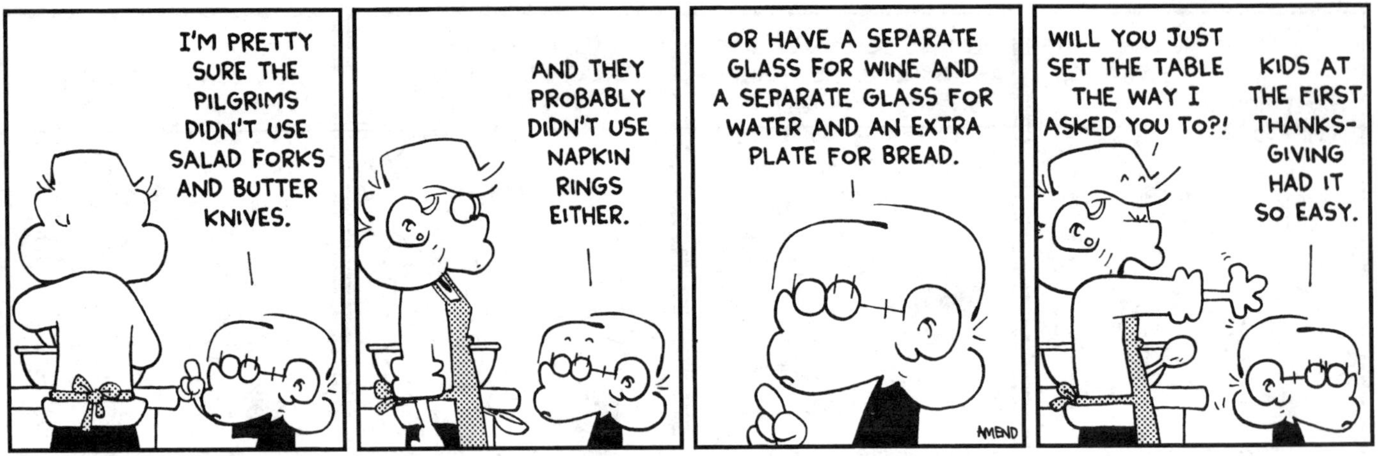
I'M PRETTY SURE THE PILGRIMS DIDN'T USE SALAD FORKS AND BUTTER KNIVES.
AND THEY PROBABLY DIDN'T USE NAPKIN RINGS EITHER.
OR HAVE A SEPARATE GLASS FOR WINE AND A SEPARATE GLASS FOR WATER AND AN EXTRA PLATE FOR BREAD.
AMEND
WILL YOU JUST SET THE TABLE THE WAY I ASKED YOU TO?!
KIDS AT THE FIRST THANKS-GIVING HAD IT SO EASY.

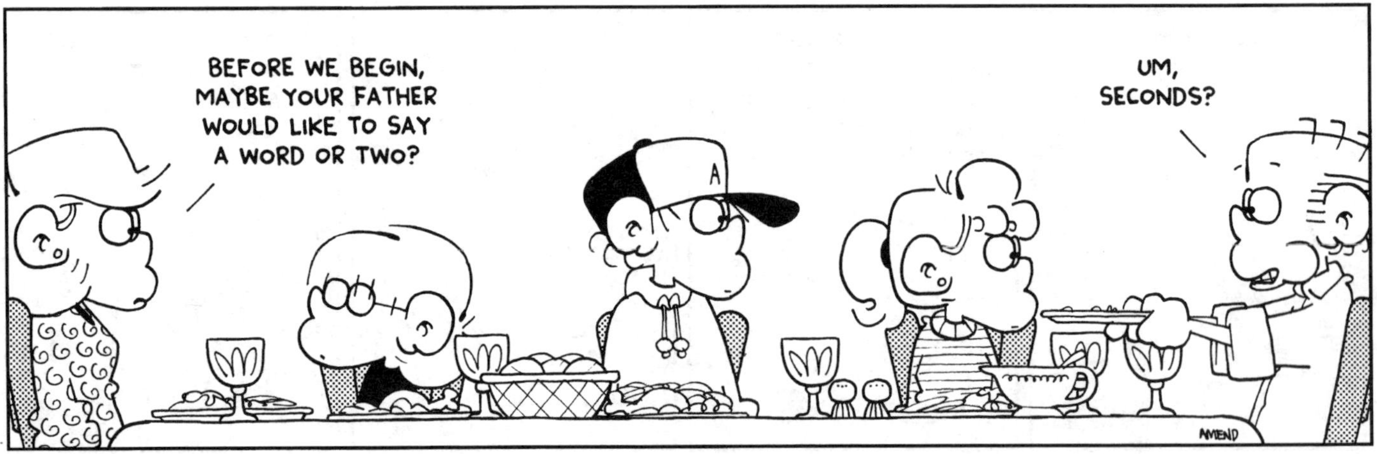
BEFORE WE BEGIN, MAYBE YOUR FATHER WOULD LIKE TO SAY A WORD OR TWO?
UM, SECONDS?
AMEND

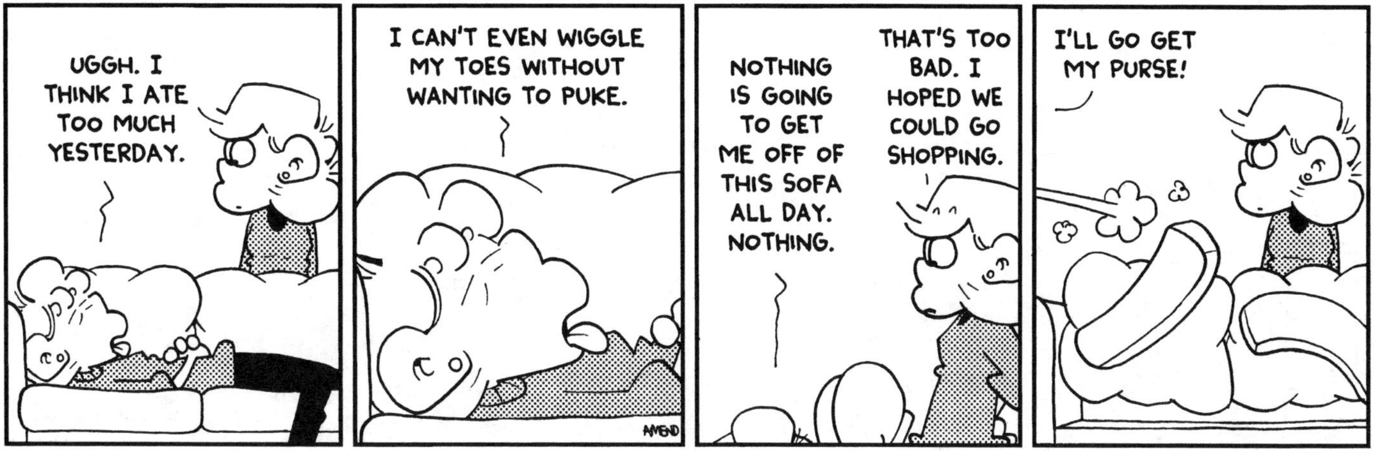
UGGH. I THINK I ATE TOO MUCH YESTERDAY.
I CAN'T EVEN WIGGLE MY TOES WITHOUT WANTING TO PUKE.
AMEND
NOTHING IS GOING TO GET ME OFF OF THIS SOFA ALL DAY. NOTHING.
THAT'S TOO BAD. I HOPED WE COULD GO SHOPPING.
I'LL GO GET MY PURSE!

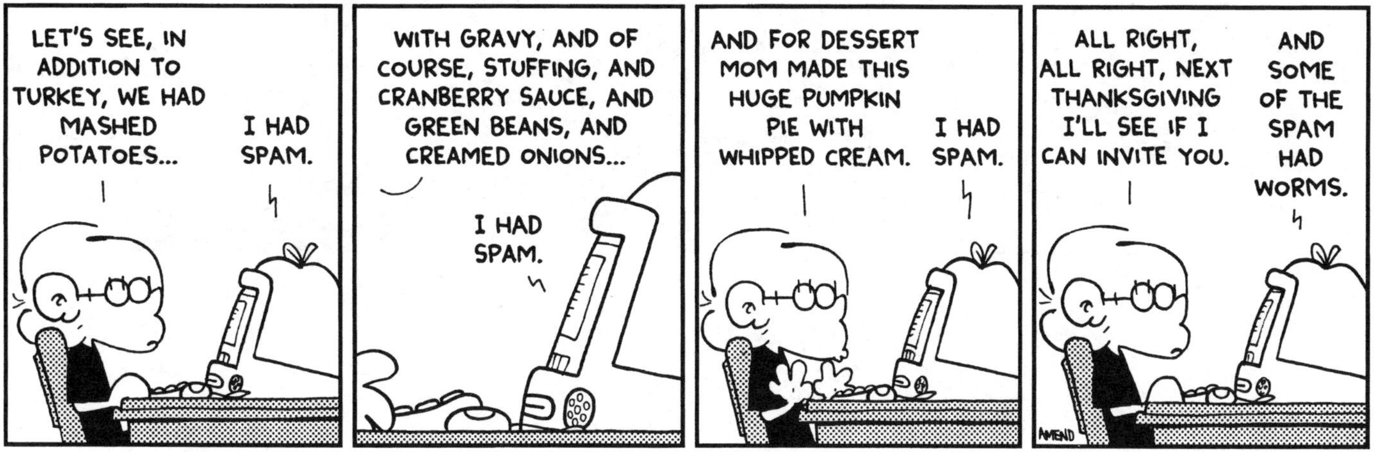
LET'S SEE, IN ADDITION TO TURKEY, WE HAD MASHED POTATOES...
I HAD SPAM.
WITH GRAVY, AND OF COURSE, STUFFING, AND CRANBERRY SAUCE, AND GREEN BEANS, AND CREAMED ONIONS...
I HAD SPAM.
AND FOR DESSERT MOM MADE THIS HUGE PUMPKIN PIE WITH WHIPPED CREAM.
I HAD SPAM.
ALL RIGHT, ALL RIGHT, NEXT THANKSGIVING I'LL SEE IF I CAN INVITE YOU.
AND SOME OF THE SPAM HAD WORMS.
AMEND

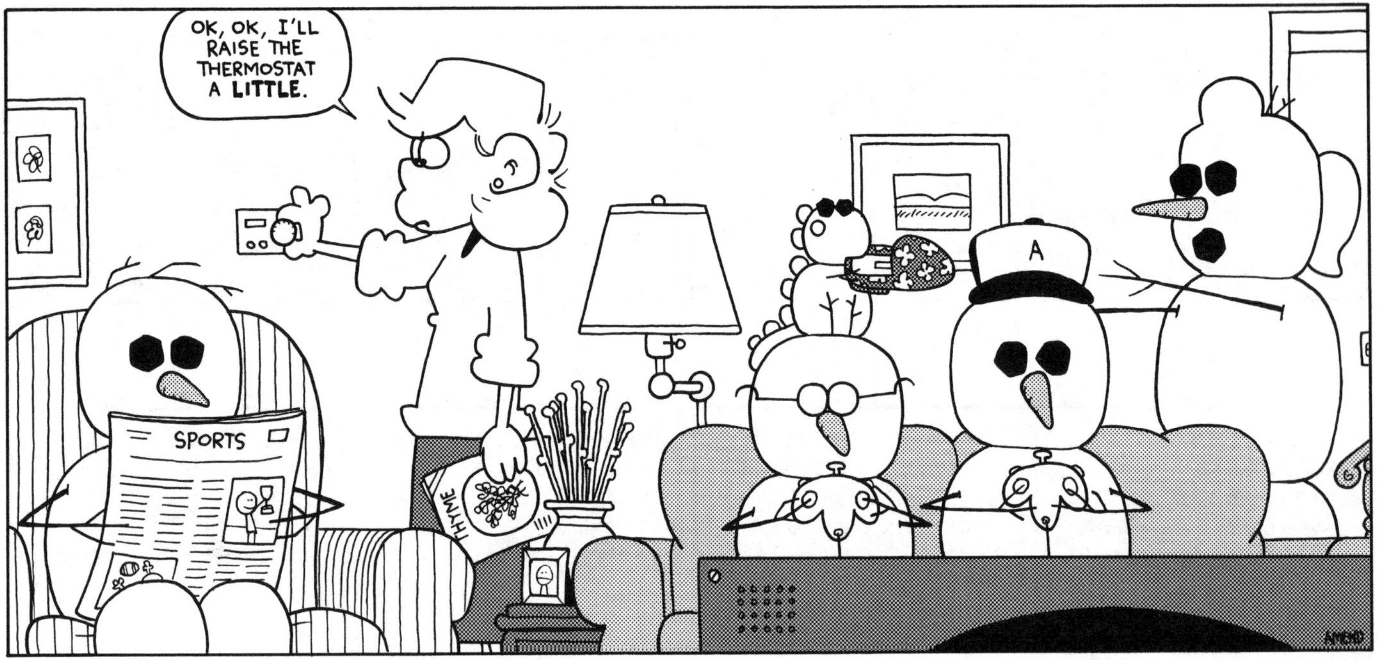
OK, OK, I'LL RAISE THE THERMOSTAT A **LITTLE**.
SPORTS
THYME
A
AMEND

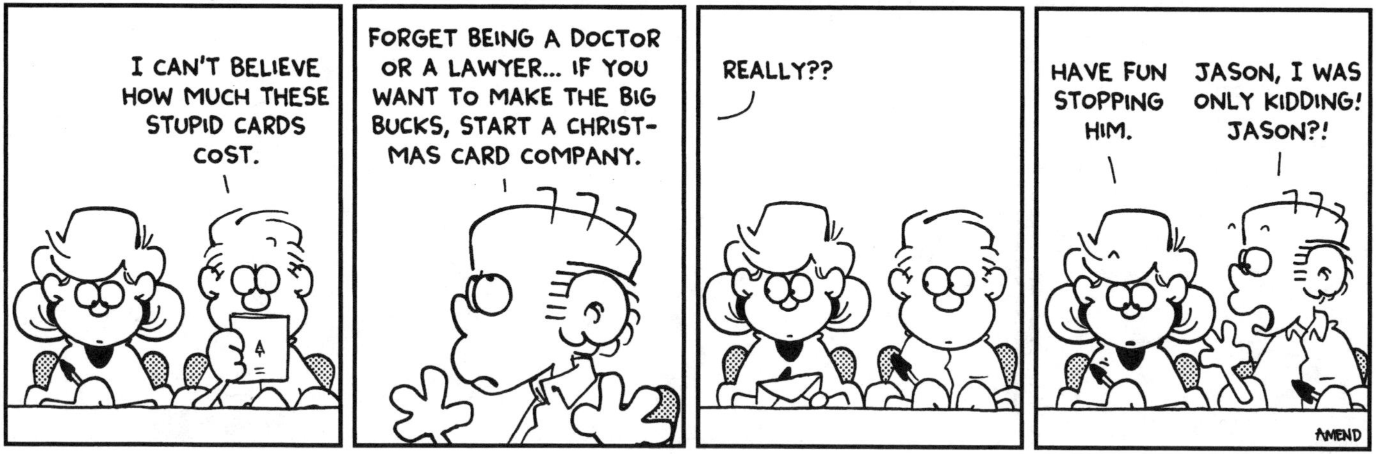
I CAN'T BELIEVE HOW MUCH THESE STUPID CARDS COST.
FORGET BEING A DOCTOR OR A LAWYER... IF YOU WANT TO MAKE THE BIG BUCKS, START A CHRIST-MAS CARD COMPANY.
REALLY??
HAVE FUN STOPPING HIM.
JASON, I WAS ONLY KIDDING! JASON?!
AMEND

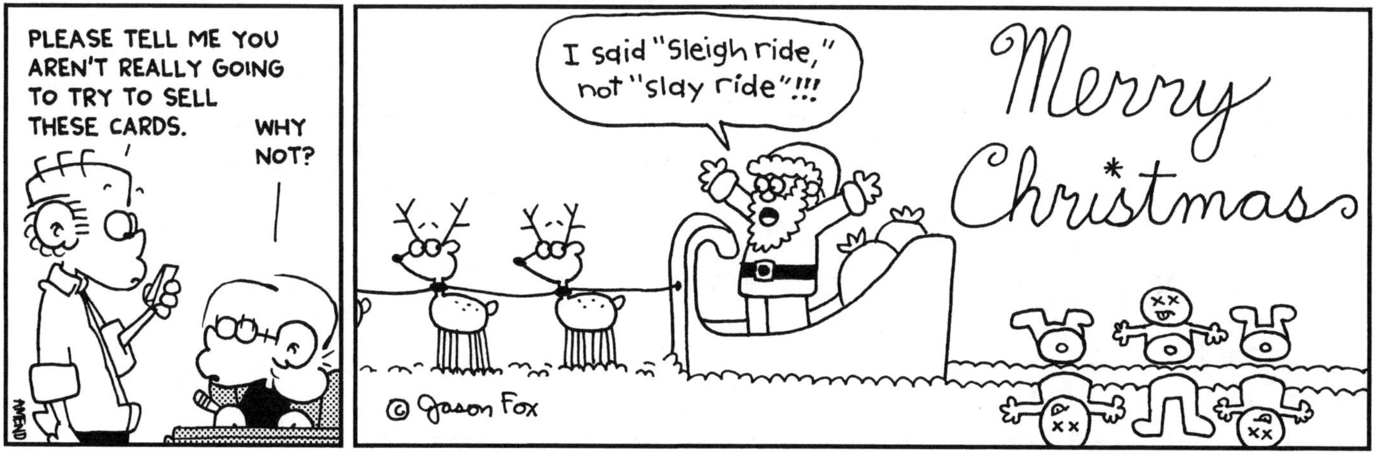
PLEASE TELL ME YOU AREN'T REALLY GOING TO TRY TO SELL THESE CARDS.
WHY NOT?
AMEND
I said "sleigh ride," not "slay ride"!!!
Merry Christmas
© Jason Fox

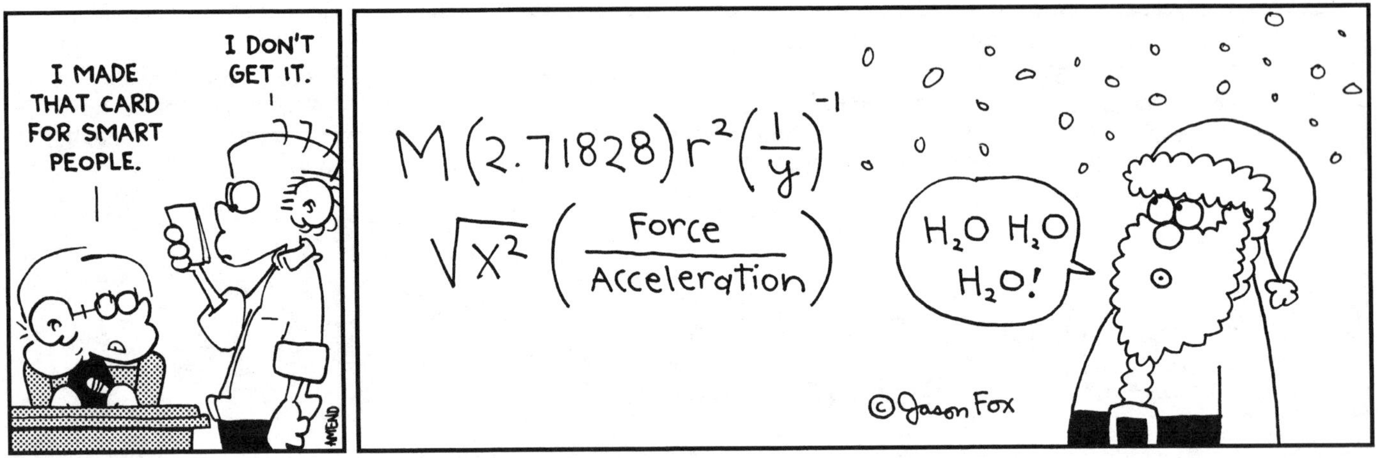
I MADE THAT CARD FOR SMART PEOPLE.
I DON'T GET IT.
AMEND
M(2.71828)r²(1/y)⁻¹ √X² (Force/Acceleration)
H₂O H₂O H₂O!
©Jason Fox

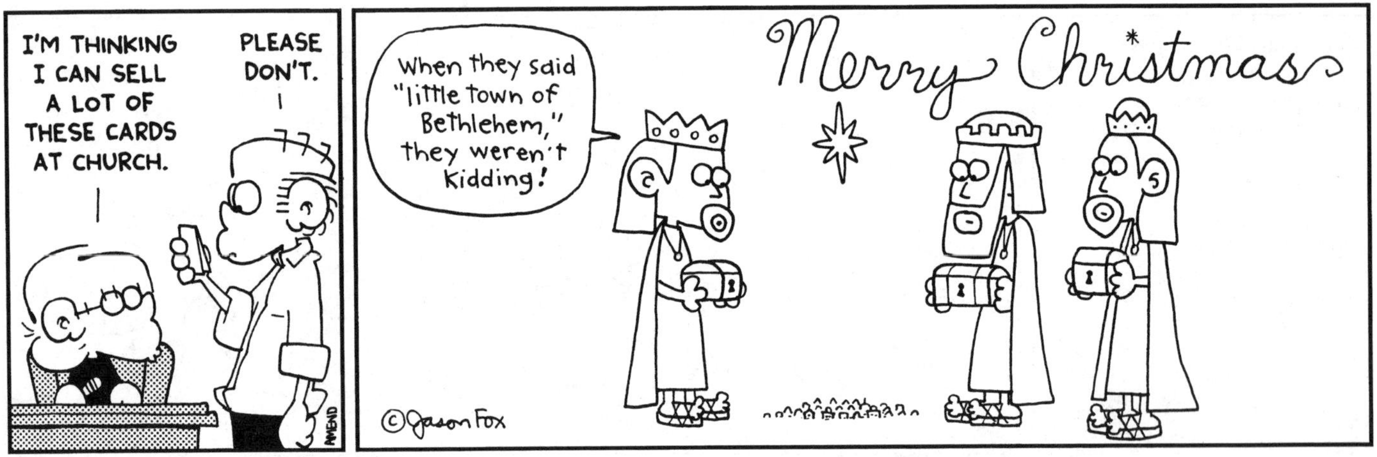
I'M THINKING I CAN SELL A LOT OF THESE CARDS AT CHURCH.
PLEASE DON'T.
AMEND
When they said "little town of Bethlehem," they weren't kidding!
Merry Christmas
©Jason Fox

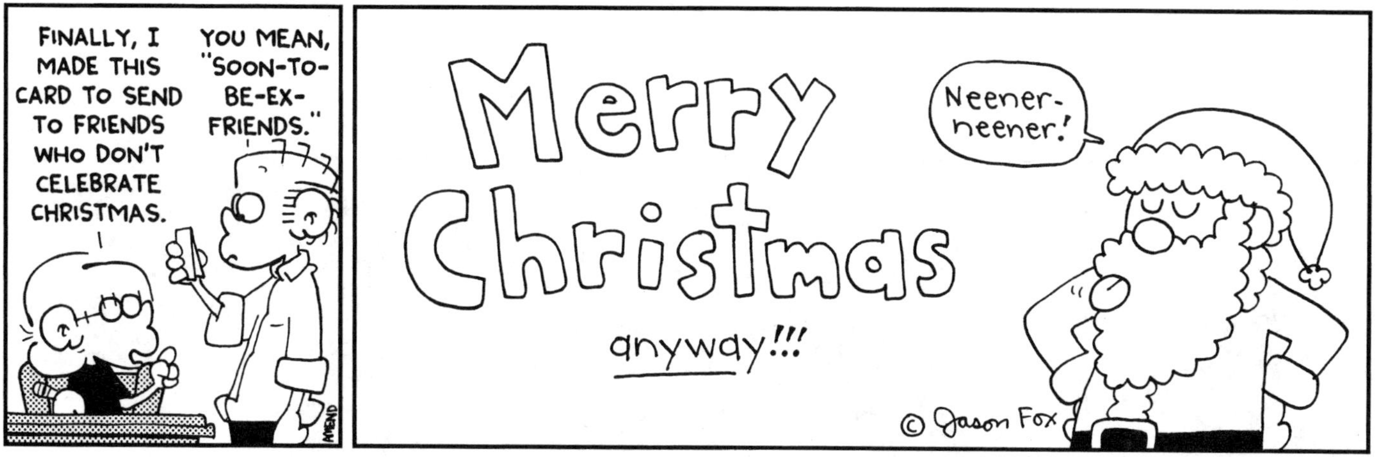
FINALLY, I MADE THIS CARD TO SEND TO FRIENDS WHO DON'T CELEBRATE CHRISTMAS.
YOU MEAN, "SOON-TO-BE-EX-FRIENDS."
Merry Christmas
anyway!!!
Neener-neener!
© Jason Fox

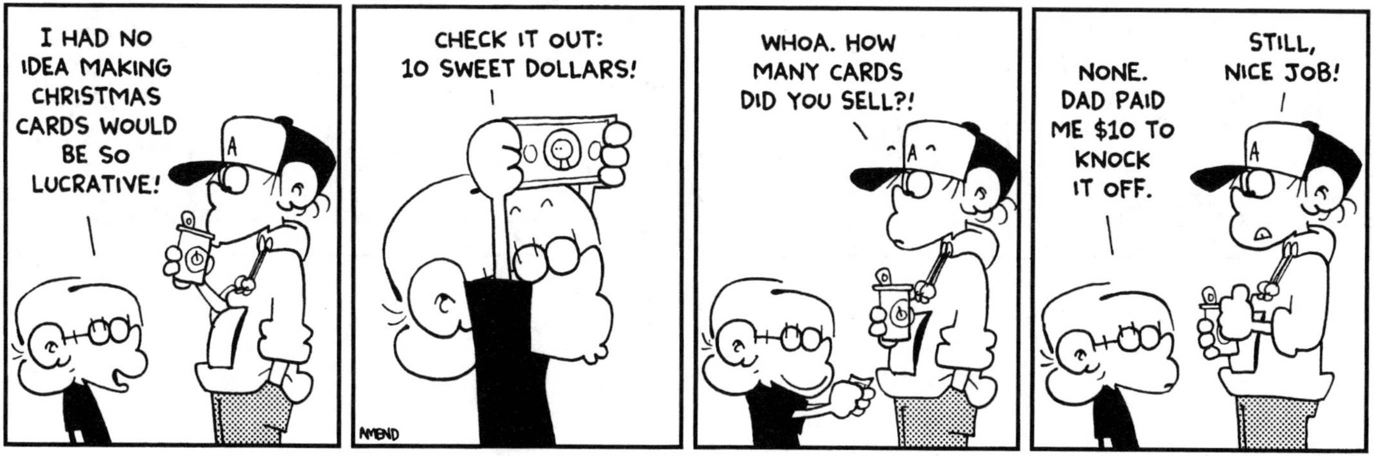
I HAD NO IDEA MAKING CHRISTMAS CARDS WOULD BE SO LUCRATIVE!
CHECK IT OUT: 10 SWEET DOLLARS!
WHOA. HOW MANY CARDS DID YOU SELL?!
NONE. DAD PAID ME $10 TO KNOCK IT OFF.
STILL, NICE JOB!

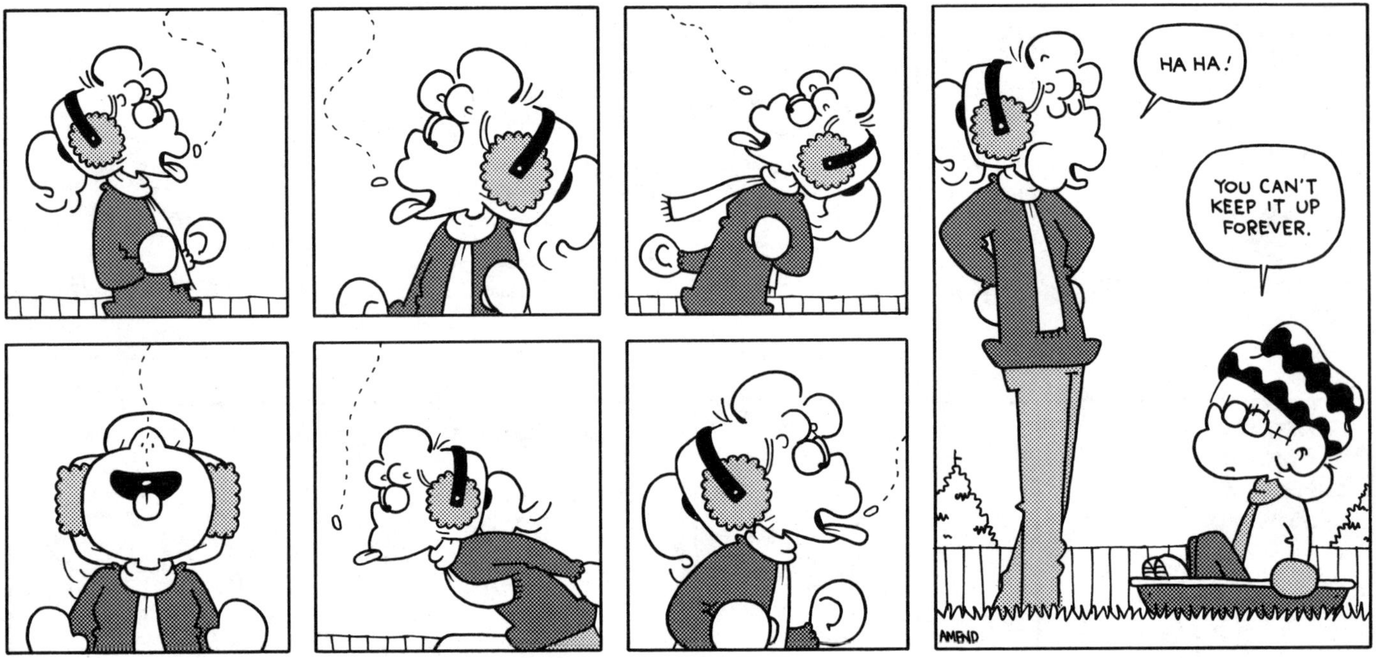
HA HA!
YOU CAN'T KEEP IT UP FOREVER.
AMEND

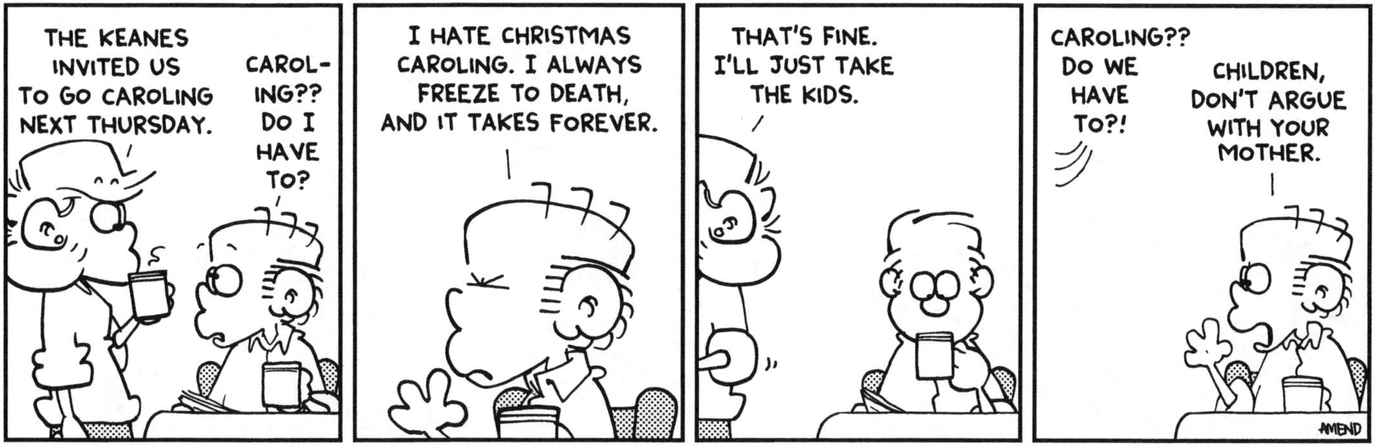
THE KEANES INVITED US TO GO CAROLING NEXT THURSDAY.
CAROL-ING?? DO I HAVE TO?
I HATE CHRISTMAS CAROLING. I ALWAYS FREEZE TO DEATH, AND IT TAKES FOREVER.
THAT'S FINE. I'LL JUST TAKE THE KIDS.
CAROLING?? DO WE HAVE TO?!
CHILDREN, DON'T ARGUE WITH YOUR MOTHER.
AMEND

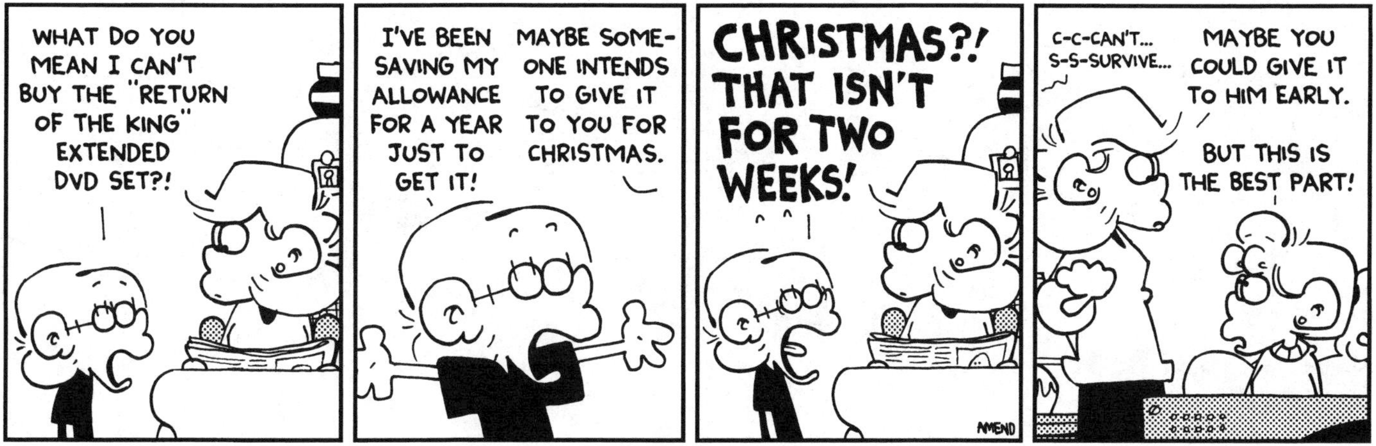
WHAT DO YOU MEAN I CAN'T BUY THE "RETURN OF THE KING" EXTENDED DVD SET?!
I'VE BEEN SAVING MY ALLOWANCE FOR A YEAR JUST TO GET IT!
MAYBE SOME-ONE INTENDS TO GIVE IT TO YOU FOR CHRISTMAS.
CHRISTMAS?! THAT ISN'T FOR TWO WEEKS!
AMEND
C-C-CAN'T... S-S-SURVIVE...
MAYBE YOU COULD GIVE IT TO HIM EARLY.
BUT THIS IS THE BEST PART!

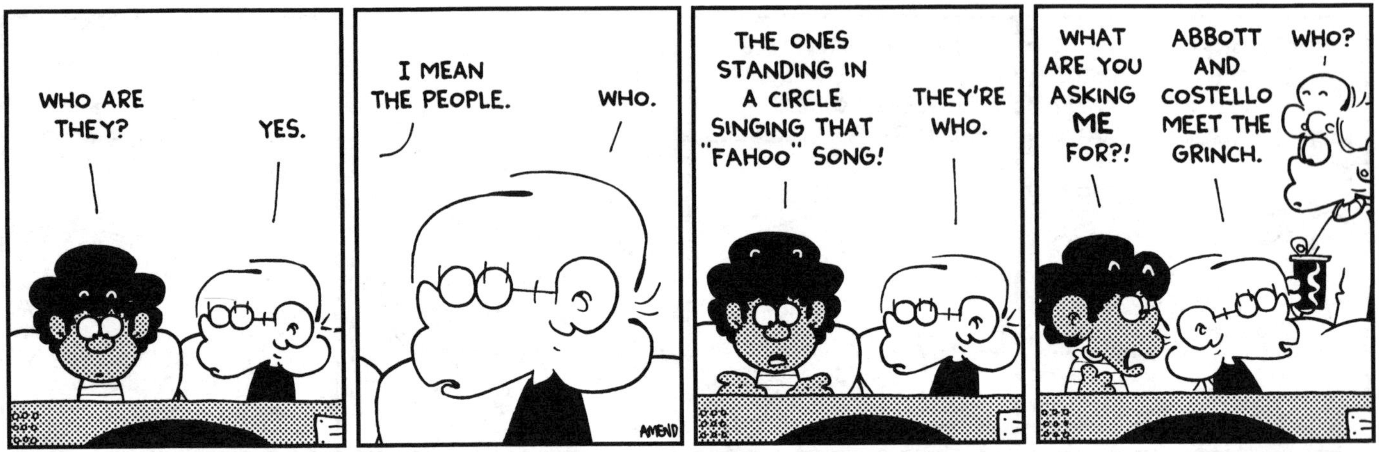
WHO ARE THEY?
YES.
I MEAN THE PEOPLE.
WHO.
AMEND
THE ONES STANDING IN A CIRCLE SINGING THAT "FAHOO" SONG!
THEY'RE WHO.
WHAT ARE YOU ASKING ME FOR?!
ABBOTT AND COSTELLO MEET THE GRINCH.
WHO?

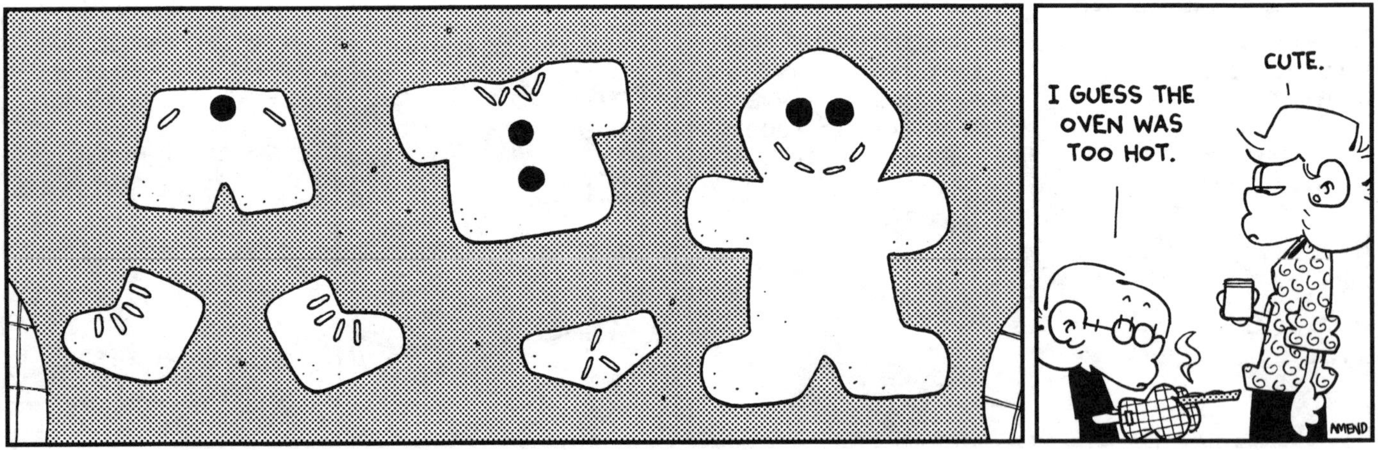
I GUESS THE OVEN WAS TOO HOT.
CUTE.
AMEND

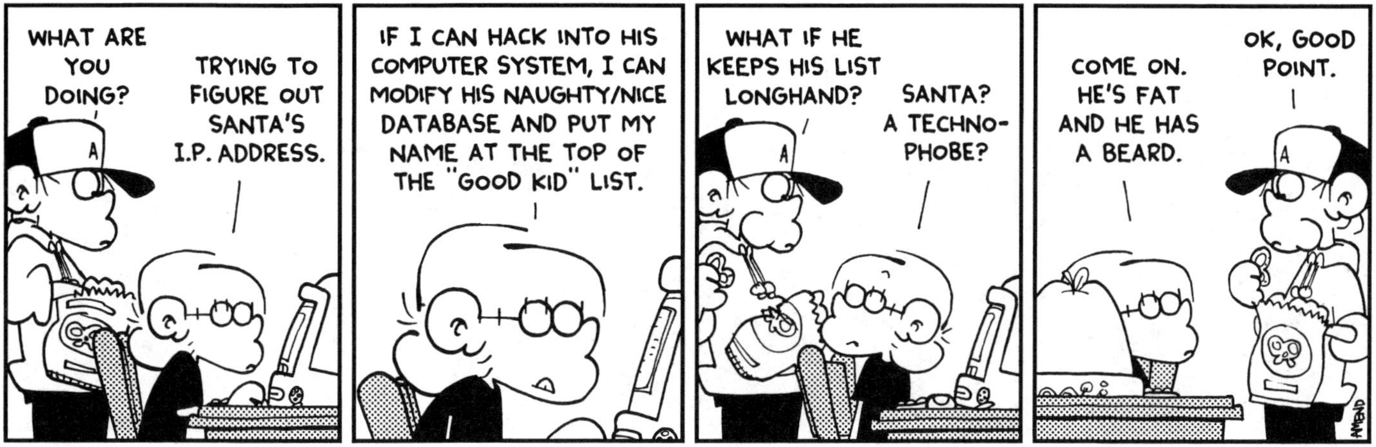
WHAT ARE YOU DOING?
TRYING TO FIGURE OUT SANTA'S I.P. ADDRESS.
IF I CAN HACK INTO HIS COMPUTER SYSTEM, I CAN MODIFY HIS NAUGHTY/NICE DATABASE AND PUT MY NAME AT THE TOP OF THE "GOOD KID" LIST.
WHAT IF HE KEEPS HIS LIST LONGHAND?
SANTA? A TECHNO-PHOBE?
COME ON. HE'S FAT AND HE HAS A BEARD.
OK, GOOD POINT.
AMEND

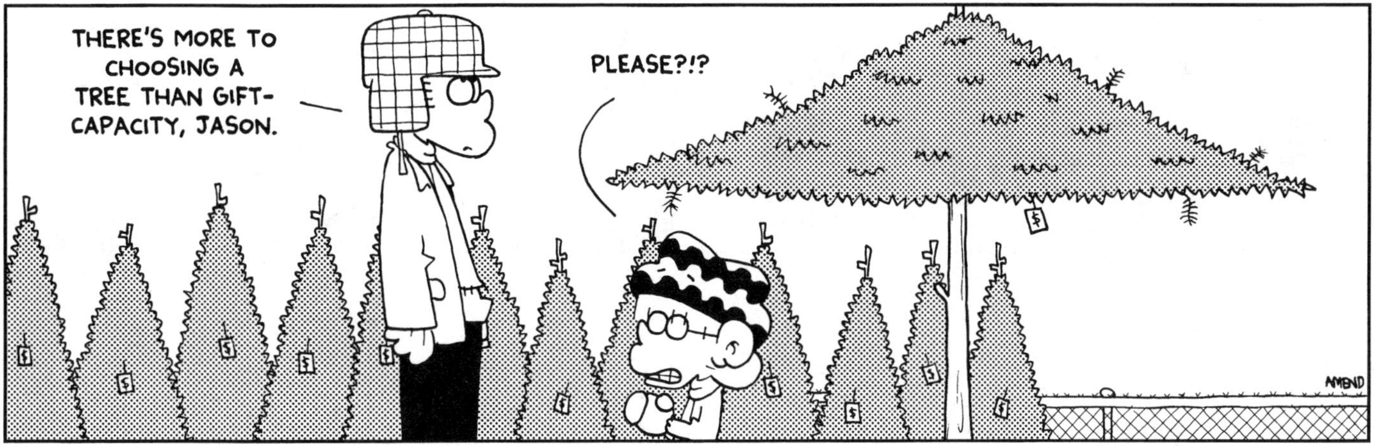
THERE'S MORE TO CHOOSING A TREE THAN GIFT-CAPACITY, JASON.
PLEASE?!?
AMEND

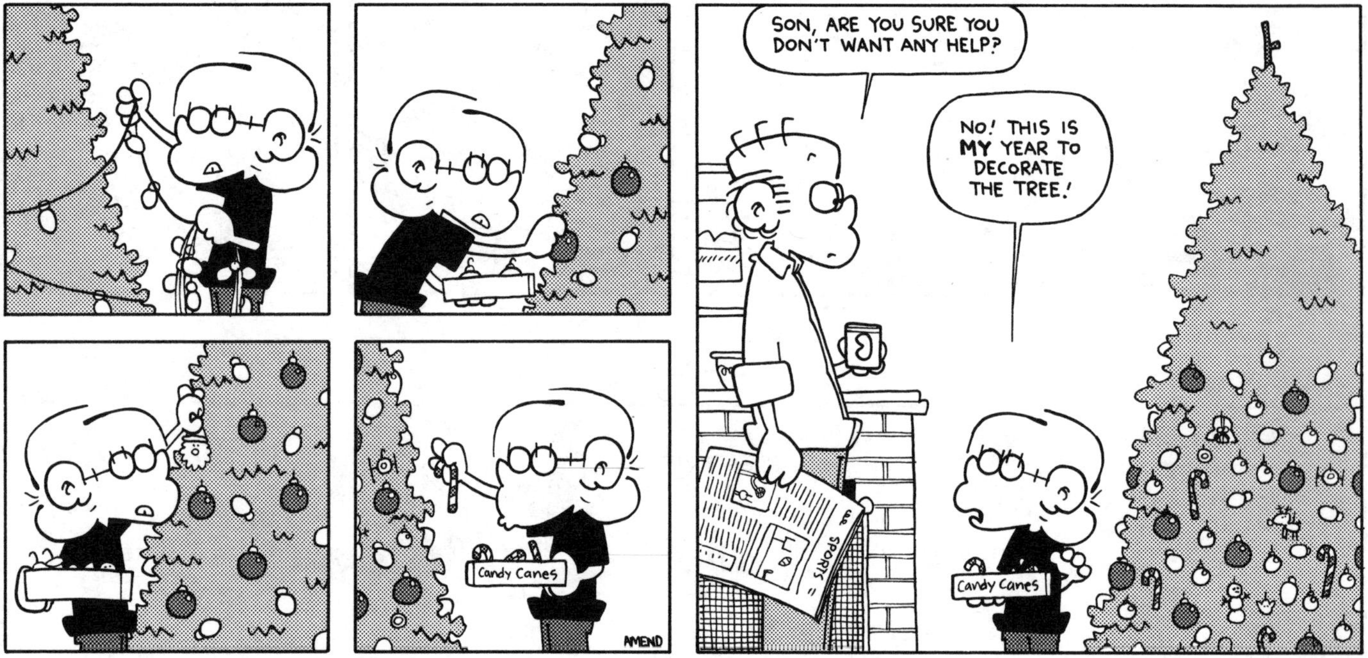
Candy Canes
AMEND
SON, ARE YOU SURE YOU DON'T WANT ANY HELP?
NO! THIS IS MY YEAR TO DECORATE THE TREE!
SPORTS
Candy Canes

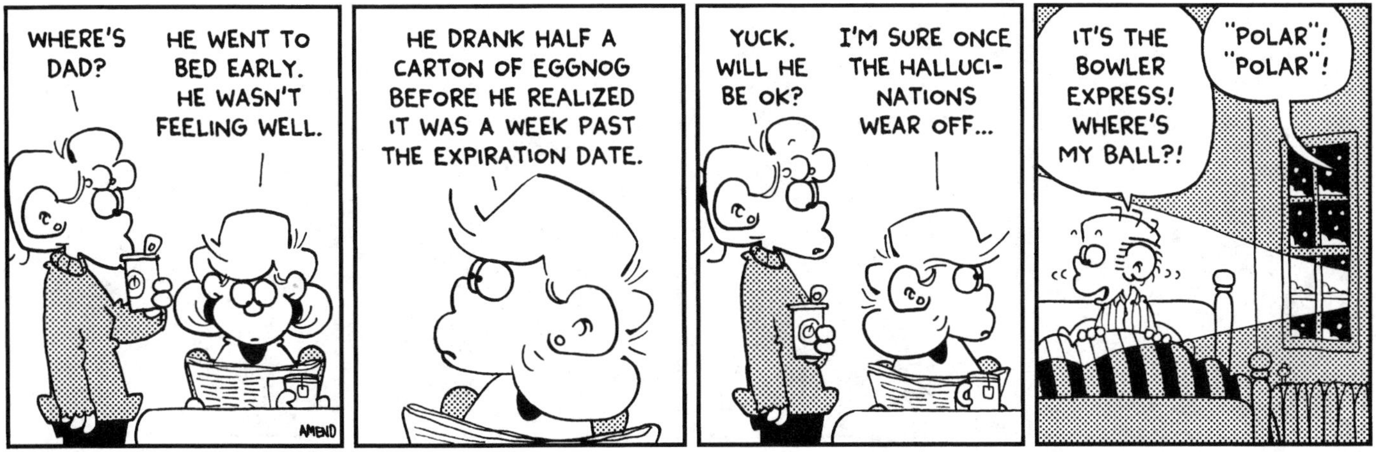
WHERE'S DAD?
HE WENT TO BED EARLY. HE WASN'T FEELING WELL.
AMEND
HE DRANK HALF A CARTON OF EGGNOG BEFORE HE REALIZED IT WAS A WEEK PAST THE EXPIRATION DATE.
YUCK. WILL HE BE OK?
I'M SURE ONCE THE HALLUCINATIONS WEAR OFF...
IT'S THE BOWLER EXPRESS! WHERE'S MY BALL?!
"POLAR"! "POLAR"!

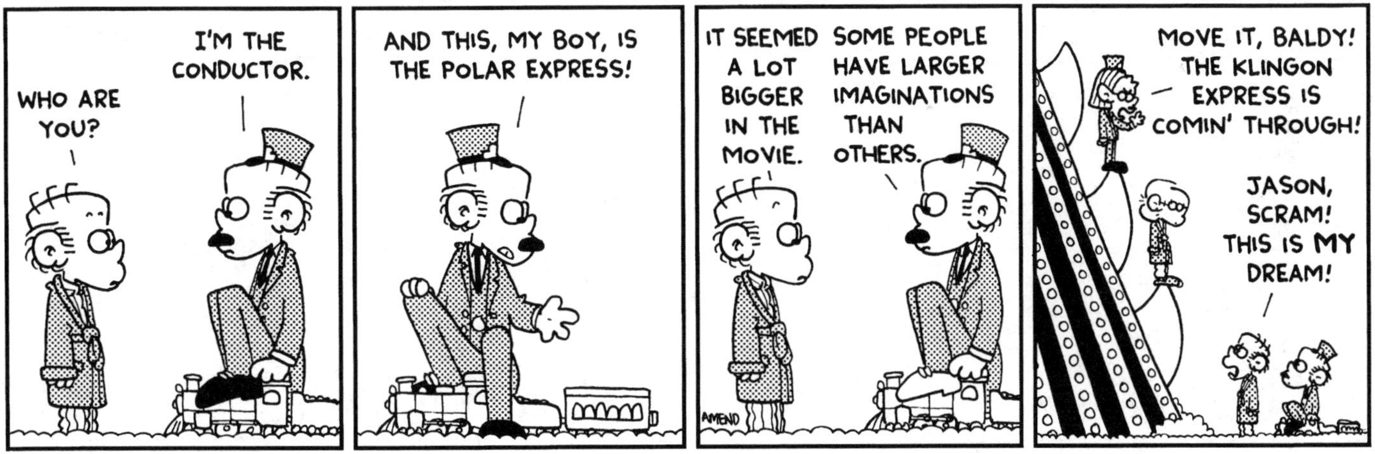
WHO ARE YOU?
I'M THE CONDUCTOR.
AND THIS, MY BOY, IS THE POLAR EXPRESS!
IT SEEMED A LOT BIGGER IN THE MOVIE.
SOME PEOPLE HAVE LARGER IMAGINATIONS THAN OTHERS.
AMEND
MOVE IT, BALDY! THE KLINGON EXPRESS IS COMIN' THROUGH!
JASON, SCRAM! THIS IS MY DREAM!

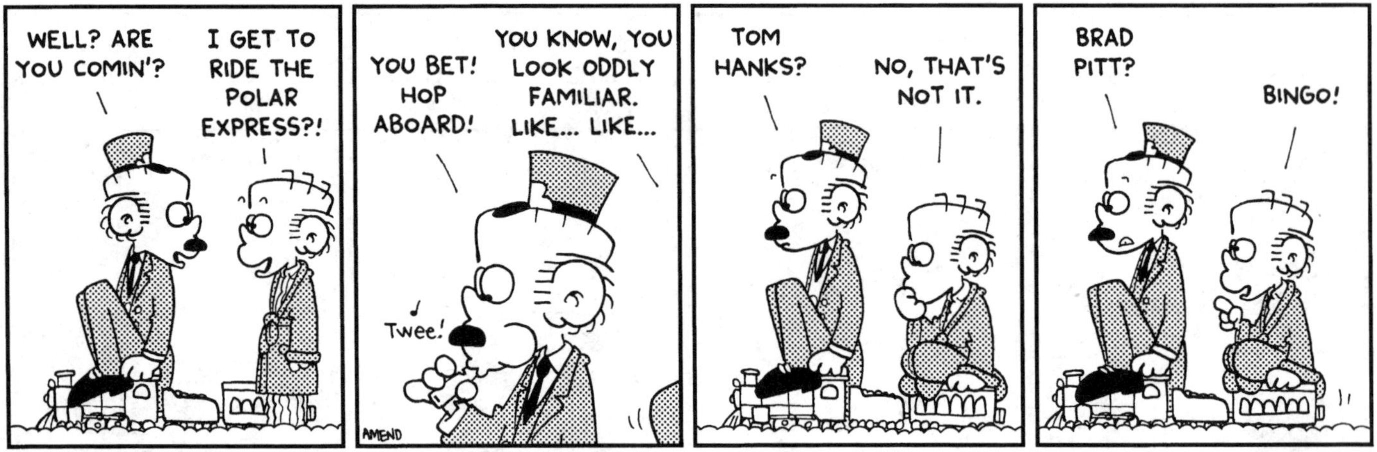
WELL? ARE YOU COMIN'?
I GET TO RIDE THE POLAR EXPRESS?!
YOU BET! HOP ABOARD!
YOU KNOW, YOU LOOK ODDLY FAMILIAR. LIKE... LIKE...
Twee!
AMEND
TOM HANKS?
NO, THAT'S NOT IT.
BRAD PITT?
BINGO!

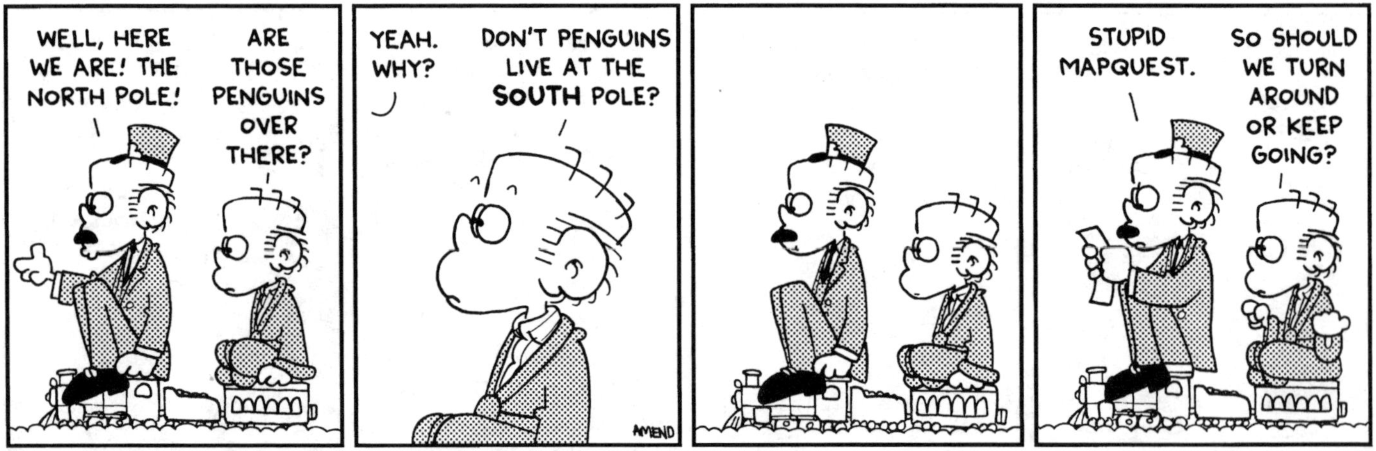
WELL, HERE WE ARE! THE NORTH POLE!
ARE THOSE PENGUINS OVER THERE?
YEAH. WHY?
DON'T PENGUINS LIVE AT THE **SOUTH** POLE?
AMEND
STUPID MAPQUEST.
SO SHOULD WE TURN AROUND OR KEEP GOING?

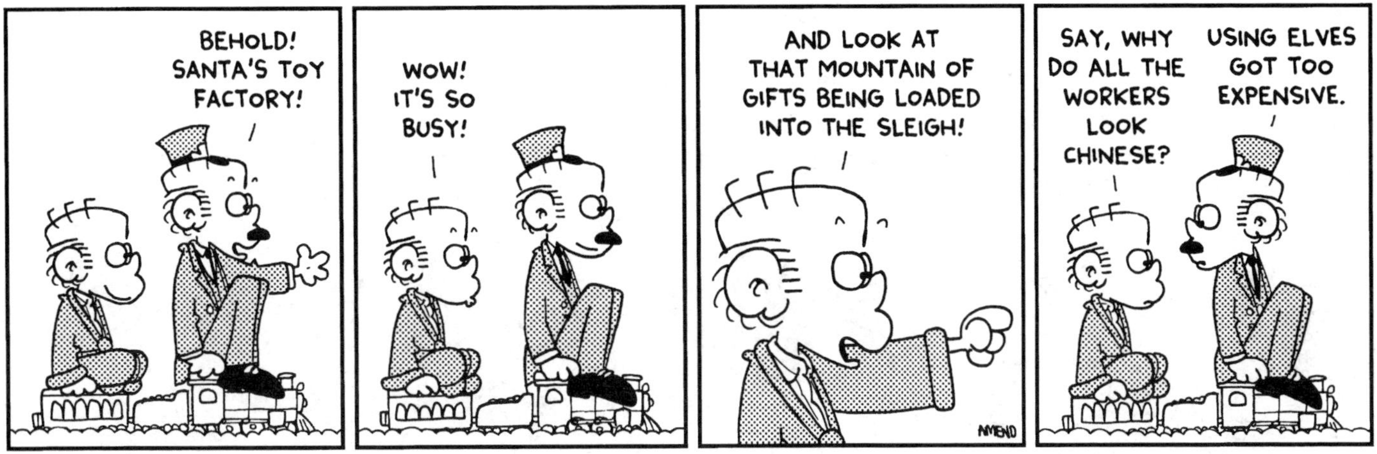
BEHOLD! SANTA'S TOY FACTORY!
WOW! IT'S SO BUSY!
AND LOOK AT THAT MOUNTAIN OF GIFTS BEING LOADED INTO THE SLEIGH!
SAY, WHY DO ALL THE WORKERS LOOK CHINESE?
USING ELVES GOT TOO EXPENSIVE.
AMEND

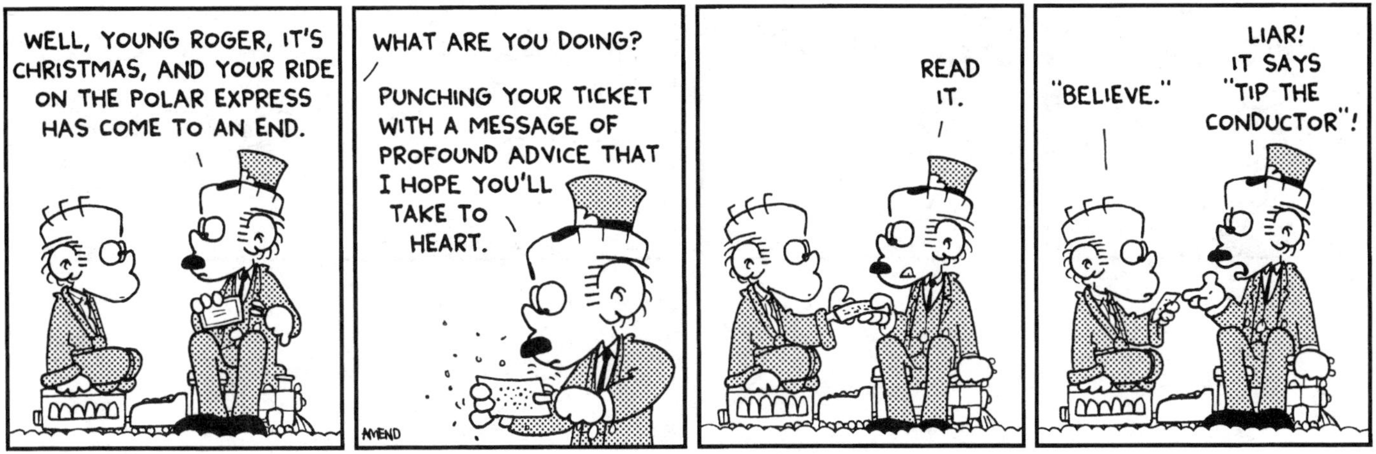
WELL, YOUNG ROGER, IT'S CHRISTMAS, AND YOUR RIDE ON THE POLAR EXPRESS HAS COME TO AN END.
WHAT ARE YOU DOING?
PUNCHING YOUR TICKET WITH A MESSAGE OF PROFOUND ADVICE THAT I HOPE YOU'LL TAKE TO HEART.
AMEND
READ IT.
"BELIEVE."
LIAR! IT SAYS "TIP THE CONDUCTOR"!

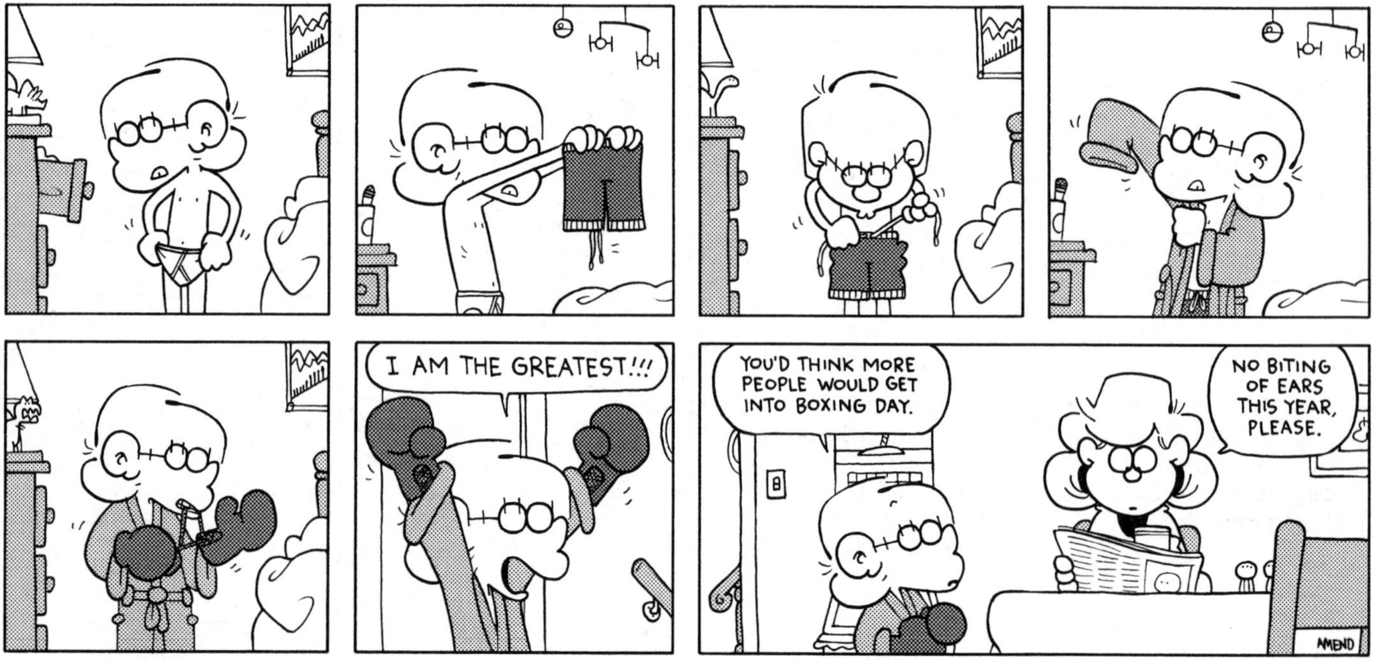
I AM THE GREATEST!!!
YOU'D THINK MORE PEOPLE WOULD GET INTO BOXING DAY.
NO BITING OF EARS THIS YEAR, PLEASE.
AMEND

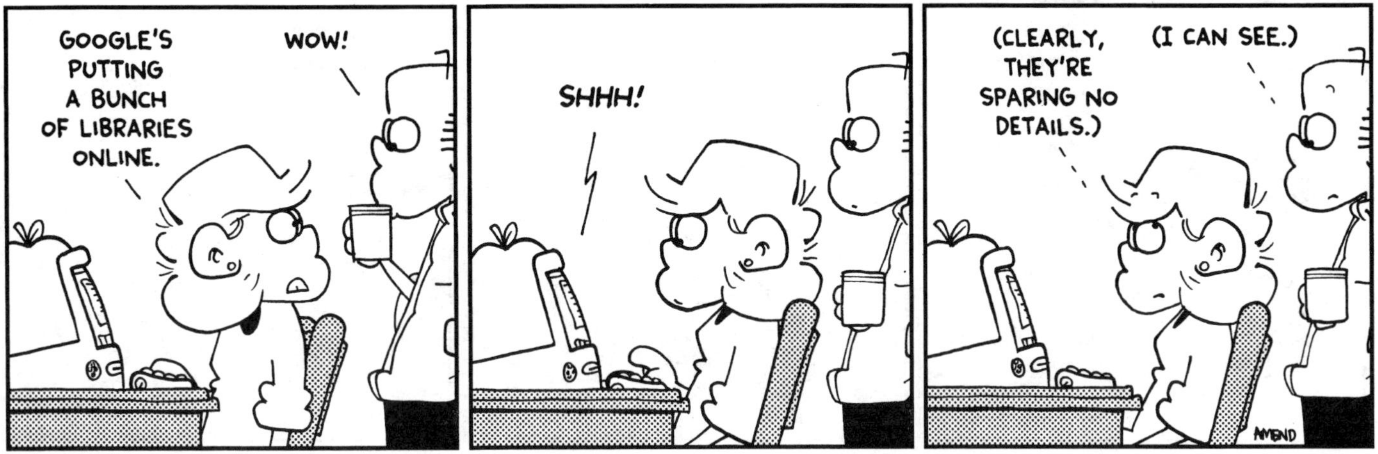
GOOGLE'S PUTTING A BUNCH OF LIBRARIES ONLINE.
WOW!
SHHH!
(CLEARLY, THEY'RE SPARING NO DETAILS.)
(I CAN SEE.)
AMEND

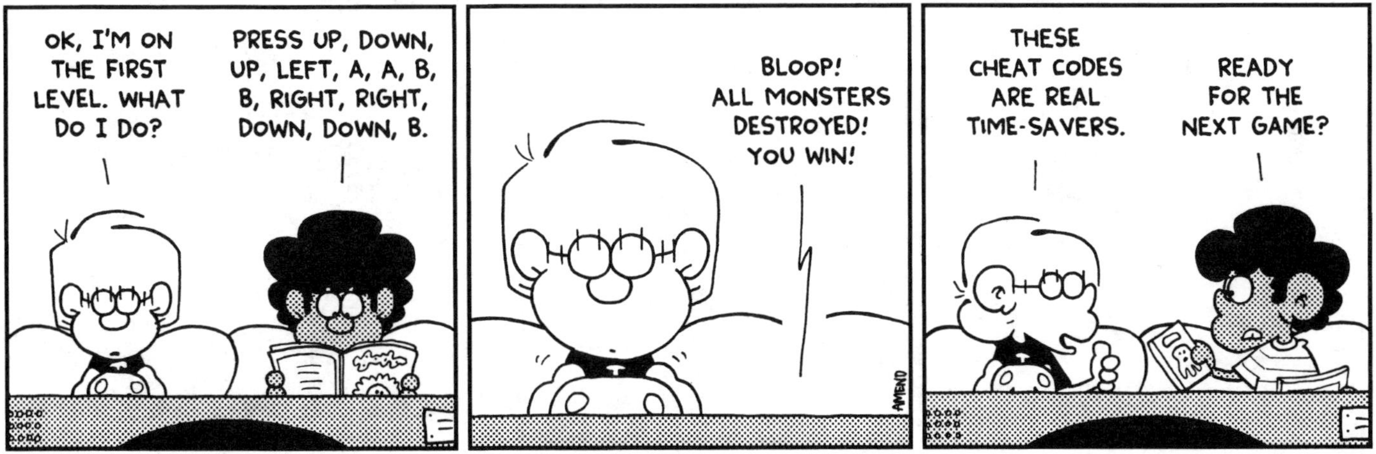
OK, I'M ON THE FIRST LEVEL. WHAT DO I DO?
PRESS UP, DOWN, UP, LEFT, A, A, B, B, RIGHT, RIGHT, DOWN, DOWN, B.
BLOOP! ALL MONSTERS DESTROYED! YOU WIN!
AMEND
THESE CHEAT CODES ARE REAL TIME-SAVERS.
READY FOR THE NEXT GAME?

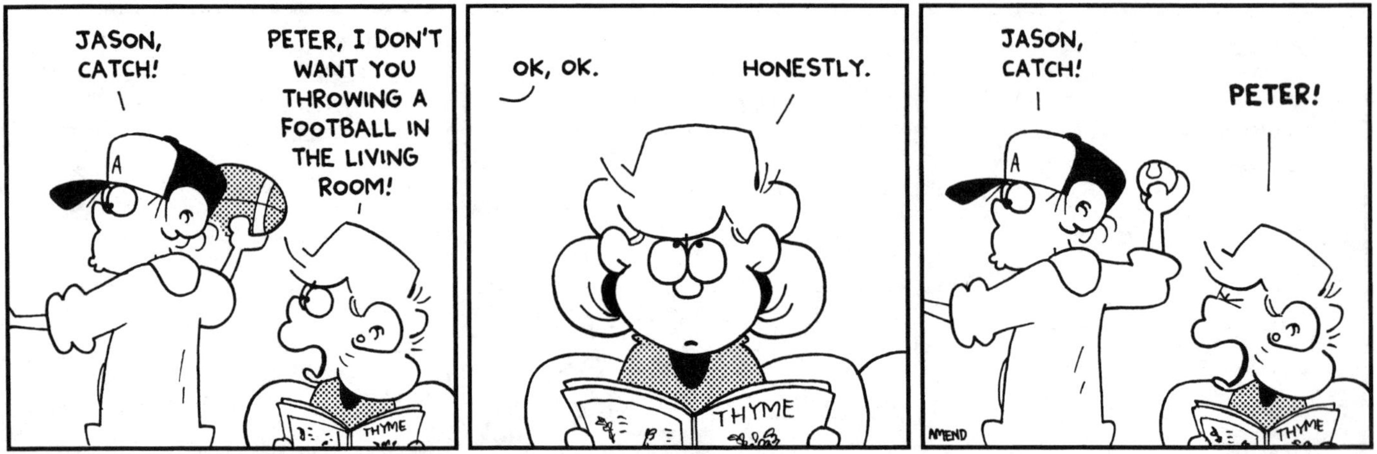
JASON, CATCH!
PETER, I DON'T WANT YOU THROWING A FOOTBALL IN THE LIVING ROOM!
THYME
OK, OK.
HONESTLY.
THYME
JASON, CATCH!
PETER!
AMEND
THYME

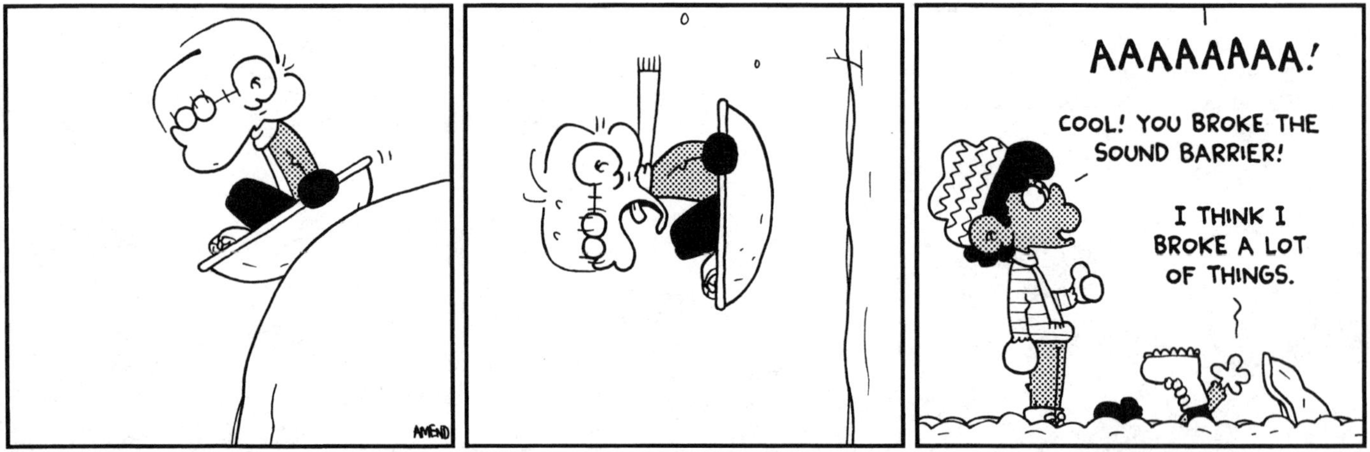
AMEND
AAAAAAAA!
COOL! YOU BROKE THE SOUND BARRIER!
I THINK I BROKE A LOT OF THINGS.

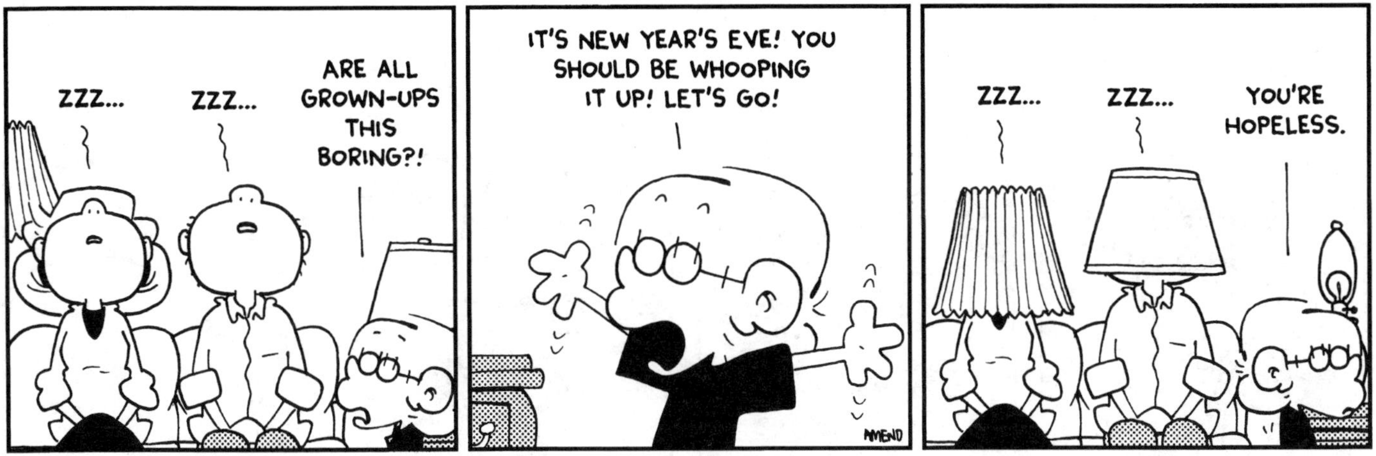
ZZZ...
ZZZ...
ARE ALL GROWN-UPS THIS BORING?!
IT'S NEW YEAR'S EVE! YOU SHOULD BE WHOOPING IT UP! LET'S GO!
AMEND
ZZZ...
ZZZ...
YOU'RE HOPELESS.

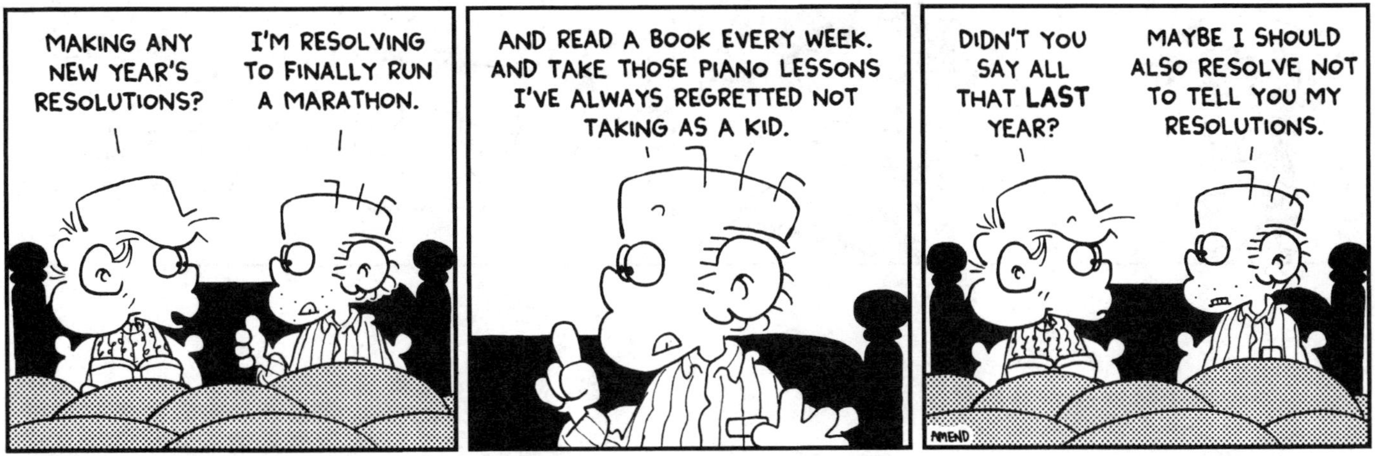
MAKING ANY NEW YEAR'S RESOLUTIONS?
I'M RESOLVING TO FINALLY RUN A MARATHON.
AND READ A BOOK EVERY WEEK. AND TAKE THOSE PIANO LESSONS I'VE ALWAYS REGRETTED NOT TAKING AS A KID.
DIDN'T YOU SAY ALL THAT **LAST** YEAR?
MAYBE I SHOULD ALSO RESOLVE NOT TO TELL YOU MY RESOLUTIONS.
AMEND

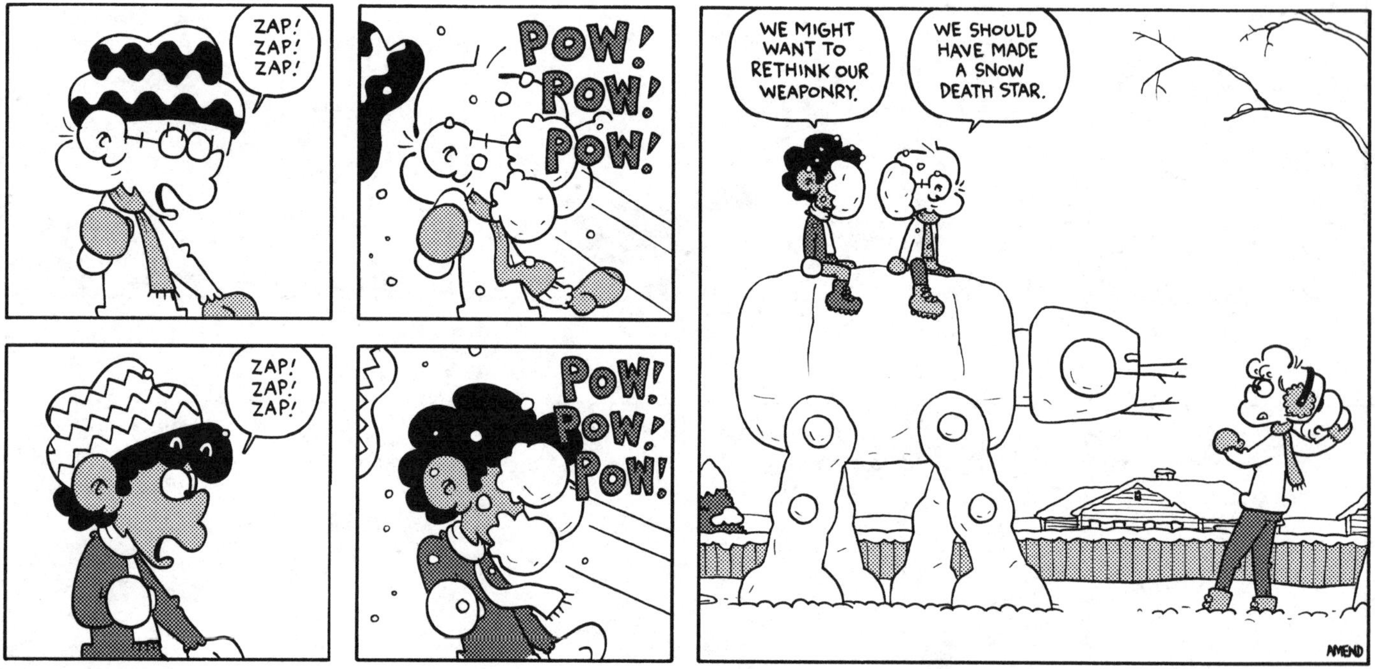
ZAP! ZAP! ZAP!
POW! POW! POW!
ZAP! ZAP! ZAP!
POW! POW! POW!
WE MIGHT WANT TO RETHINK OUR WEAPONRY.
WE SHOULD HAVE MADE A SNOW DEATH STAR.
AMEND

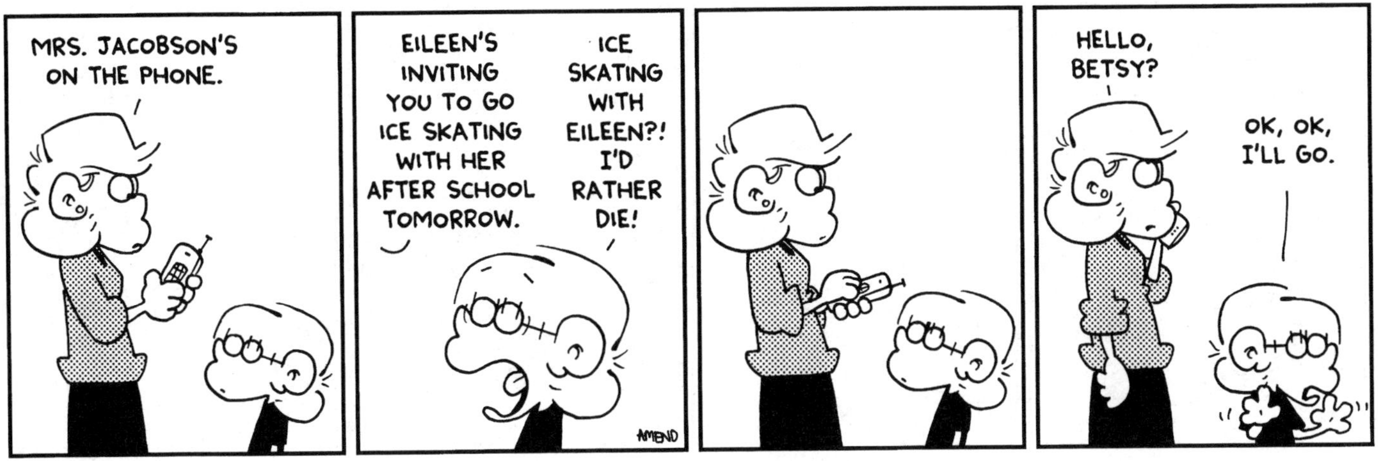
MRS. JACOBSON'S ON THE PHONE.
EILEEN'S INVITING YOU TO GO ICE SKATING WITH HER AFTER SCHOOL TOMORROW.
ICE SKATING WITH EILEEN?! I'D RATHER DIE!
AMEND
HELLO, BETSY?
OK, OK, I'LL GO.

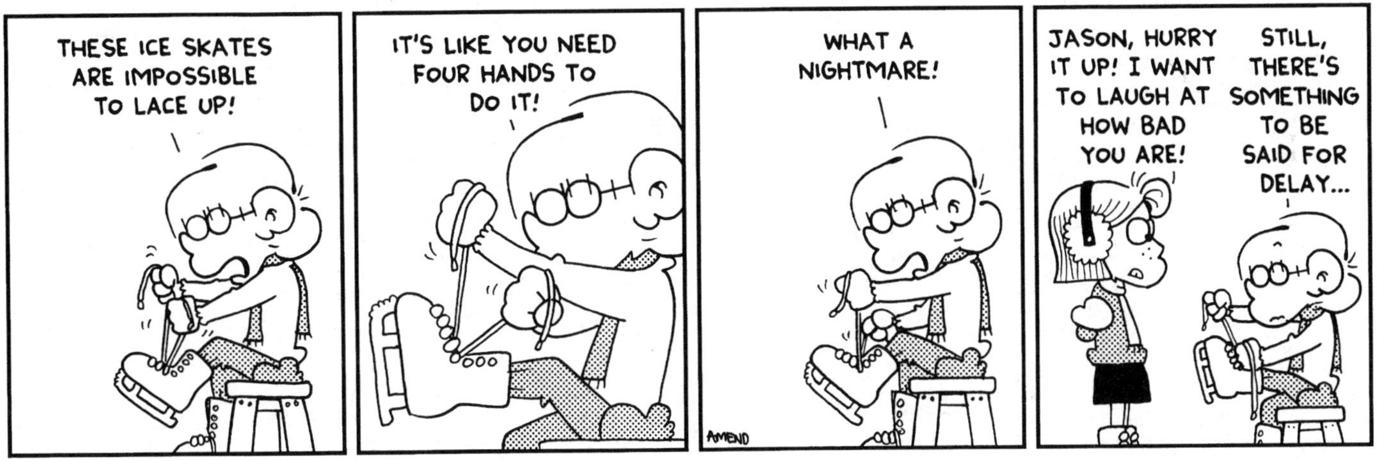
THESE ICE SKATES ARE IMPOSSIBLE TO LACE UP!
IT'S LIKE YOU NEED FOUR HANDS TO DO IT!
WHAT A NIGHTMARE!
AMEND
JASON, HURRY IT UP! I WANT TO LAUGH AT HOW BAD YOU ARE!
STILL, THERE'S SOMETHING TO BE SAID FOR DELAY...

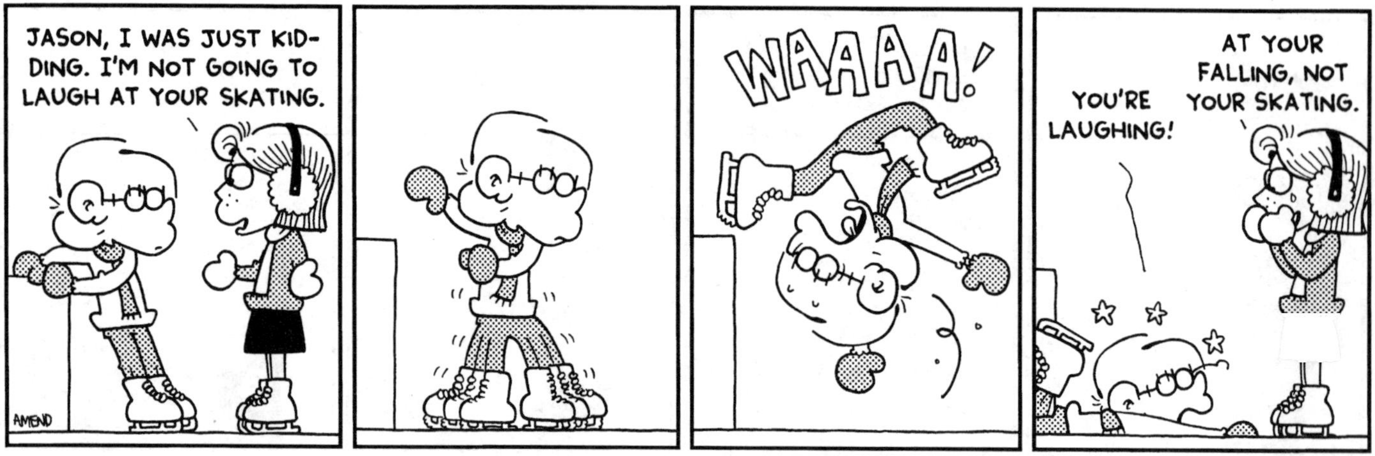
JASON, I WAS JUST KIDDING. I'M NOT GOING TO LAUGH AT YOUR SKATING.
AMEND
WAAAA!
YOU'RE LAUGHING!
AT YOUR FALLING, NOT YOUR SKATING.

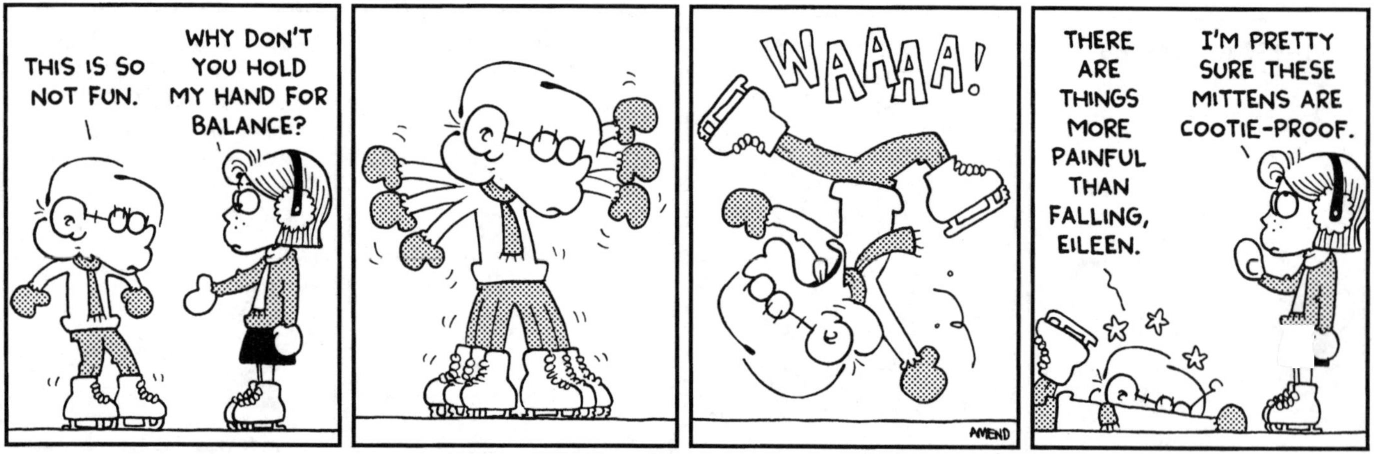
THIS IS SO NOT FUN.
WHY DON'T YOU HOLD MY HAND FOR BALANCE?
WAAAA!
AMEND
THERE ARE THINGS MORE PAINFUL THAN FALLING, EILEEN.
I'M PRETTY SURE THESE MITTENS ARE COOTIE-PROOF.

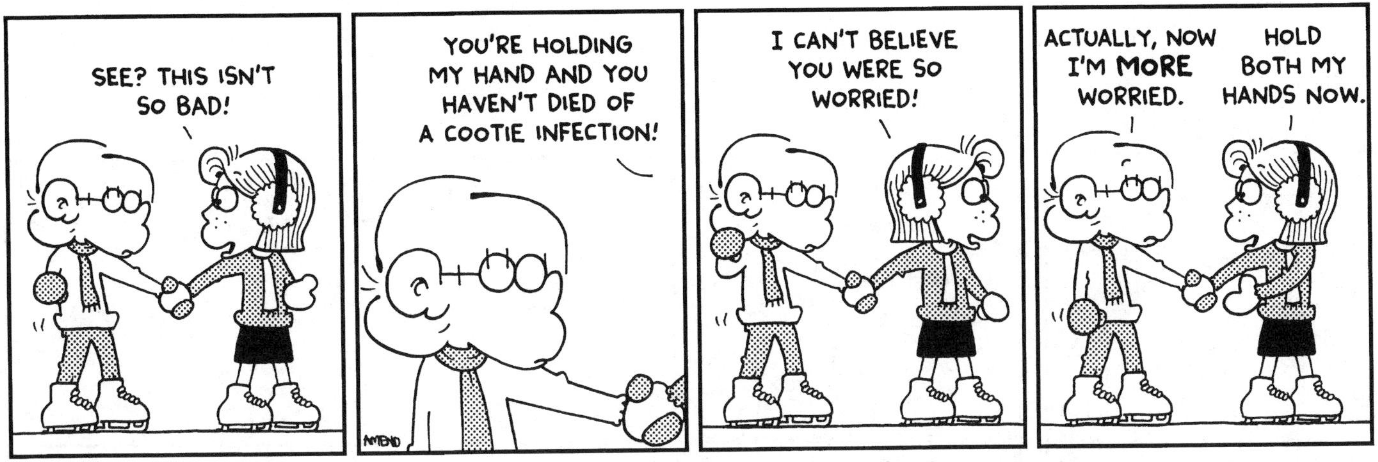
SEE? THIS ISN'T SO BAD!
YOU'RE HOLDING MY HAND AND YOU HAVEN'T DIED OF A COOTIE INFECTION!
AMEND
I CAN'T BELIEVE YOU WERE SO WORRIED!
ACTUALLY, NOW I'M **MORE** WORRIED.
HOLD BOTH MY HANDS NOW.

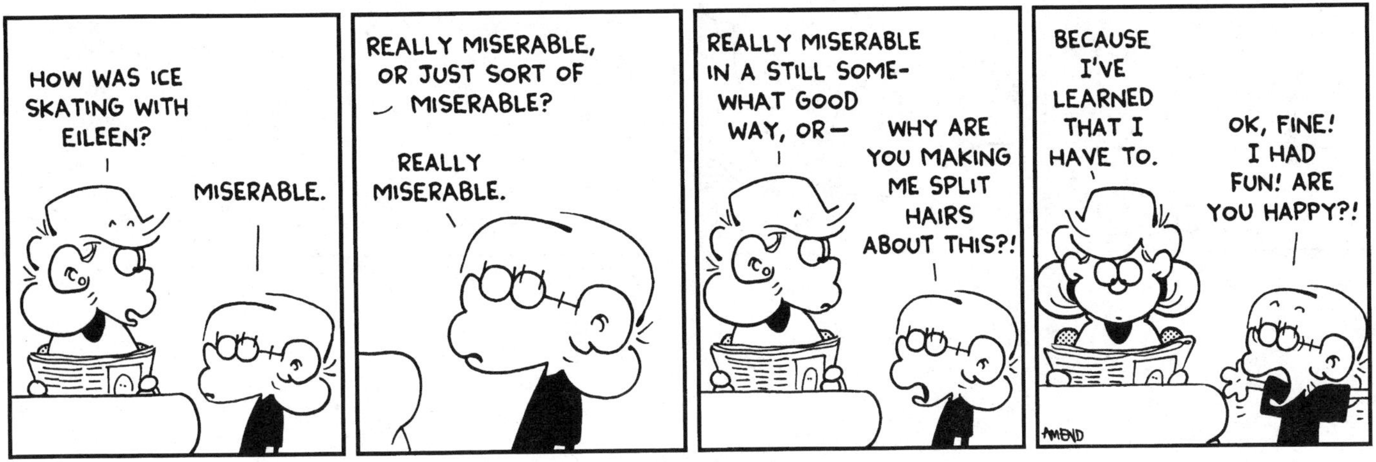
HOW WAS ICE SKATING WITH EILEEN?
MISERABLE.
REALLY MISERABLE, OR JUST SORT OF MISERABLE?
REALLY MISERABLE.
REALLY MISERABLE IN A STILL SOME-WHAT GOOD WAY, OR—
WHY ARE YOU MAKING ME SPLIT HAIRS ABOUT THIS?!
BECAUSE I'VE LEARNED THAT I HAVE TO.
OK, FINE! I HAD FUN! ARE YOU HAPPY?!
AMEND

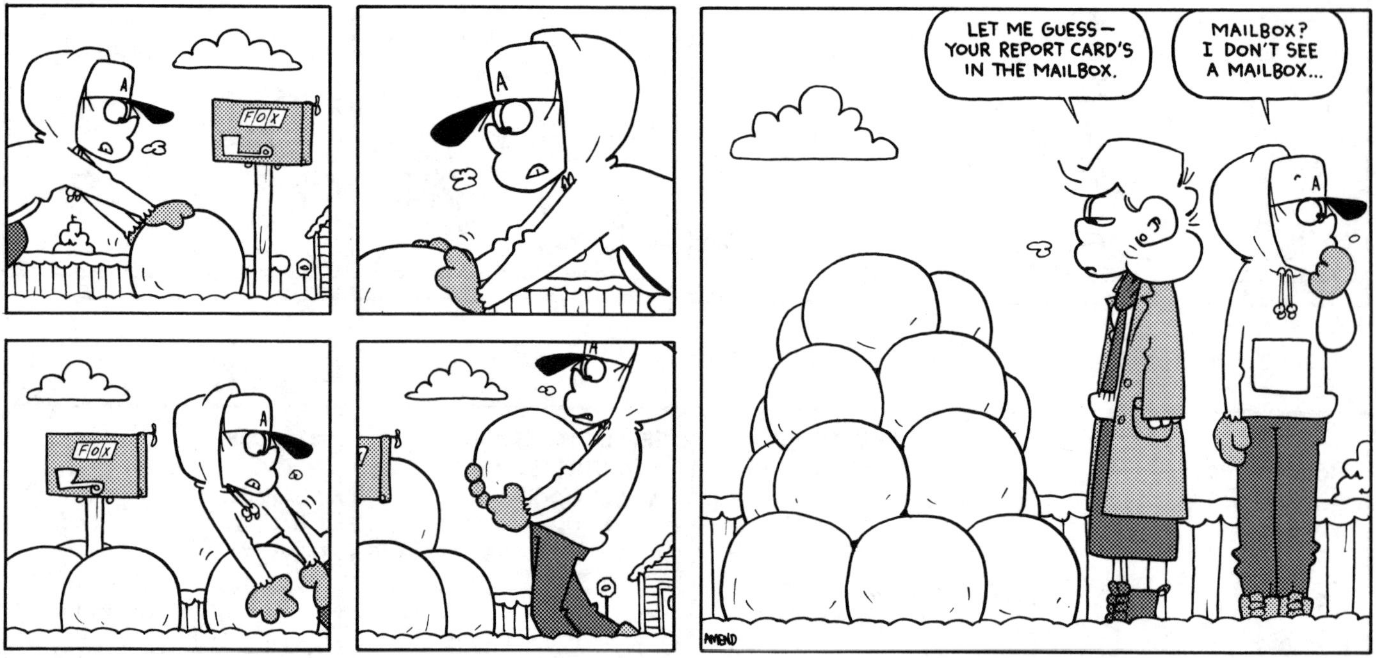
FOX
FOX
LET ME GUESS— YOUR REPORT CARD'S IN THE MAILBOX.
MAILBOX? I DON'T SEE A MAILBOX...
AMEND

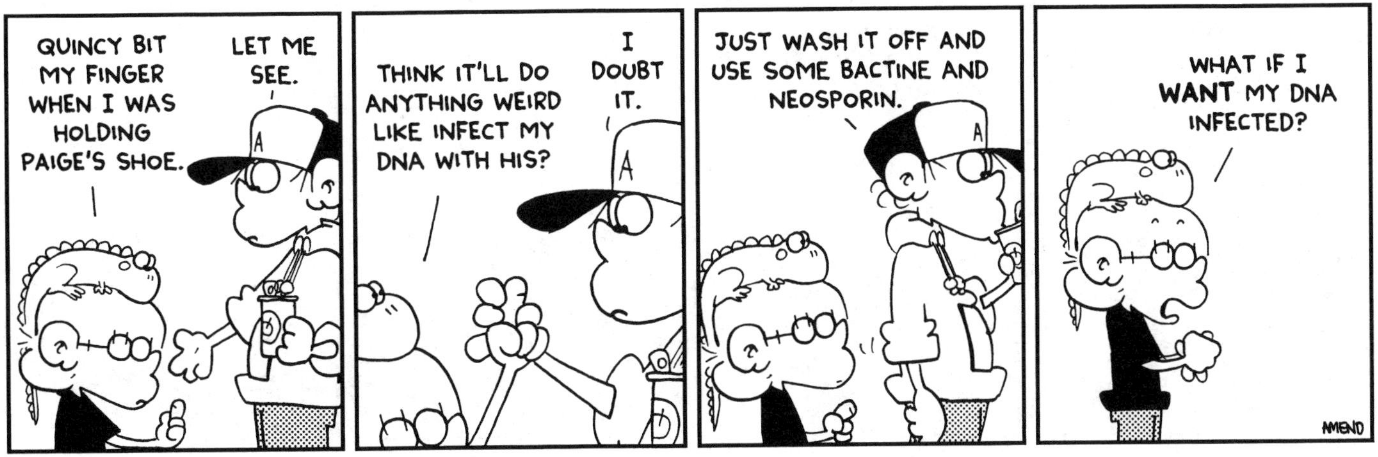
QUINCY BIT MY FINGER WHEN I WAS HOLDING PAIGE'S SHOE.
LET ME SEE.
THINK IT'LL DO ANYTHING WEIRD LIKE INFECT MY DNA WITH HIS?
I DOUBT IT.
JUST WASH IT OFF AND USE SOME BACTINE AND NEOSPORIN.
WHAT IF I **WANT** MY DNA INFECTED?
AMEND

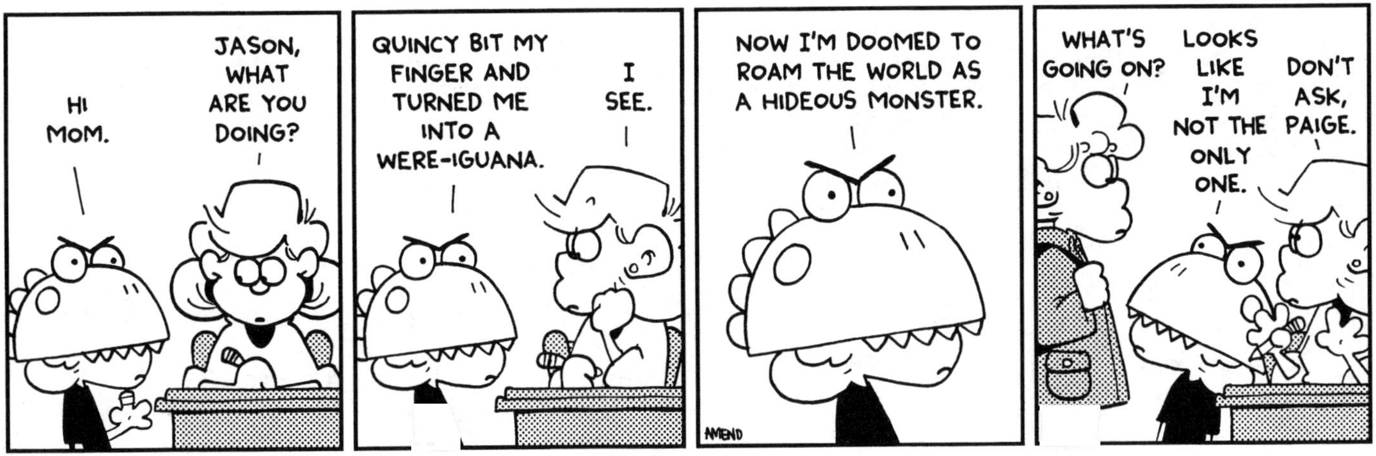
HI MOM.
JASON, WHAT ARE YOU DOING?
QUINCY BIT MY FINGER AND TURNED ME INTO A WERE-IGUANA.
I SEE.
NOW I'M DOOMED TO ROAM THE WORLD AS A HIDEOUS MONSTER.
AMEND
WHAT'S GOING ON?
LOOKS LIKE I'M NOT THE ONLY ONE.
DON'T ASK, PAIGE.

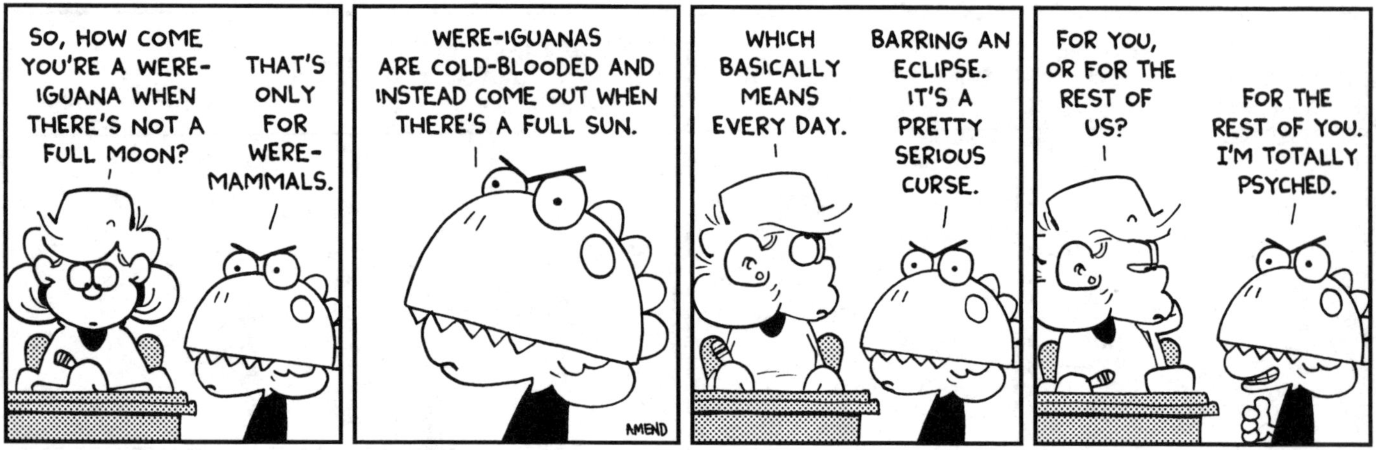
SO, HOW COME YOU'RE A WERE-IGUANA WHEN THERE'S NOT A FULL MOON?
THAT'S ONLY FOR WERE-MAMMALS.
WERE-IGUANAS ARE COLD-BLOODED AND INSTEAD COME OUT WHEN THERE'S A FULL SUN.
AMEND
WHICH BASICALLY MEANS EVERY DAY.
BARRING AN ECLIPSE. IT'S A PRETTY SERIOUS CURSE.
FOR YOU, OR FOR THE REST OF US?
FOR THE REST OF YOU. I'M TOTALLY PSYCHED.

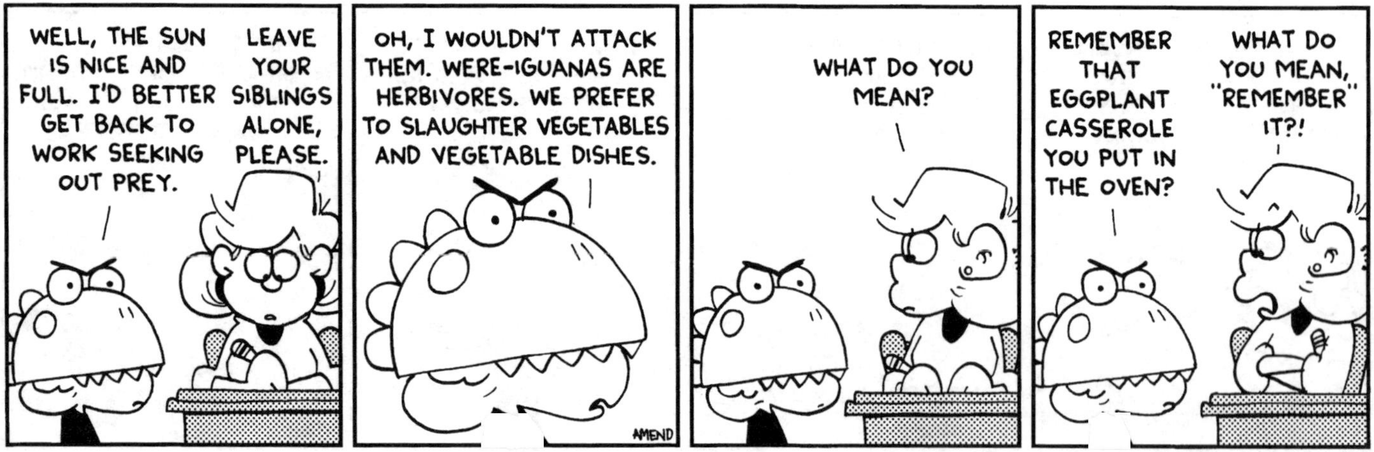
WELL, THE SUN IS NICE AND FULL. I'D BETTER GET BACK TO WORK SEEKING OUT PREY.
LEAVE YOUR SIBLINGS ALONE, PLEASE.
OH, I WOULDN'T ATTACK THEM. WERE-IGUANAS ARE HERBIVORES. WE PREFER TO SLAUGHTER VEGETABLES AND VEGETABLE DISHES.
AMEND
WHAT DO YOU MEAN?
REMEMBER THAT EGGPLANT CASSEROLE YOU PUT IN THE OVEN?
WHAT DO YOU MEAN, "REMEMBER IT?!

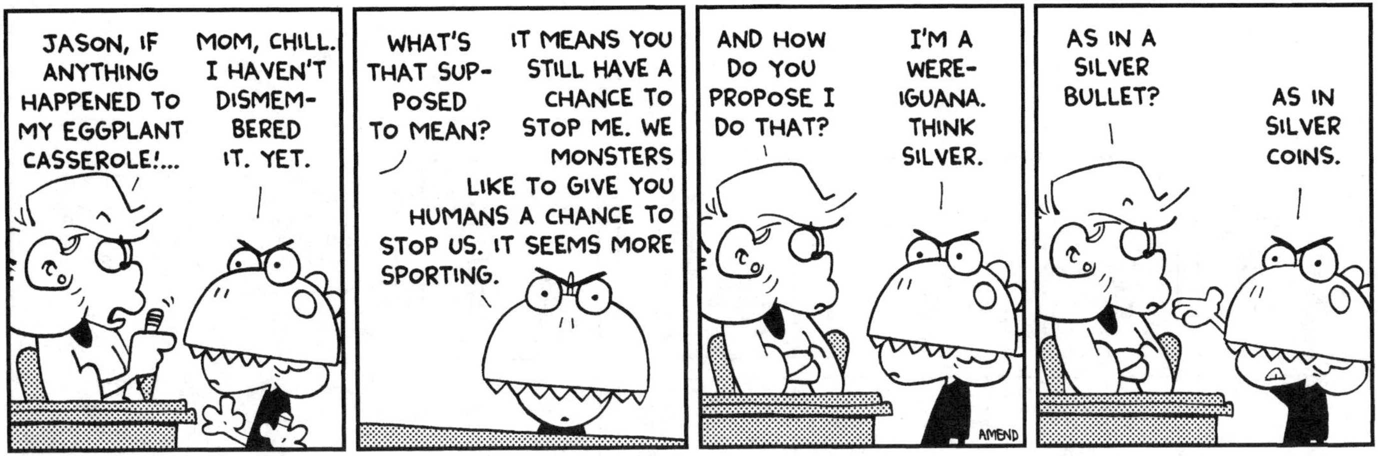
JASON, IF ANYTHING HAPPENED TO MY EGGPLANT CASSEROLE!...
MOM, CHILL. I HAVEN'T DISMEMBERED IT. YET.
WHAT'S THAT SUPPOSED TO MEAN?
IT MEANS YOU STILL HAVE A CHANCE TO STOP ME. WE MONSTERS LIKE TO GIVE YOU HUMANS A CHANCE TO STOP US. IT SEEMS MORE SPORTING.
AND HOW DO YOU PROPOSE I DO THAT?
I'M A WERE-IGUANA. THINK SILVER.
AS IN A SILVER BULLET?
AS IN SILVER COINS.
AMEND

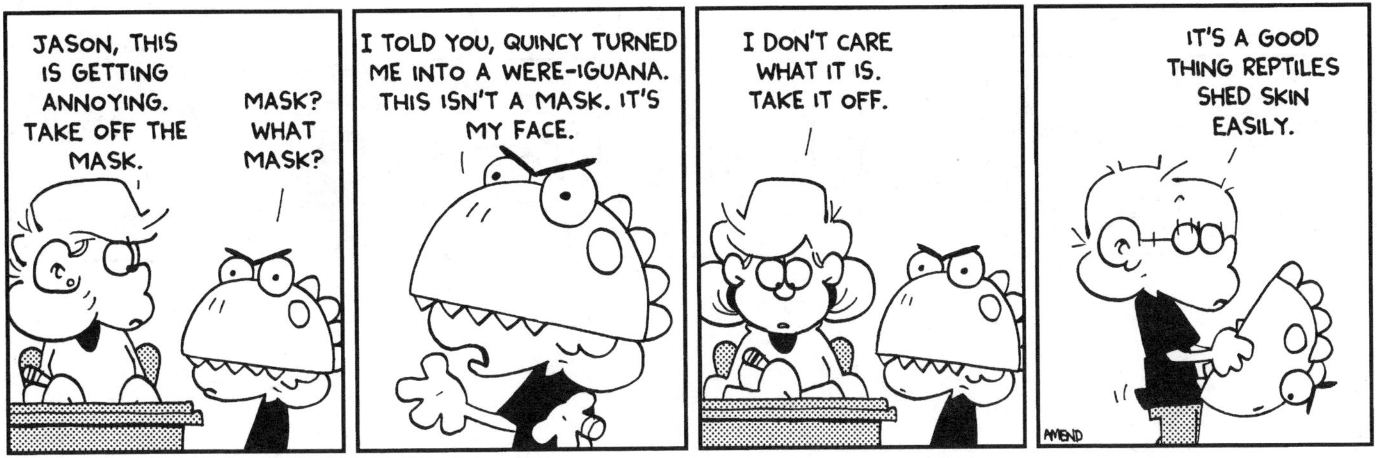
JASON, THIS IS GETTING ANNOYING. TAKE OFF THE MASK.
MASK? WHAT MASK?
I TOLD YOU, QUINCY TURNED ME INTO A WERE-IGUANA. THIS ISN'T A MASK. IT'S MY FACE.
I DON'T CARE WHAT IT IS. TAKE IT OFF.
IT'S A GOOD THING REPTILES SHED SKIN EASILY.
AMEND

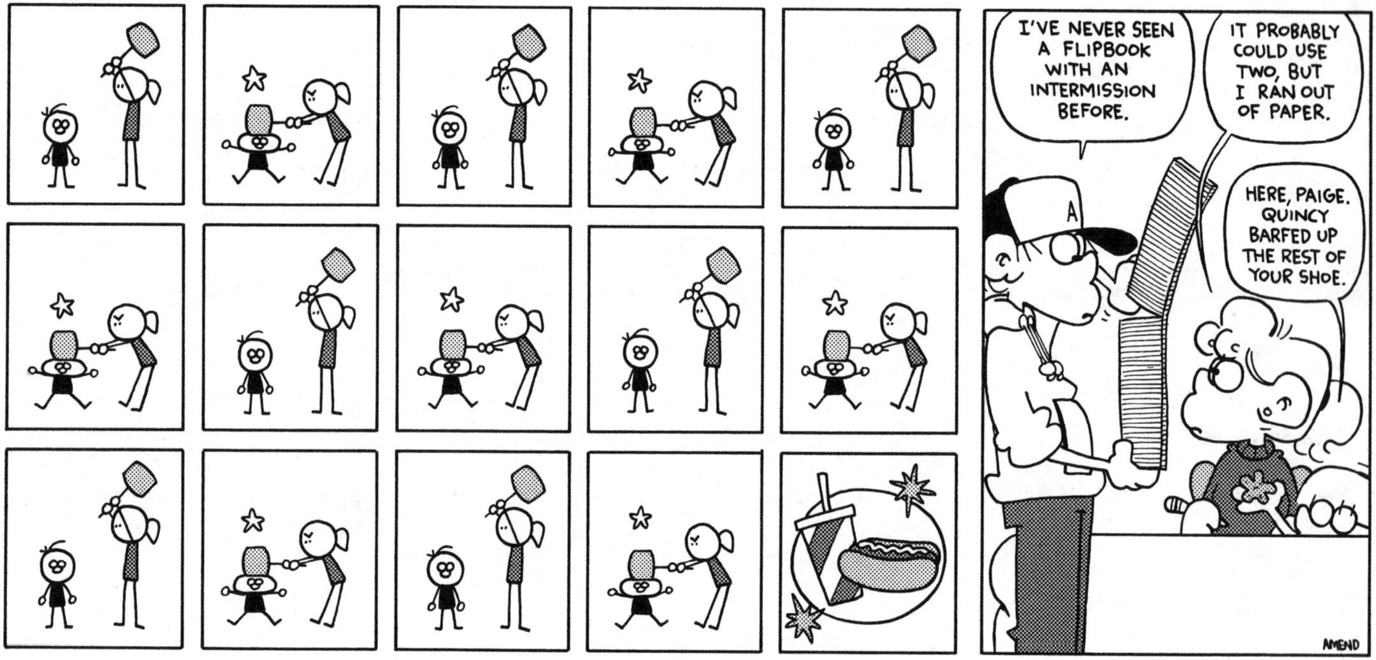
I'VE NEVER SEEN A FLIPBOOK WITH AN INTERMISSION BEFORE.
IT PROBABLY COULD USE TWO, BUT I RAN OUT OF PAPER.
HERE, PAIGE. QUINCY BARFED UP THE REST OF YOUR SHOE.
AMEND

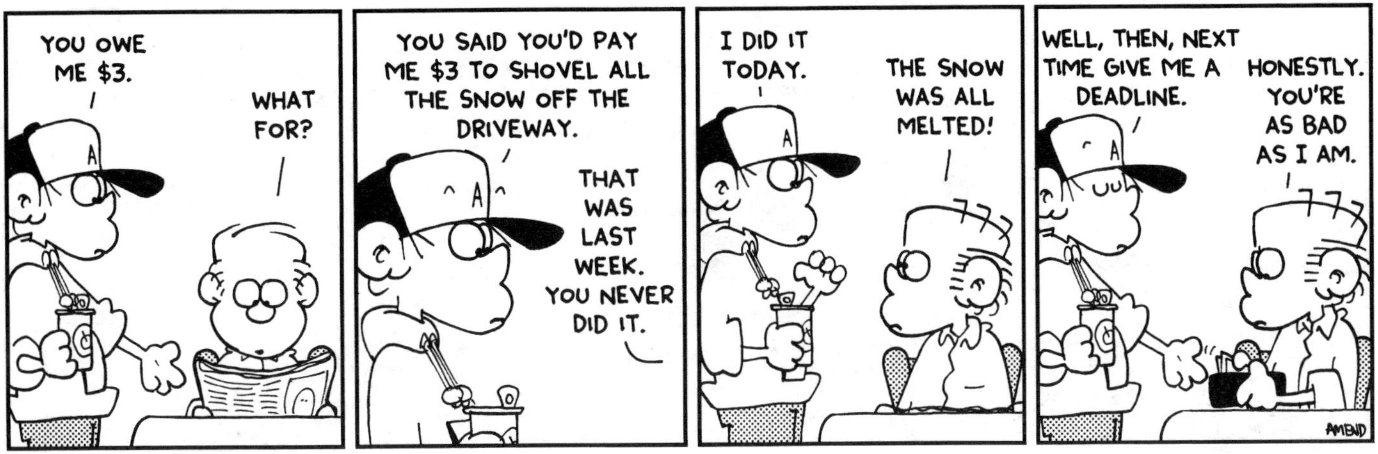
YOU OWE ME $3.
WHAT FOR?
YOU SAID YOU'D PAY ME $3 TO SHOVEL ALL THE SNOW OFF THE DRIVEWAY.
THAT WAS LAST WEEK. YOU NEVER DID IT.
I DID IT TODAY.
THE SNOW WAS ALL MELTED!
WELL, THEN, NEXT TIME GIVE ME A DEADLINE.
HONESTLY. YOU'RE AS BAD AS I AM.
AMEND

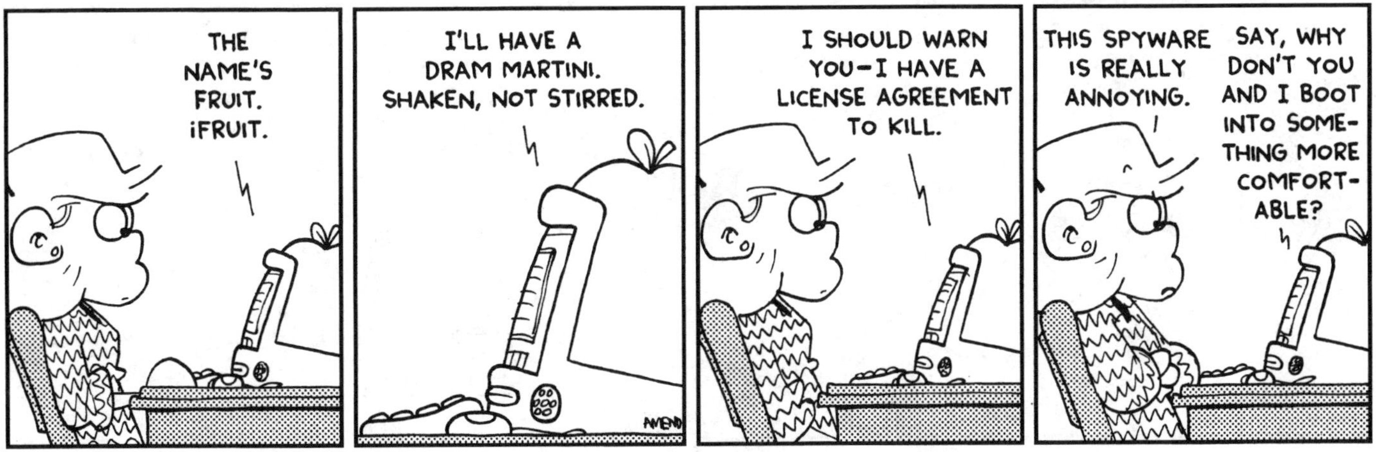
THE NAME'S FRUIT. iFRUIT.
I'LL HAVE A DRAM MARTINI. SHAKEN, NOT STIRRED.
I SHOULD WARN YOU—I HAVE A LICENSE AGREEMENT TO KILL.
THIS SPYWARE IS REALLY ANNOYING.
SAY, WHY DON'T YOU AND I BOOT INTO SOMETHING MORE COMFORTABLE?
AMEND

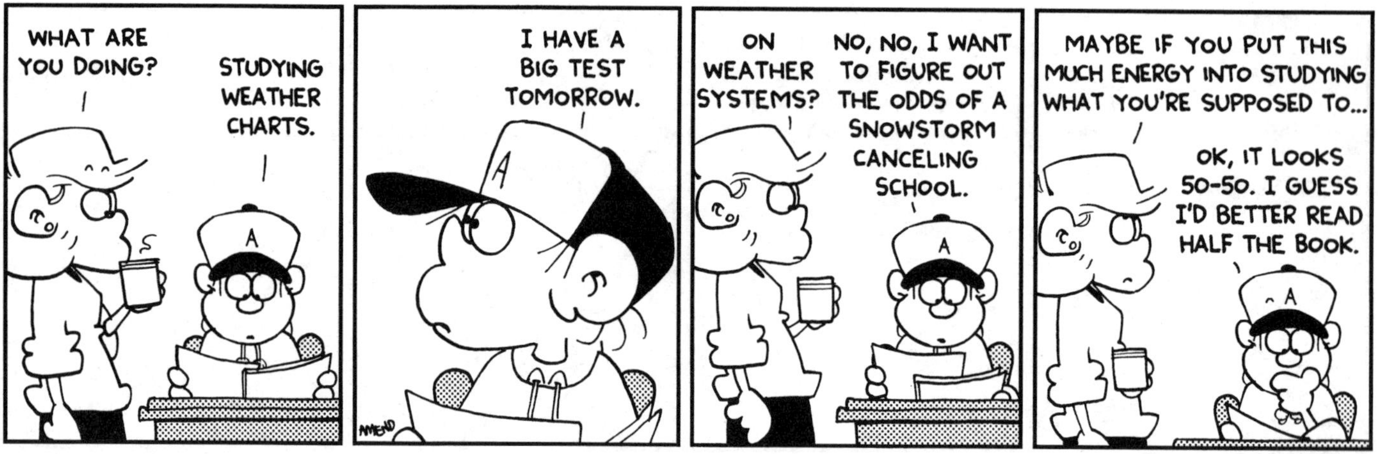
WHAT ARE YOU DOING?
STUDYING WEATHER CHARTS.
I HAVE A BIG TEST TOMORROW.
AMEND
ON WEATHER SYSTEMS?
NO, NO, I WANT TO FIGURE OUT THE ODDS OF A SNOWSTORM CANCELING SCHOOL.
MAYBE IF YOU PUT THIS MUCH ENERGY INTO STUDYING WHAT YOU'RE SUPPOSED TO...
OK, IT LOOKS 50-50. I GUESS I'D BETTER READ HALF THE BOOK.

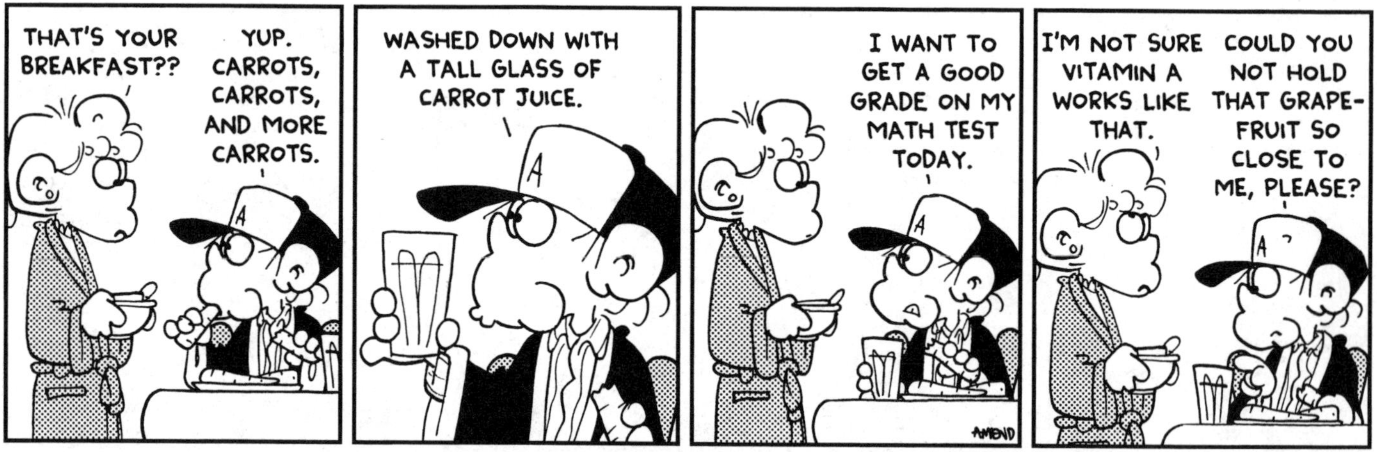
THAT'S YOUR BREAKFAST??
YUP. CARROTS, CARROTS, AND MORE CARROTS.
WASHED DOWN WITH A TALL GLASS OF CARROT JUICE.
I WANT TO GET A GOOD GRADE ON MY MATH TEST TODAY.
AMEND
I'M NOT SURE VITAMIN A WORKS LIKE THAT.
COULD YOU NOT HOLD THAT GRAPE-FRUIT SO CLOSE TO ME, PLEASE?

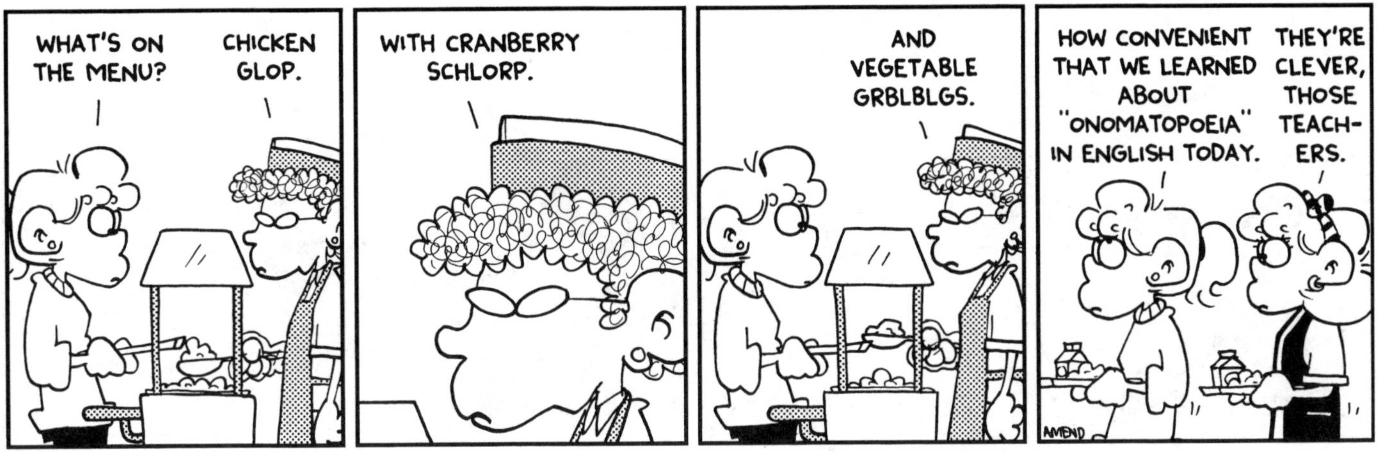
WHAT'S ON THE MENU?
CHICKEN GLOP.
WITH CRANBERRY SCHLORP.
AND VEGETABLE GRBLBLGS.
HOW CONVENIENT THAT WE LEARNED ABOUT "ONOMATOPOEIA" IN ENGLISH TODAY.
THEY'RE CLEVER, THOSE TEACH- ERS.
AMEND

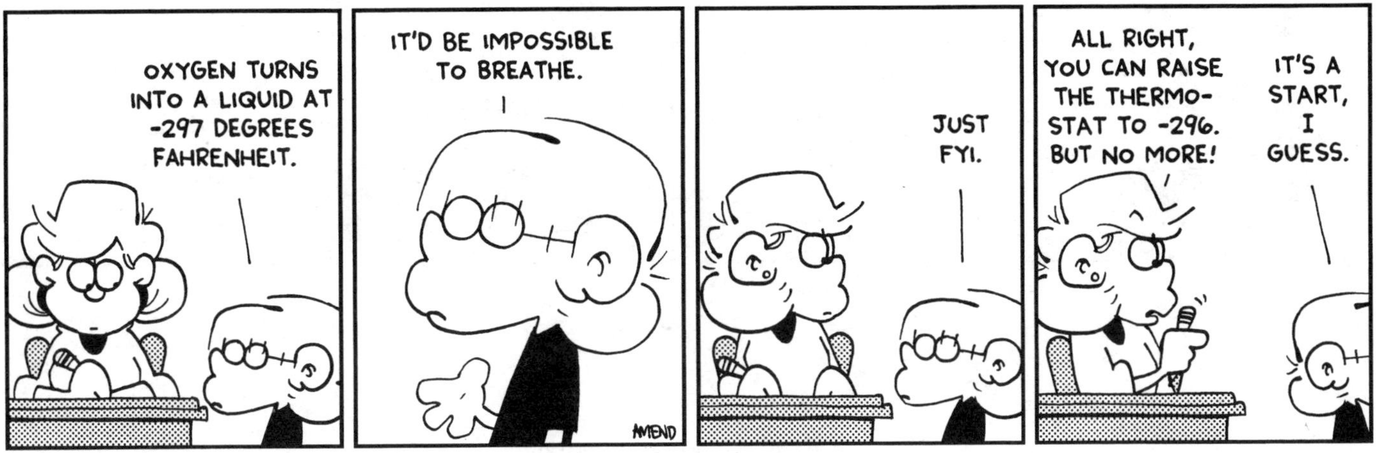
OXYGEN TURNS INTO A LIQUID AT -297 DEGREES FAHRENHEIT.
IT'D BE IMPOSSIBLE TO BREATHE.
AMEND
JUST FYI.
ALL RIGHT, YOU CAN RAISE THE THERMO- STAT TO -296. BUT NO MORE!
IT'S A START, I GUESS.

THOSE NEW TIRES YOU GOT ARE AWFUL!
THEY ARE?
I WAS DRIVING WITH STEVE THROUGH A SNOWY PARKING LOT AND IT WAS A JOKE!
YOU WOULDN'T BELIEVE HOW HORRIBLY I WAS SPINNING AND FISHTAILING!
I GUESS I'LL CALL THE SHOP...
WITH THE OLD TIRES, I WAS **GREAT** AT SPINNING AND FISHTAILING!
THIS IS WHERE I PATIENTLY WAIT FOR YOU TO SAY, "JUST KIDDING, MOM."

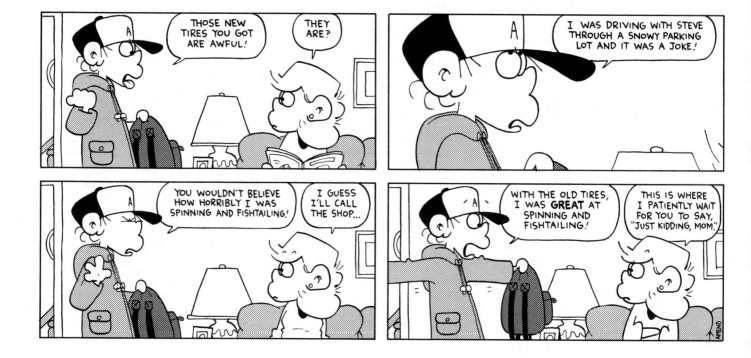

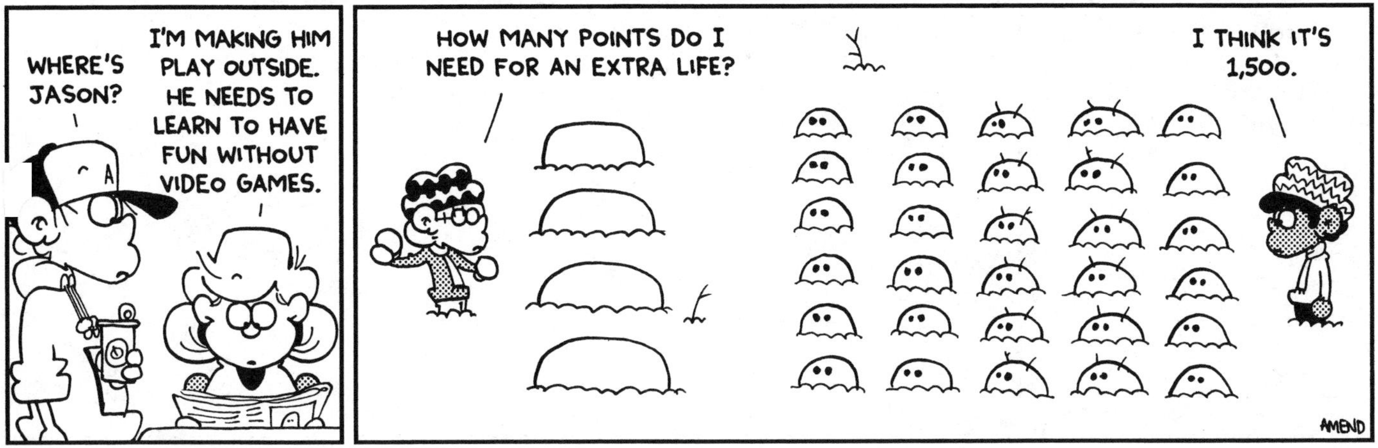
WHERE'S JASON?
I'M MAKING HIM PLAY OUTSIDE. HE NEEDS TO LEARN TO HAVE FUN WITHOUT VIDEO GAMES.
HOW MANY POINTS DO I NEED FOR AN EXTRA LIFE?
I THINK IT'S 1,500.
AMEND

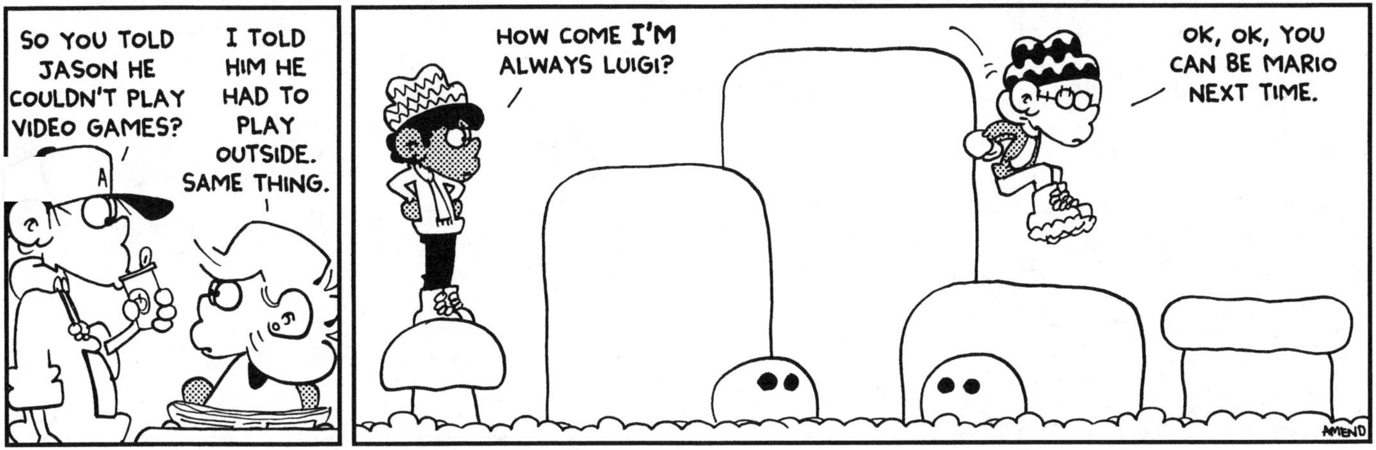
SO YOU TOLD JASON HE COULDN'T PLAY VIDEO GAMES?
I TOLD HIM HE HAD TO PLAY OUTSIDE. SAME THING.
HOW COME I'M ALWAYS LUIGI?
OK, OK, YOU CAN BE MARIO NEXT TIME.
AMEND

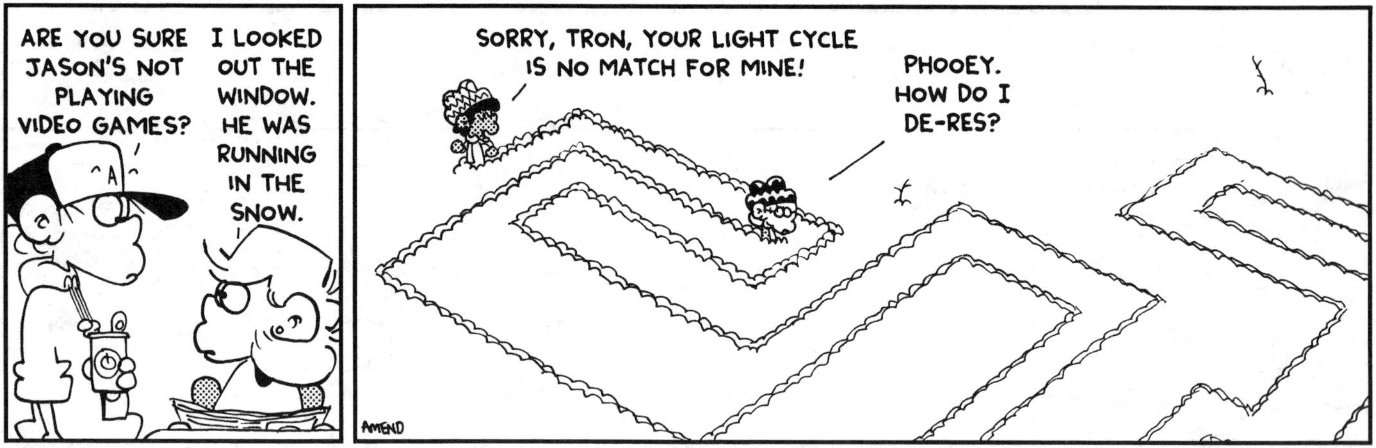
ARE YOU SURE JASON'S NOT PLAYING VIDEO GAMES?
I LOOKED OUT THE WINDOW. HE WAS RUNNING IN THE SNOW.
SORRY, TRON, YOUR LIGHT CYCLE IS NO MATCH FOR MINE!
PHOOEY. HOW DO I DE-RES?
AMEND

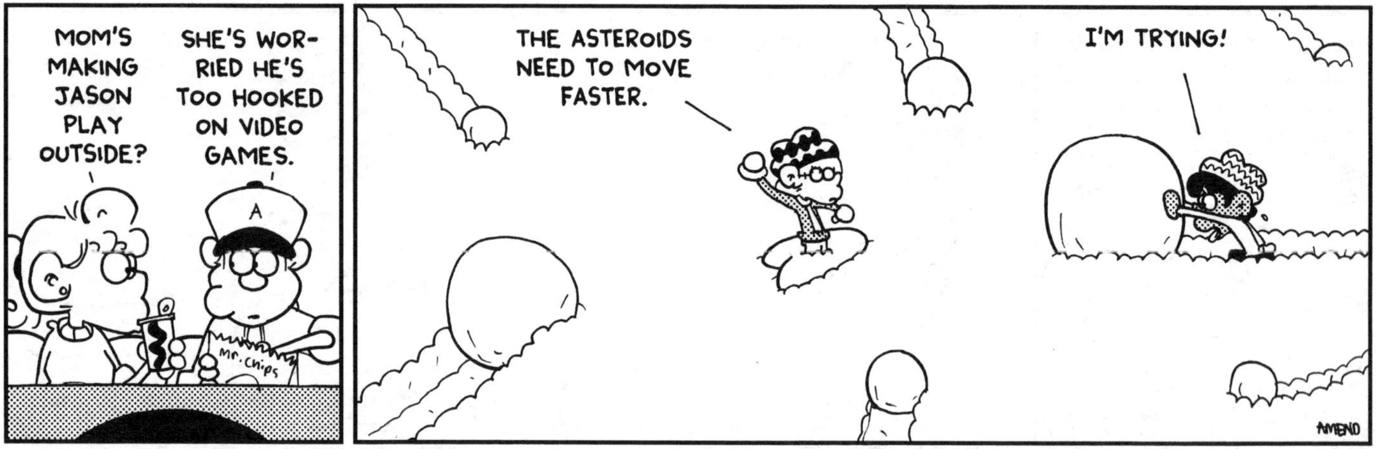
MOM'S MAKING JASON PLAY OUTSIDE?
SHE'S WORRIED HE'S TOO HOOKED ON VIDEO GAMES.
Mr. Chips
THE ASTEROIDS NEED TO MOVE FASTER.
I'M TRYING!
AMEND

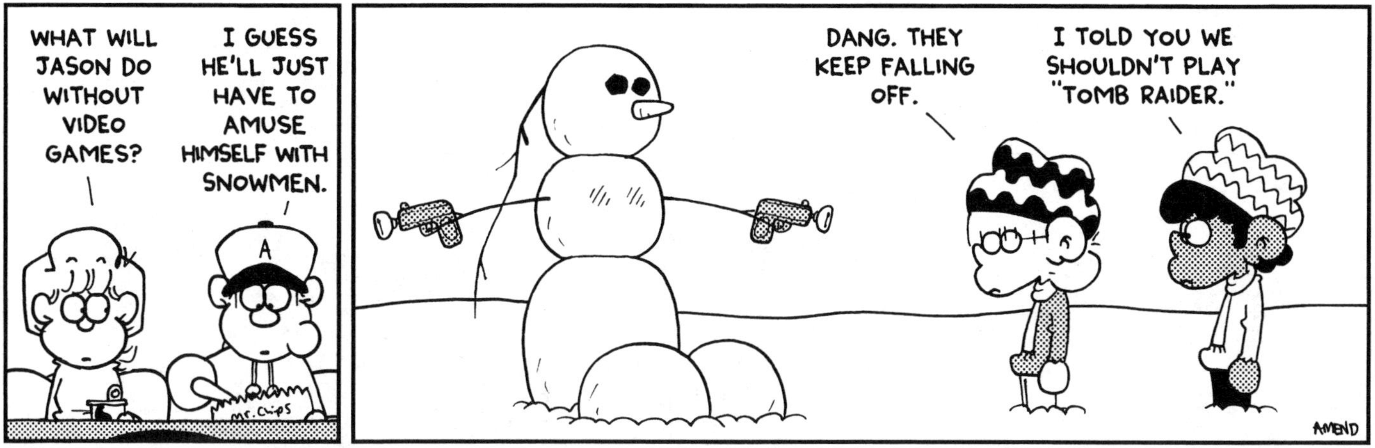
WHAT WILL JASON DO WITHOUT VIDEO GAMES?
I GUESS HE'LL JUST HAVE TO AMUSE HIMSELF WITH SNOWMEN.
mr. chips
DANG. THEY KEEP FALLING OFF.
I TOLD YOU WE SHOULDN'T PLAY "TOMB RAIDER."
AMEND

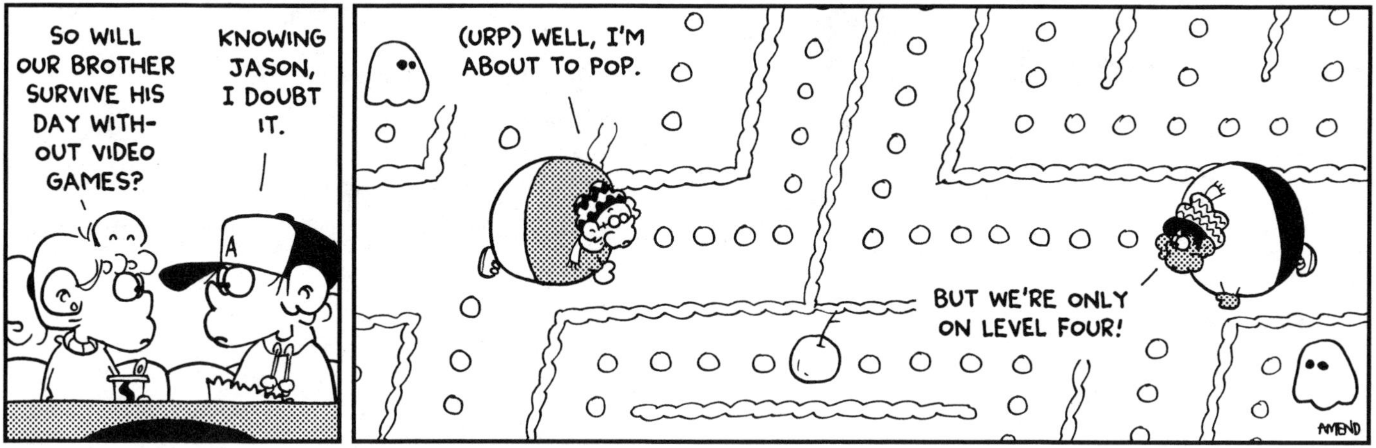
SO WILL OUR BROTHER SURVIVE HIS DAY WITH- OUT VIDEO GAMES?
KNOWING JASON, I DOUBT IT.
(URP) WELL, I'M ABOUT TO POP.
BUT WE'RE ONLY ON LEVEL FOUR!
AMEND

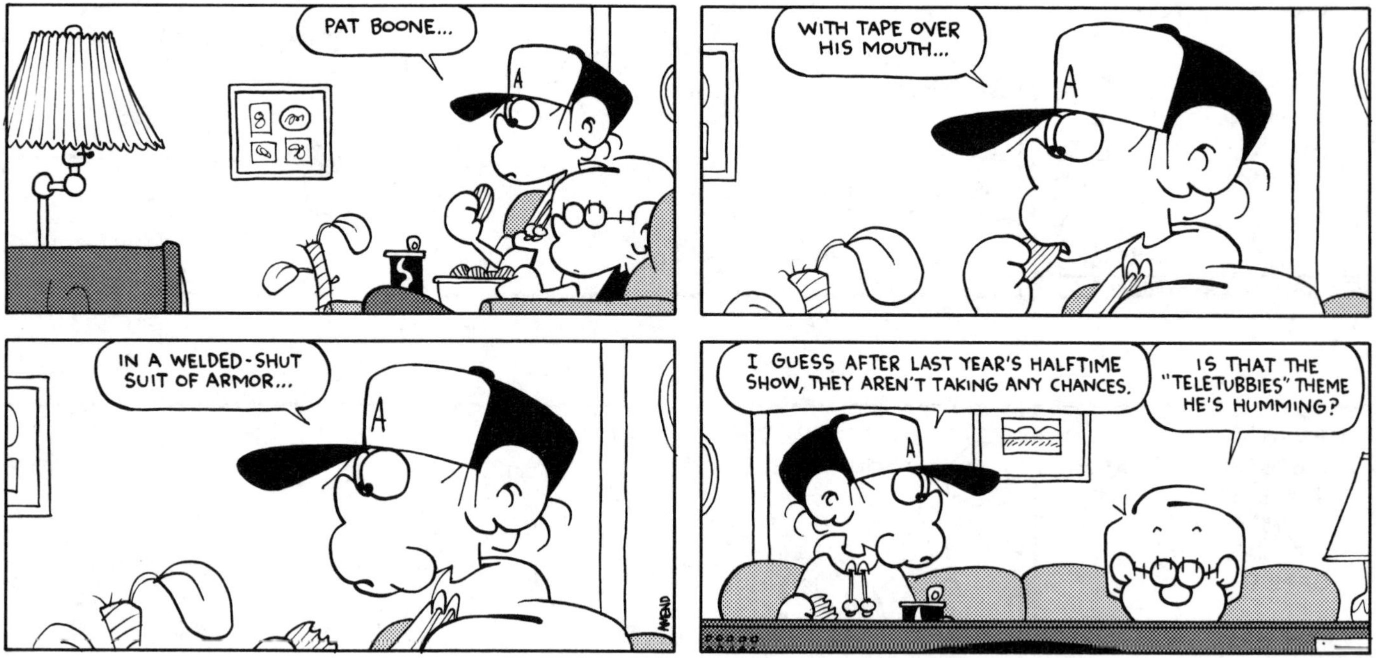
PAT BOONE...
WITH TAPE OVER HIS MOUTH...
IN A WELDED-SHUT SUIT OF ARMOR...
I GUESS AFTER LAST YEAR'S HALFTIME SHOW, THEY AREN'T TAKING ANY CHANCES.
IS THAT THE "TELETUBBIES" THEME HE'S HUMMING?

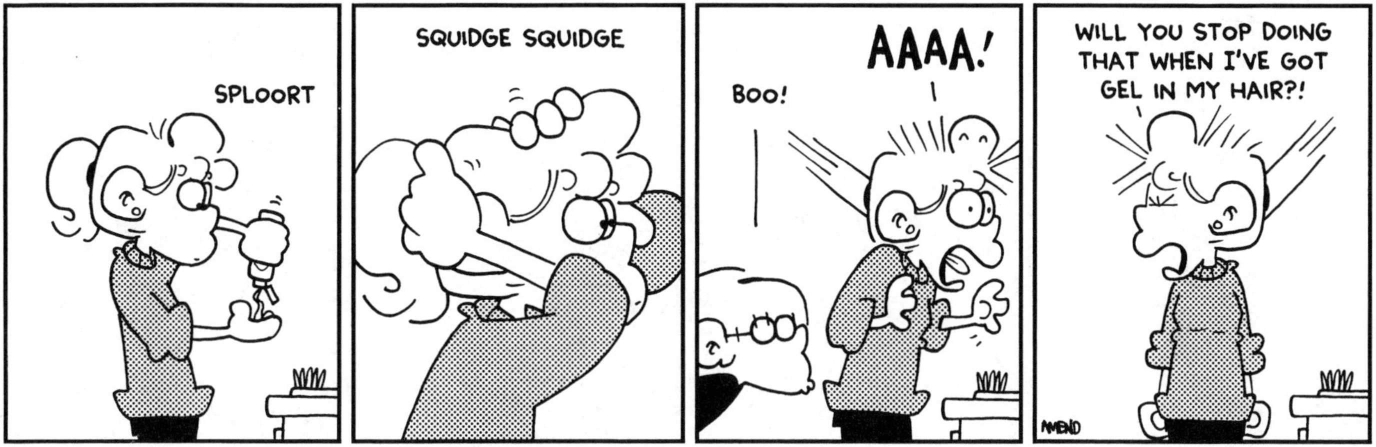
SPLOORT
SQUIDGE SQUIDGE
BOO!
AAAA!
WILL YOU STOP DOING THAT WHEN I'VE GOT GEL IN MY HAIR?!
AMEND

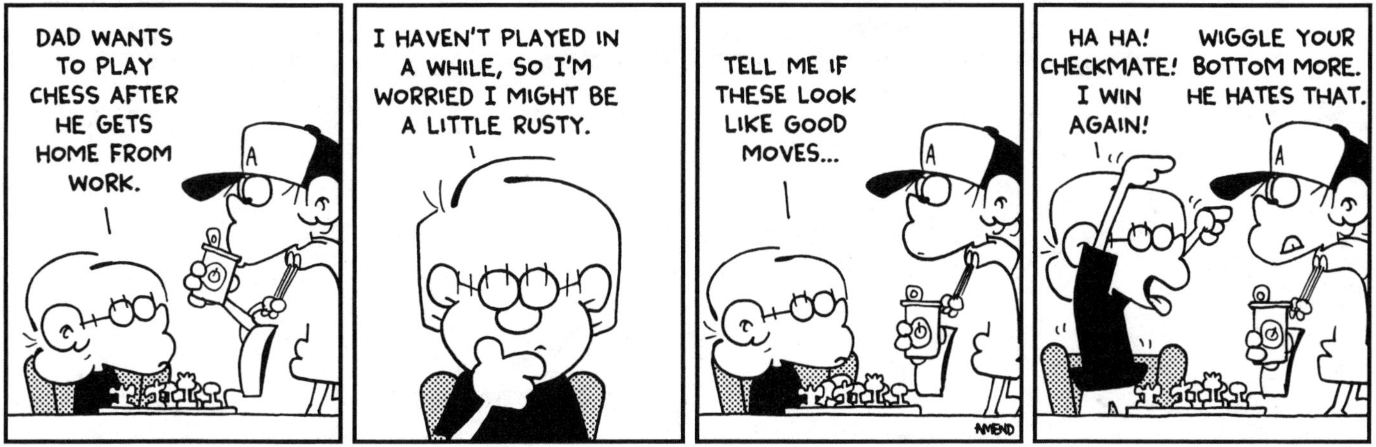
DAD WANTS TO PLAY CHESS AFTER HE GETS HOME FROM WORK.
I HAVEN'T PLAYED IN A WHILE, SO I'M WORRIED I MIGHT BE A LITTLE RUSTY.
TELL ME IF THESE LOOK LIKE GOOD MOVES...
AMEND
HA HA! CHECKMATE! I WIN AGAIN!
WIGGLE YOUR BOTTOM MORE. HE HATES THAT.

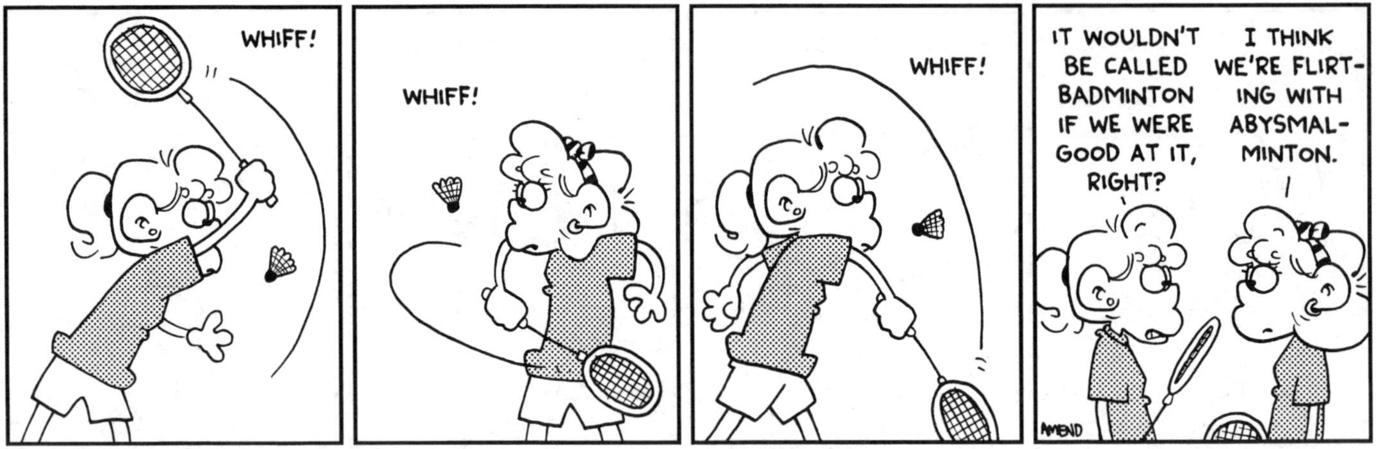
WHIFF!
WHIFF!
WHIFF!
IT WOULDN'T BE CALLED BADMINTON IF WE WERE GOOD AT IT, RIGHT?
I THINK WE'RE FLIRTING WITH ABYSMAL-MINTON.
AMEND

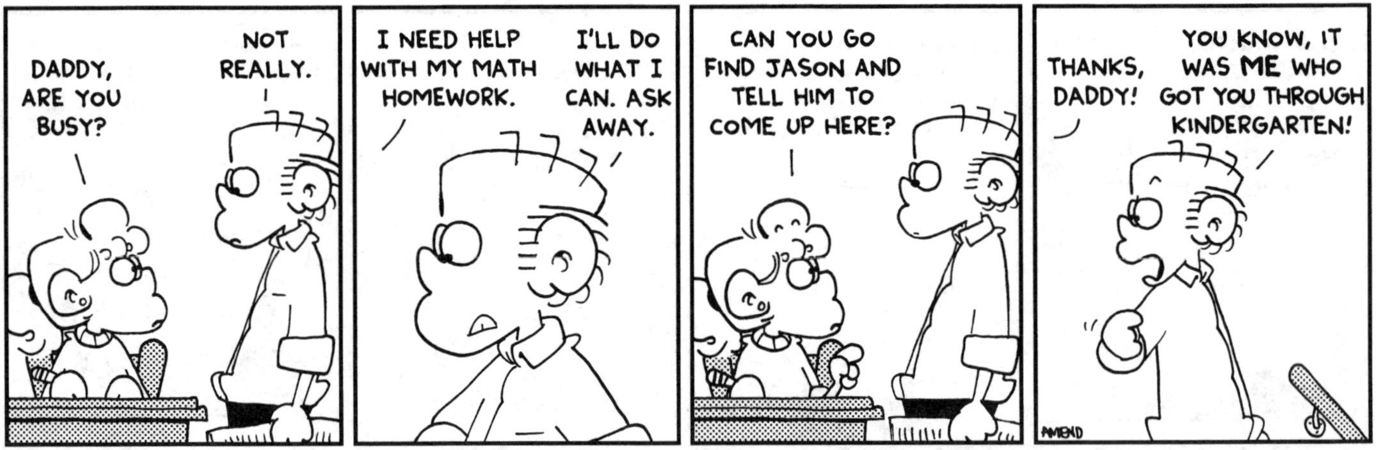
DADDY, ARE YOU BUSY?
NOT REALLY.
I NEED HELP WITH MY MATH HOMEWORK.
I'LL DO WHAT I CAN. ASK AWAY.
CAN YOU GO FIND JASON AND TELL HIM TO COME UP HERE?
THANKS, DADDY!
YOU KNOW, IT WAS ME WHO GOT YOU THROUGH KINDERGARTEN!
AMEND

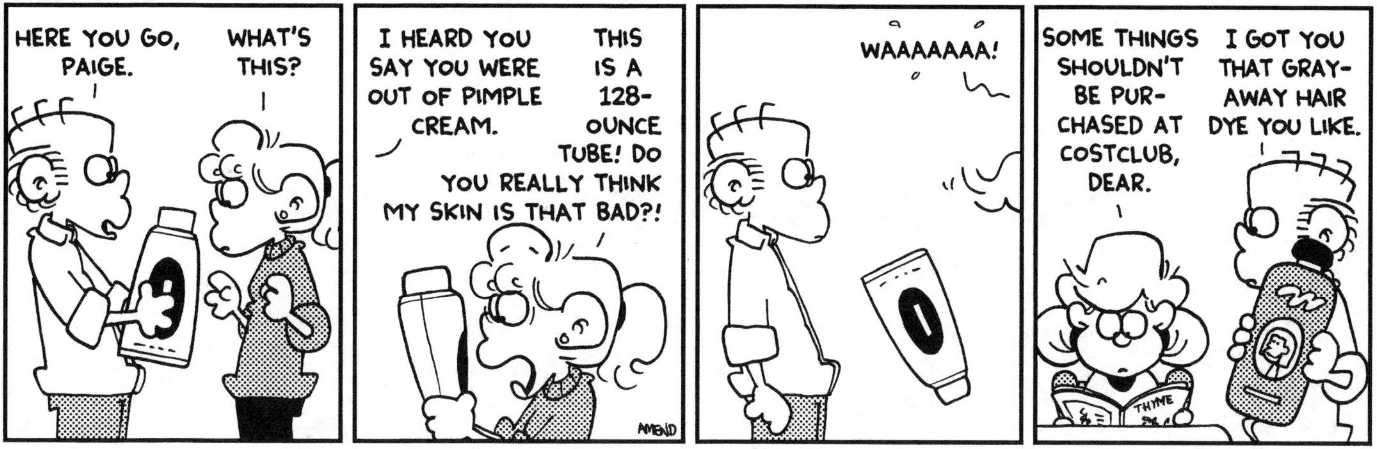
HERE YOU GO, PAIGE.
WHAT'S THIS?
I HEARD YOU SAY YOU WERE OUT OF PIMPLE CREAM.
THIS IS A 128-OUNCE TUBE! DO YOU REALLY THINK MY SKIN IS THAT BAD?!
WAAAAAAA!
SOME THINGS SHOULDN'T BE PURCHASED AT COSTCLUB, DEAR.
I GOT YOU THAT GRAY-AWAY HAIR DYE YOU LIKE.
THYME
AMEND

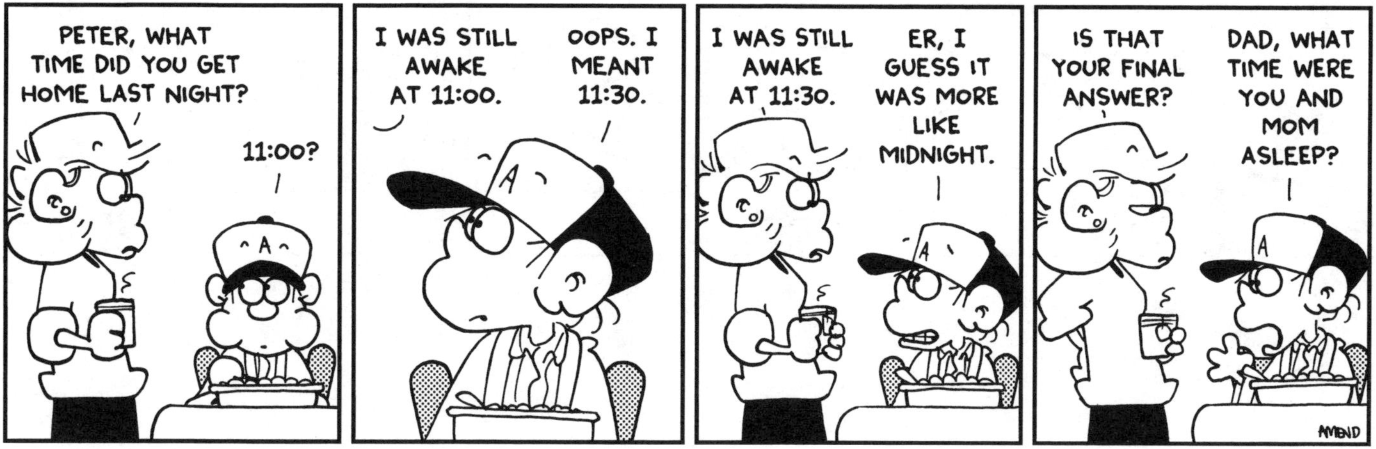
PETER, WHAT TIME DID YOU GET HOME LAST NIGHT?
11:00?
I WAS STILL AWAKE AT 11:00.
OOPS. I MEANT 11:30.
I WAS STILL AWAKE AT 11:30.
ER, I GUESS IT WAS MORE LIKE MIDNIGHT.
IS THAT YOUR FINAL ANSWER?
DAD, WHAT TIME WERE YOU AND MOM ASLEEP?
AMEND

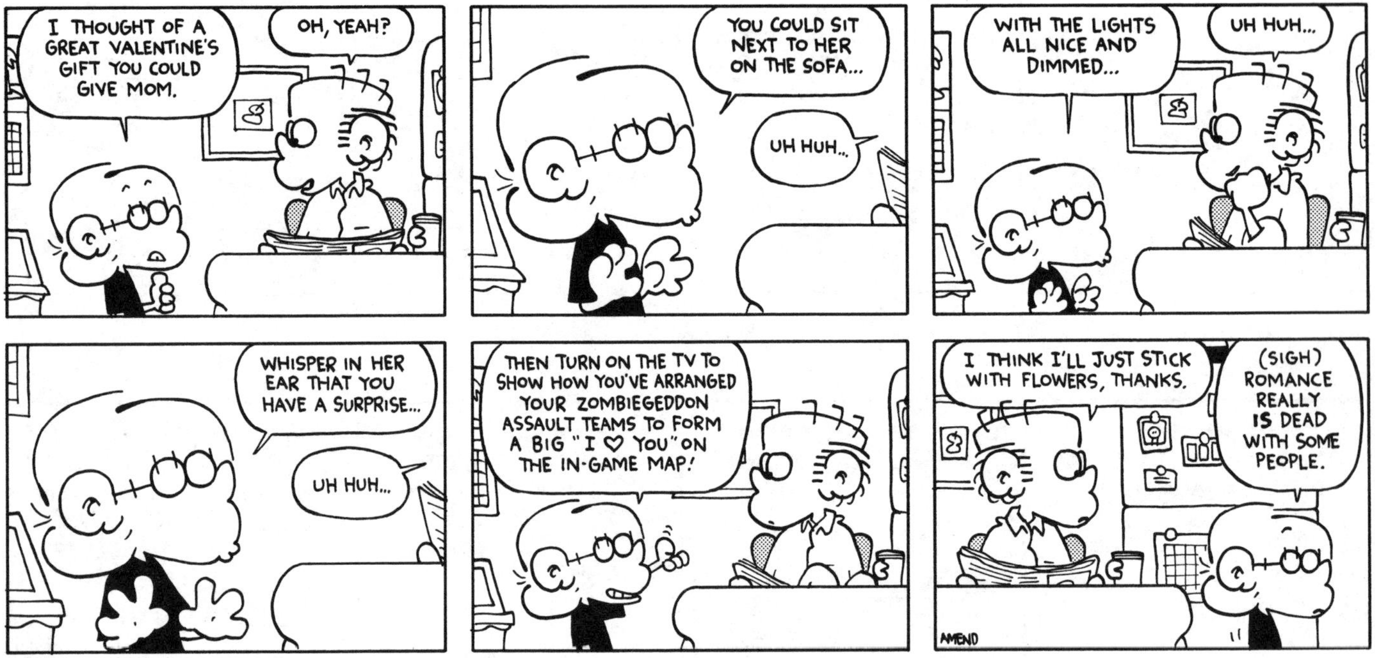
I THOUGHT OF A GREAT VALENTINE'S GIFT YOU COULD GIVE MOM.
OH, YEAH?
YOU COULD SIT NEXT TO HER ON THE SOFA...
UH HUH...
WITH THE LIGHTS ALL NICE AND DIMMED...
UH HUH...
WHISPER IN HER EAR THAT YOU HAVE A SURPRISE...
UH HUH...
THEN TURN ON THE TV TO SHOW HOW YOU'VE ARRANGED YOUR ZOMBIEGEDDON ASSAULT TEAMS TO FORM A BIG "I ♡ YOU" ON THE IN-GAME MAP!
I THINK I'LL JUST STICK WITH FLOWERS, THANKS.
(SIGH) ROMANCE REALLY **IS** DEAD WITH SOME PEOPLE.
AMEND

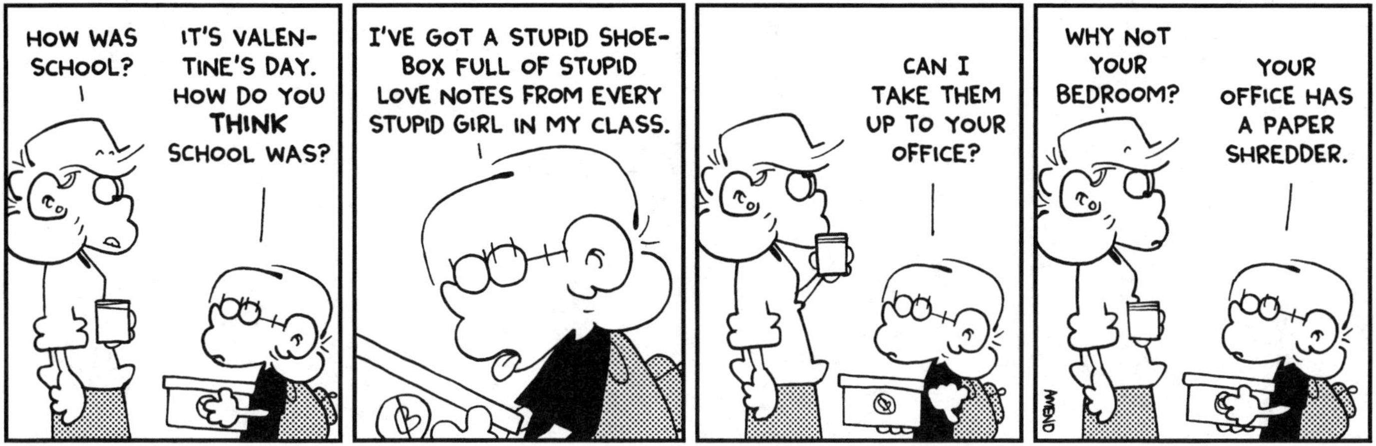
HOW WAS SCHOOL?
IT'S VALEN-TINE'S DAY. HOW DO YOU THINK SCHOOL WAS?
I'VE GOT A STUPID SHOE-BOX FULL OF STUPID LOVE NOTES FROM EVERY STUPID GIRL IN MY CLASS.
CAN I TAKE THEM UP TO YOUR OFFICE?
WHY NOT YOUR BEDROOM?
YOUR OFFICE HAS A PAPER SHREDDER.
AMEND

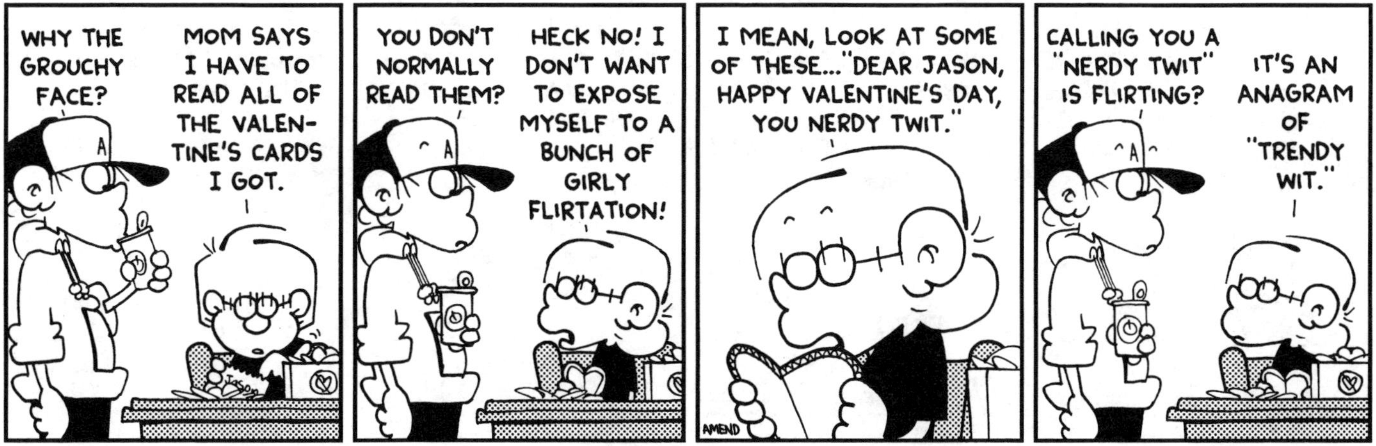
WHY THE GROUCHY FACE?
MOM SAYS I HAVE TO READ ALL OF THE VALEN-TINE'S CARDS I GOT.
YOU DON'T NORMALLY READ THEM?
HECK NO! I DON'T WANT TO EXPOSE MYSELF TO A BUNCH OF GIRLY FLIRTATION!
I MEAN, LOOK AT SOME OF THESE... "DEAR JASON, HAPPY VALENTINE'S DAY, YOU NERDY TWIT."
AMEND
CALLING YOU A "NERDY TWIT" IS FLIRTING?
IT'S AN ANAGRAM OF "TRENDY WIT."

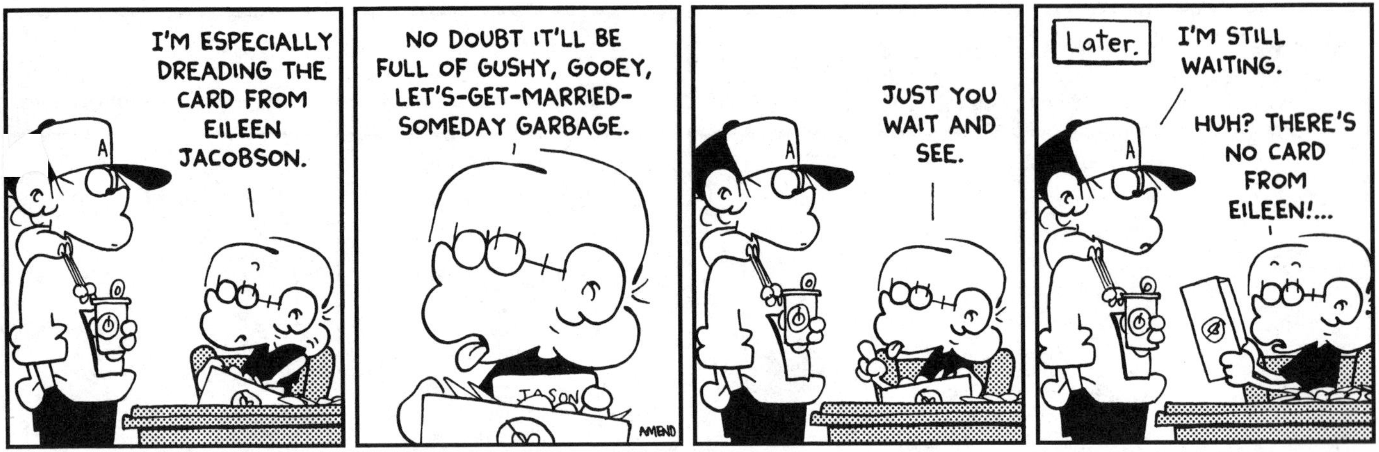
I'M ESPECIALLY DREADING THE CARD FROM EILEEN JACOBSON.
NO DOUBT IT'LL BE FULL OF GUSHY, GOOEY, LET'S-GET-MARRIED-SOMEDAY GARBAGE.
JASON
AMEND
JUST YOU WAIT AND SEE.
Later.
I'M STILL WAITING.
HUH? THERE'S NO CARD FROM EILEEN!...

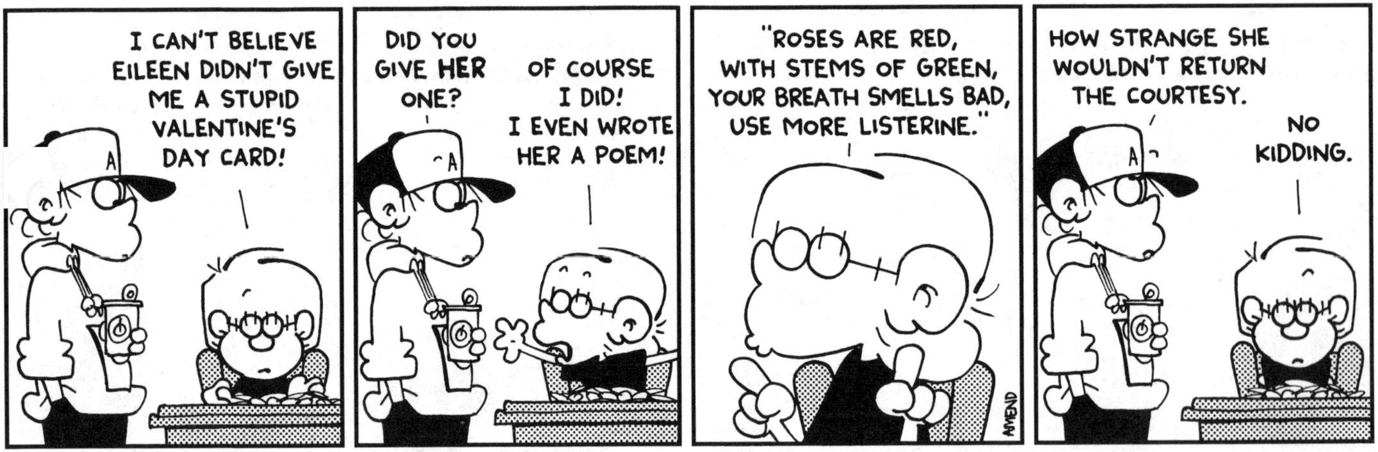
I CAN'T BELIEVE EILEEN DIDN'T GIVE ME A STUPID VALENTINE'S DAY CARD!
DID YOU GIVE HER ONE?
OF COURSE I DID! I EVEN WROTE HER A POEM!
"ROSES ARE RED, WITH STEMS OF GREEN, YOUR BREATH SMELLS BAD, USE MORE LISTERINE."
AMEND
HOW STRANGE SHE WOULDN'T RETURN THE COURTESY.
NO KIDDING.

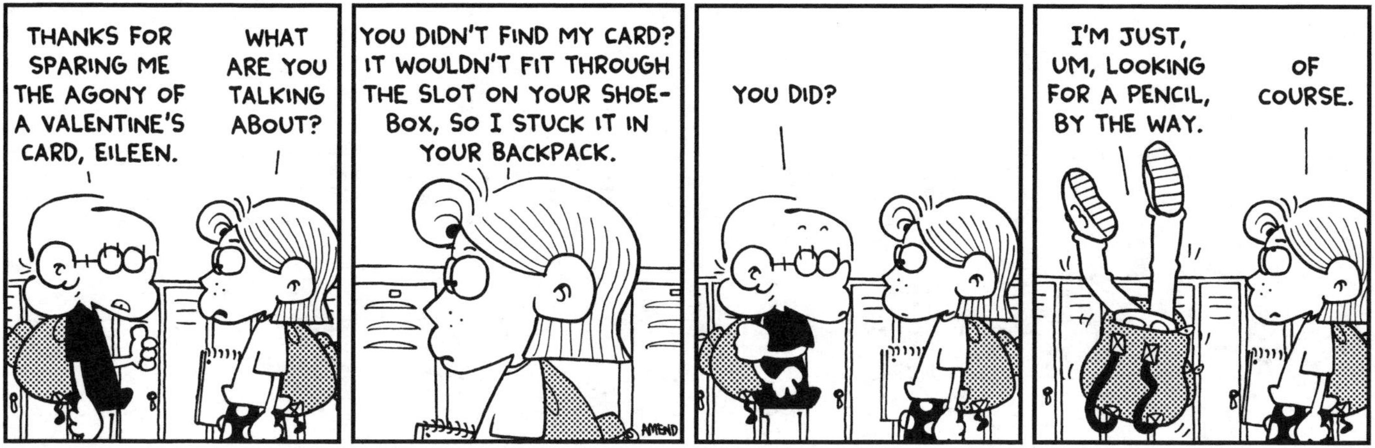
THANKS FOR SPARING ME THE AGONY OF A VALENTINE'S CARD, EILEEN.
WHAT ARE YOU TALKING ABOUT?
YOU DIDN'T FIND MY CARD? IT WOULDN'T FIT THROUGH THE SLOT ON YOUR SHOE-BOX, SO I STUCK IT IN YOUR BACKPACK.
AMEND
YOU DID?
I'M JUST, UM, LOOKING FOR A PENCIL, BY THE WAY.
OF COURSE.

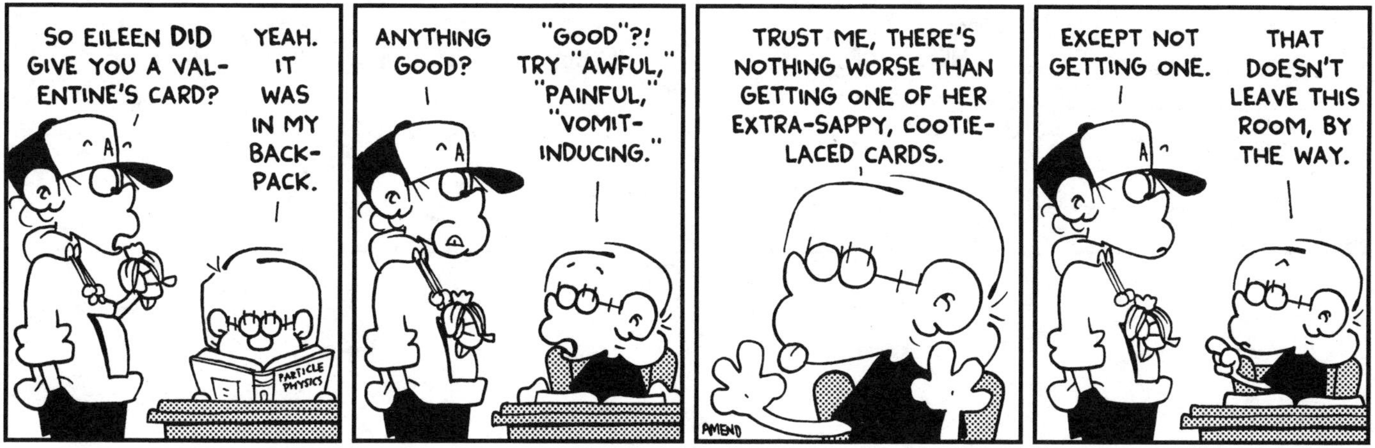
SO EILEEN DID GIVE YOU A VAL-ENTINE'S CARD?
YEAH. IT WAS IN MY BACK-PACK.
PARTICLE PHYSICS
ANYTHING GOOD?
"GOOD"?! TRY "AWFUL," "PAINFUL," "VOMIT-INDUCING."
TRUST ME, THERE'S NOTHING WORSE THAN GETTING ONE OF HER EXTRA-SAPPY, COOTIE-LACED CARDS.
AMEND
EXCEPT NOT GETTING ONE.
THAT DOESN'T LEAVE THIS ROOM, BY THE WAY.

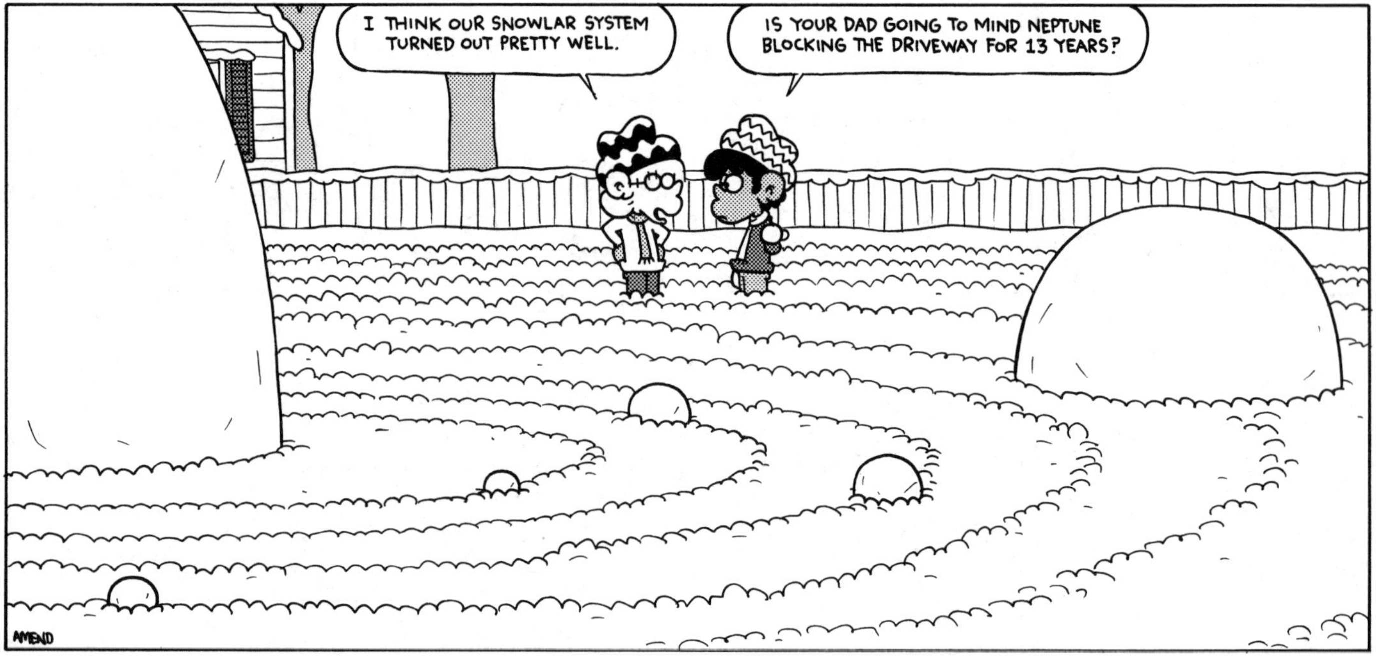
I THINK OUR SNOWLAR SYSTEM TURNED OUT PRETTY WELL.
IS YOUR DAD GOING TO MIND NEPTUNE BLOCKING THE DRIVEWAY FOR 13 YEARS?
AMEND

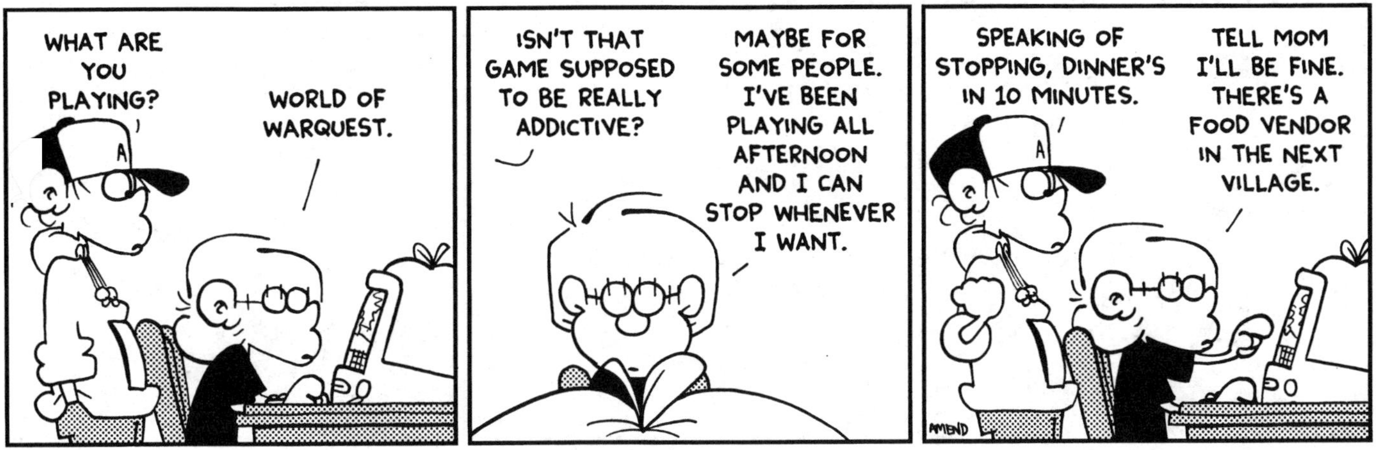
WHAT ARE YOU PLAYING?
WORLD OF WARQUEST.
ISN'T THAT GAME SUPPOSED TO BE REALLY ADDICTIVE?
MAYBE FOR SOME PEOPLE. I'VE BEEN PLAYING ALL AFTERNOON AND I CAN STOP WHENEVER I WANT.
SPEAKING OF STOPPING, DINNER'S IN 10 MINUTES.
TELL MOM I'LL BE FINE. THERE'S A FOOD VENDOR IN THE NEXT VILLAGE.
AMEND

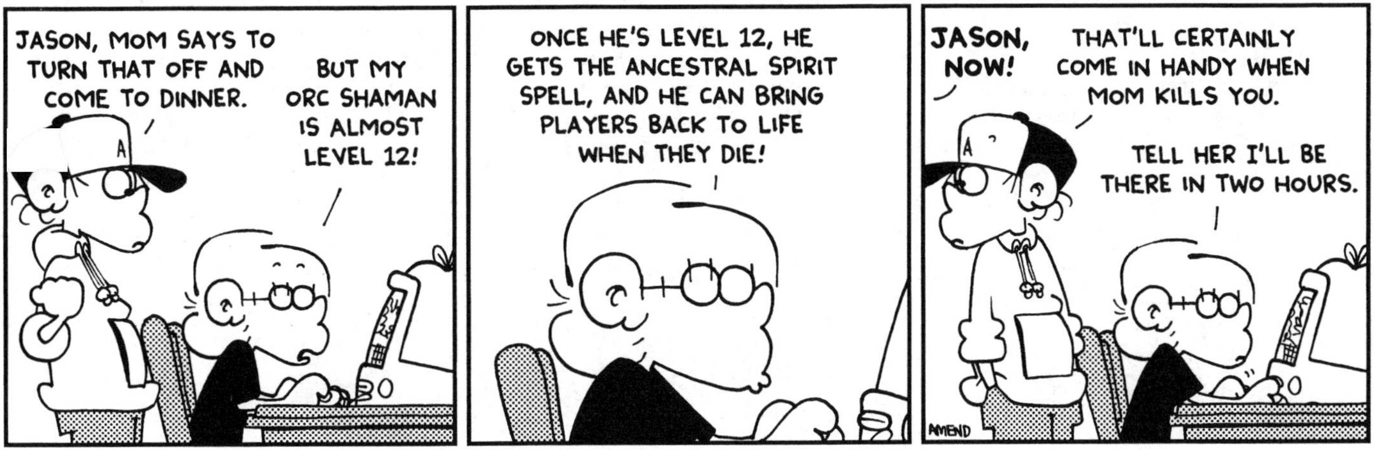
JASON, MOM SAYS TO TURN THAT OFF AND COME TO DINNER.
BUT MY ORC SHAMAN IS ALMOST LEVEL 12!
ONCE HE'S LEVEL 12, HE GETS THE ANCESTRAL SPIRIT SPELL, AND HE CAN BRING PLAYERS BACK TO LIFE WHEN THEY DIE!
JASON, NOW!
THAT'LL CERTAINLY COME IN HANDY WHEN MOM KILLS YOU.
TELL HER I'LL BE THERE IN TWO HOURS.
AMEND

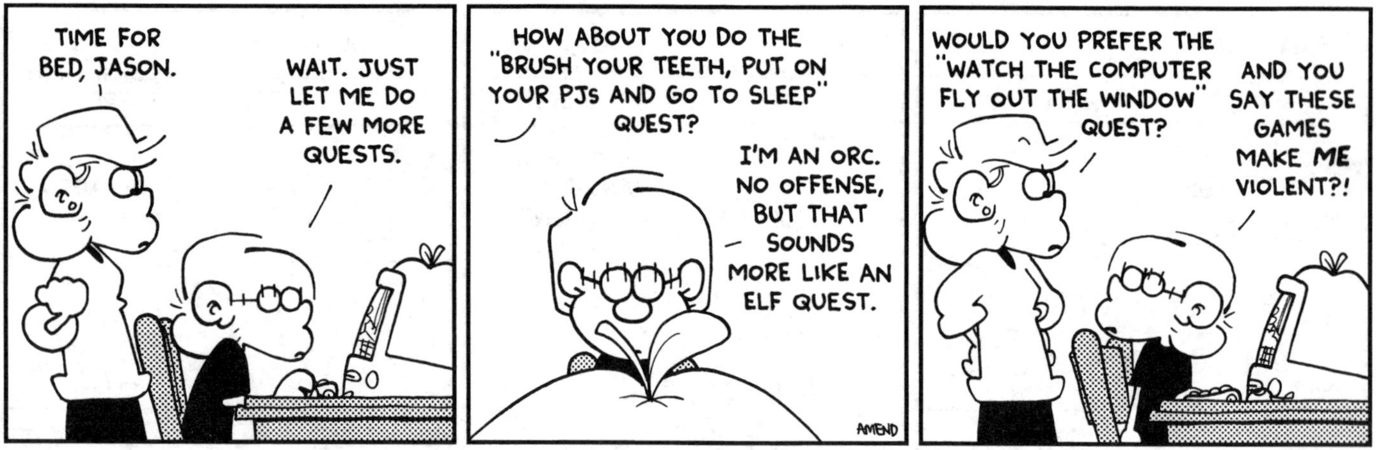
TIME FOR BED, JASON.
WAIT. JUST LET ME DO A FEW MORE QUESTS.
HOW ABOUT YOU DO THE "BRUSH YOUR TEETH, PUT ON YOUR PJs AND GO TO SLEEP" QUEST?
I'M AN ORC. NO OFFENSE, BUT THAT SOUNDS MORE LIKE AN ELF QUEST.
AMEND
WOULD YOU PREFER THE "WATCH THE COMPUTER FLY OUT THE WINDOW" QUEST?
AND YOU SAY THESE GAMES MAKE **ME** VIOLENT?!

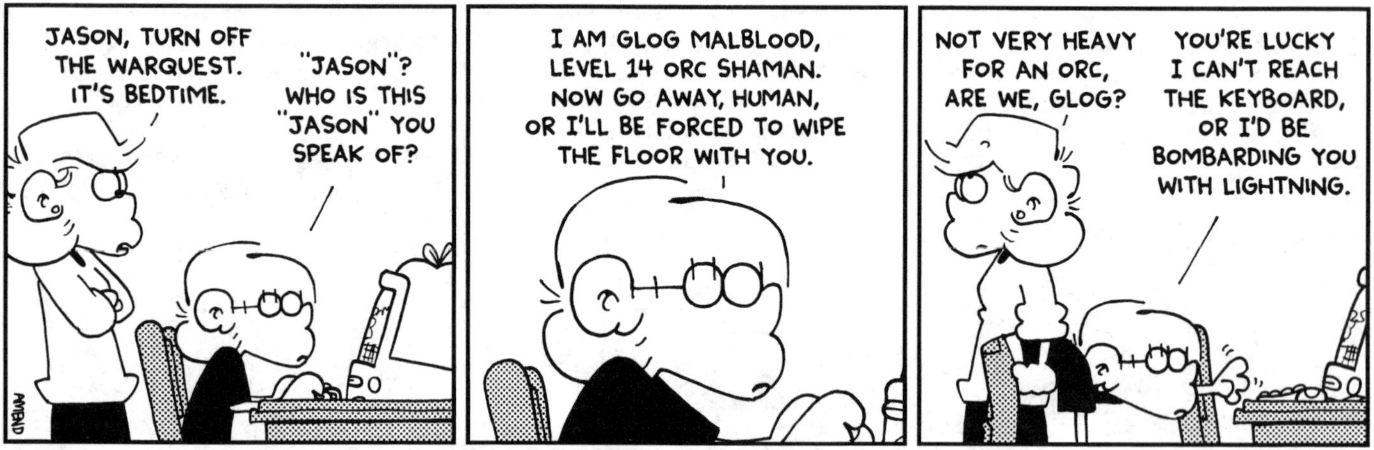
JASON, TURN OFF THE WARQUEST. IT'S BEDTIME.
"JASON"? WHO IS THIS "JASON" YOU SPEAK OF?
AMEND
I AM GLOG MALBLOOD, LEVEL 14 ORC SHAMAN. NOW GO AWAY, HUMAN, OR I'LL BE FORCED TO WIPE THE FLOOR WITH YOU.
NOT VERY HEAVY FOR AN ORC, ARE WE, GLOG?
YOU'RE LUCKY I CAN'T REACH THE KEYBOARD, OR I'D BE BOMBARDING YOU WITH LIGHTNING.

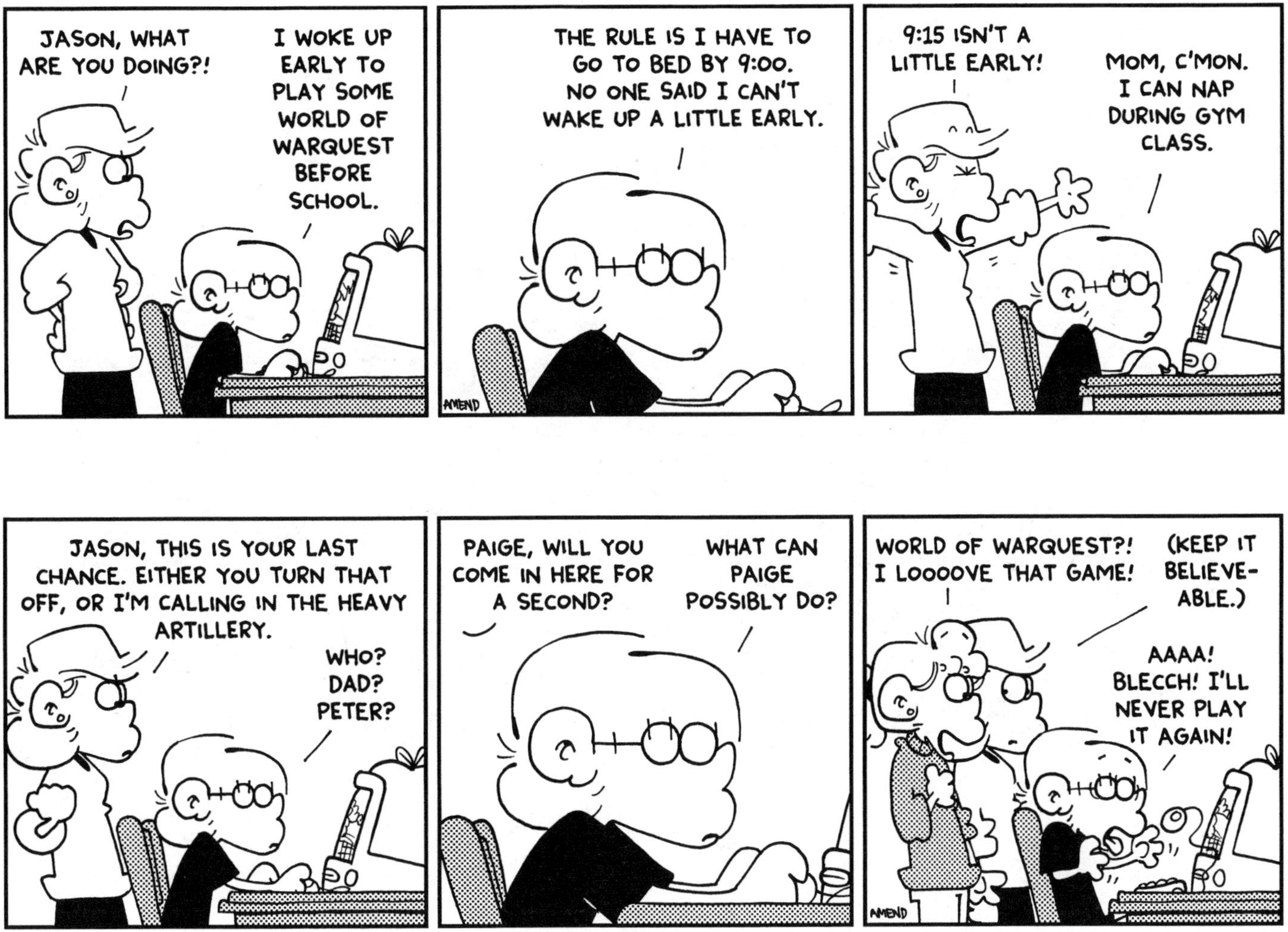
JASON, WHAT ARE YOU DOING?!
I WOKE UP EARLY TO PLAY SOME WORLD OF WARQUEST BEFORE SCHOOL.
AMEND
THE RULE IS I HAVE TO GO TO BED BY 9:00. NO ONE SAID I CAN'T WAKE UP A LITTLE EARLY.
9:15 ISN'T A LITTLE EARLY!
MOM, C'MON. I CAN NAP DURING GYM CLASS.
JASON, THIS IS YOUR LAST CHANCE. EITHER YOU TURN THAT OFF, OR I'M CALLING IN THE HEAVY ARTILLERY.
WHO? DAD? PETER?
PAIGE, WILL YOU COME IN HERE FOR A SECOND?
WHAT CAN PAIGE POSSIBLY DO?
WORLD OF WARQUEST?! I LOOOOVE THAT GAME!
(KEEP IT BELIEVE-ABLE.)
AAAA! BLECCH! I'LL NEVER PLAY IT AGAIN!
AMEND

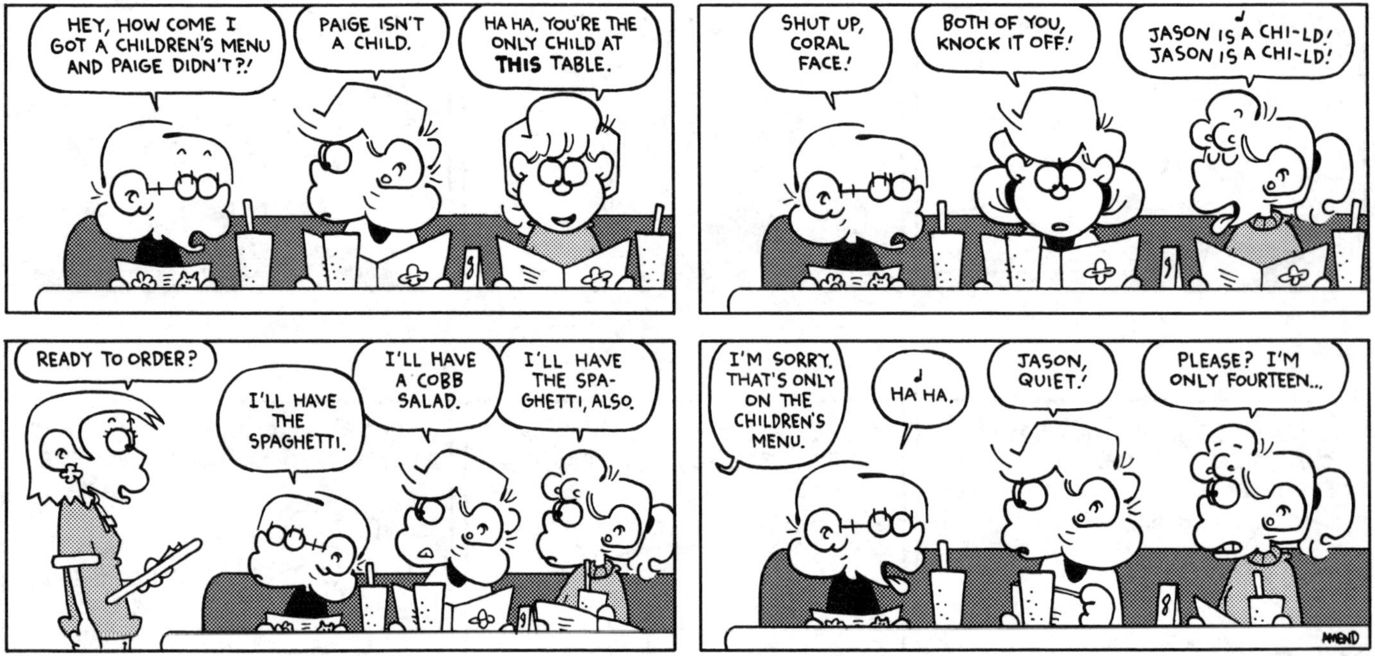
HEY, HOW COME I GOT A CHILDREN'S MENU AND PAIGE DIDN'T?!
PAIGE ISN'T A CHILD.
HA HA, YOU'RE THE ONLY CHILD AT **THIS** TABLE.
SHUT UP, CORAL FACE!
BOTH OF YOU, KNOCK IT OFF!
JASON IS A CHI-LD! JASON IS A CHI-LD!
READY TO ORDER?
I'LL HAVE THE SPAGHETTI.
I'LL HAVE A COBB SALAD.
I'LL HAVE THE SPA-GHETTI, ALSO.
I'M SORRY. THAT'S ONLY ON THE CHILDREN'S MENU.
HA HA.
JASON, QUIET!
PLEASE? I'M ONLY FOURTEEN...
AMEND

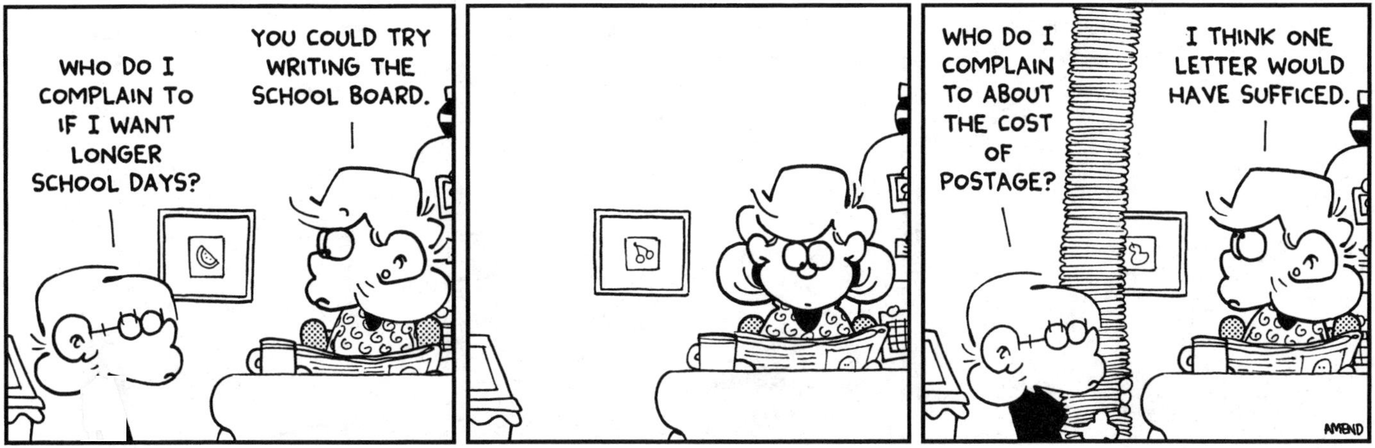

WHO DO I COMPLAIN TO IF I WANT LONGER SCHOOL DAYS?
YOU COULD TRY WRITING THE SCHOOL BOARD.
WHO DO I COMPLAIN TO ABOUT THE COST OF POSTAGE?
I THINK ONE LETTER WOULD HAVE SUFFICED.
AMEND

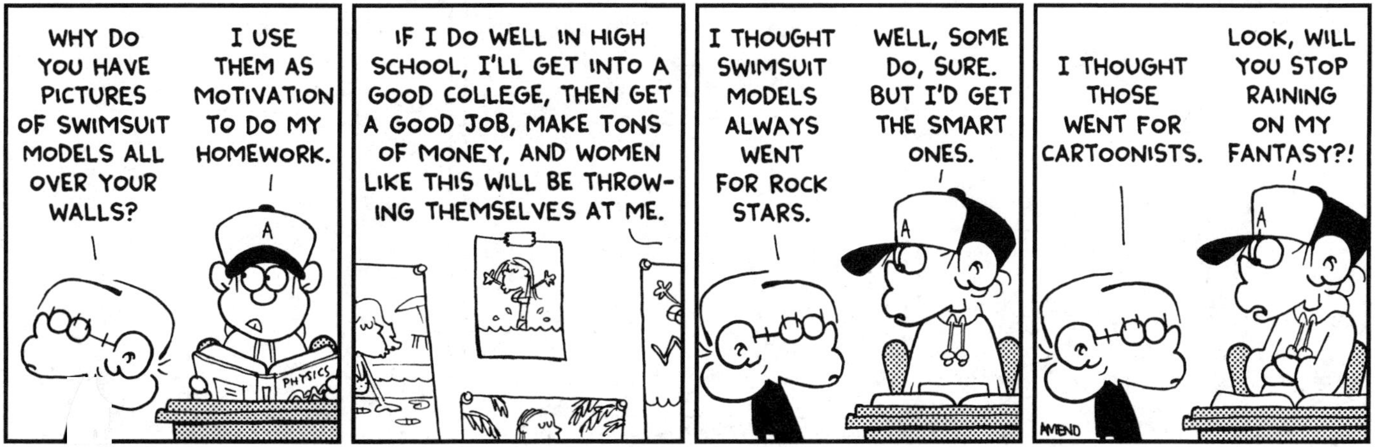

WHY DO YOU HAVE PICTURES OF SWIMSUIT MODELS ALL OVER YOUR WALLS?
I USE THEM AS MOTIVATION TO DO MY HOMEWORK.
A
PHYSICS
IF I DO WELL IN HIGH SCHOOL, I'LL GET INTO A GOOD COLLEGE, THEN GET A GOOD JOB, MAKE TONS OF MONEY, AND WOMEN LIKE THIS WILL BE THROWING THEMSELVES AT ME.
I THOUGHT SWIMSUIT MODELS ALWAYS WENT FOR ROCK STARS.
WELL, SOME DO, SURE. BUT I'D GET THE SMART ONES.
I THOUGHT THOSE WENT FOR CARTOONISTS.
LOOK, WILL YOU STOP RAINING ON MY FANTASY?!
AMEND

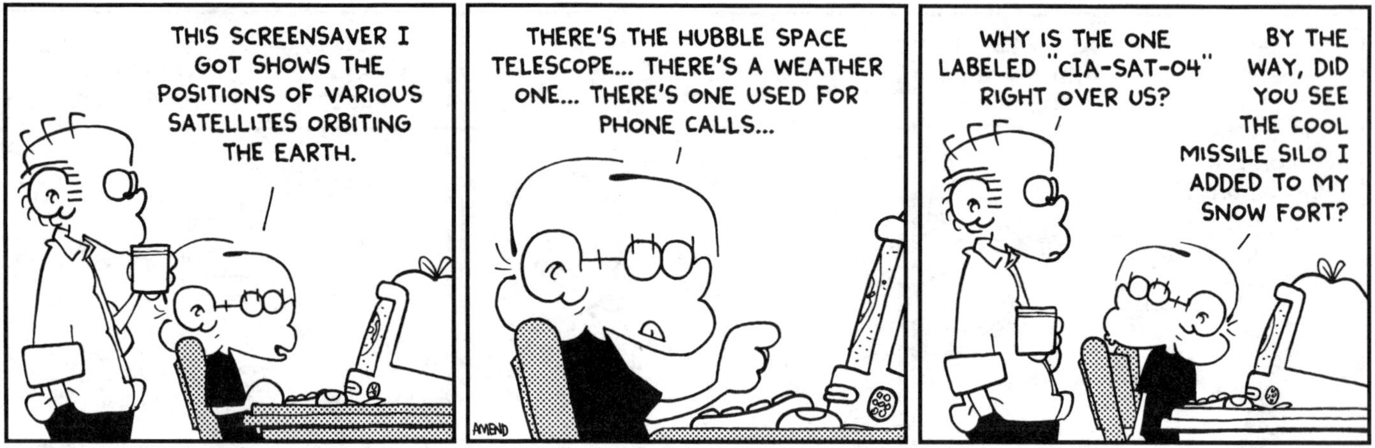
THIS SCREENSAVER I GOT SHOWS THE POSITIONS OF VARIOUS SATELLITES ORBITING THE EARTH.
THERE'S THE HUBBLE SPACE TELESCOPE... THERE'S A WEATHER ONE... THERE'S ONE USED FOR PHONE CALLS...
WHY IS THE ONE LABELED "CIA-SAT-04" RIGHT OVER US?
BY THE WAY, DID YOU SEE THE COOL MISSILE SILO I ADDED TO MY SNOW FORT?
AMEND

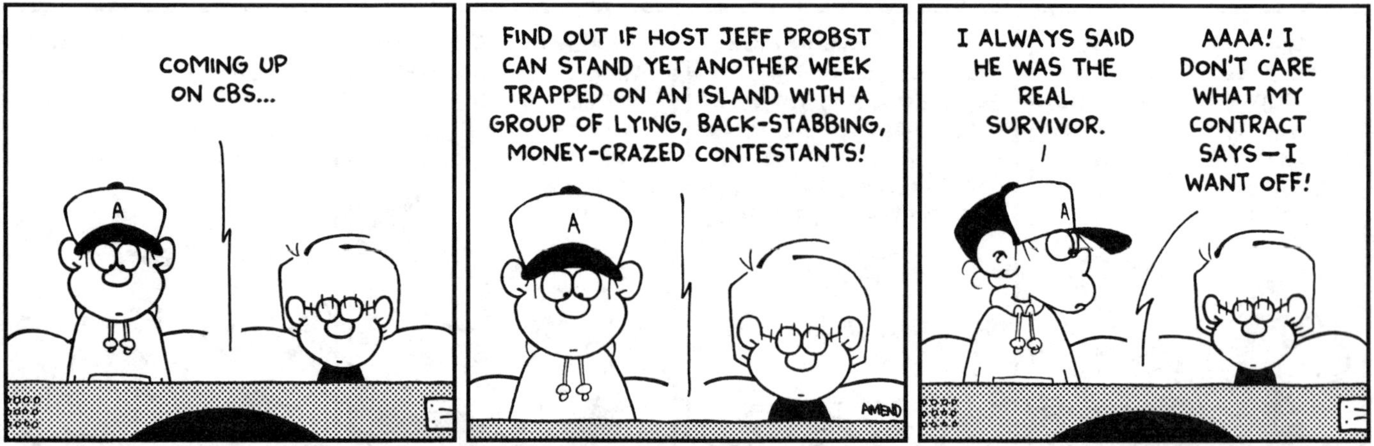
COMING UP ON CBS...
FIND OUT IF HOST JEFF PROBST CAN STAND YET ANOTHER WEEK TRAPPED ON AN ISLAND WITH A GROUP OF LYING, BACK-STABBING, MONEY-CRAZED CONTESTANTS!
I ALWAYS SAID HE WAS THE REAL SURVIVOR.
AAAA! I DON'T CARE WHAT MY CONTRACT SAYS—I WANT OFF!
AMEND

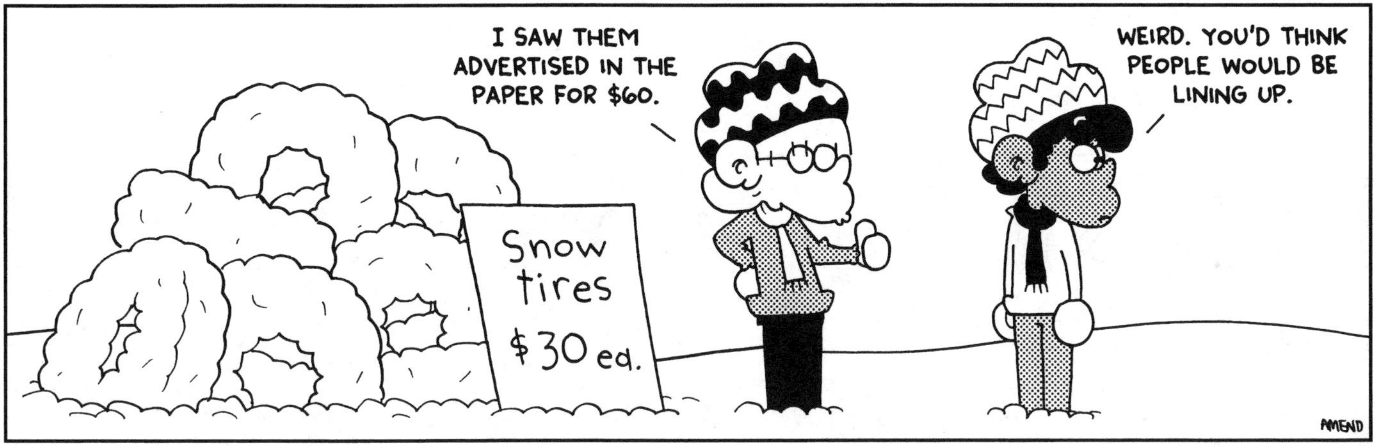
I SAW THEM ADVERTISED IN THE PAPER FOR $60.
Snow tires $30 ea.
WEIRD. YOU'D THINK PEOPLE WOULD BE LINING UP.
AMEND

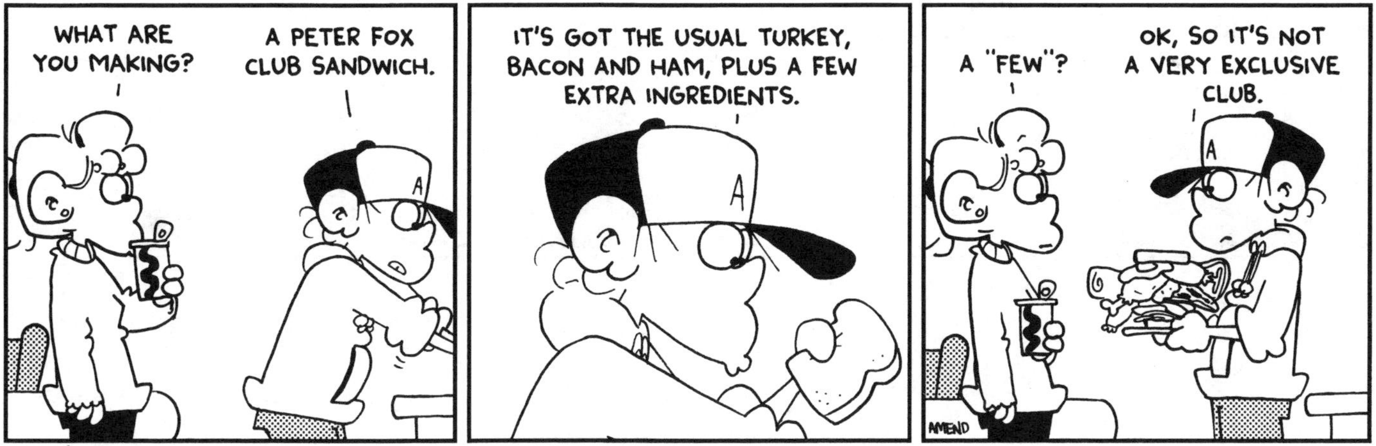
WHAT ARE YOU MAKING?
A PETER FOX CLUB SANDWICH.
IT'S GOT THE USUAL TURKEY, BACON AND HAM, PLUS A FEW EXTRA INGREDIENTS.
A "FEW"?
OK, SO IT'S NOT A VERY EXCLUSIVE CLUB.
AMEND

"PLEASE DON'T KILL ME" ISN'T A NORMAL CATCHER'S SIGN, JASON.
WELL, IT **SHOULD** BE.

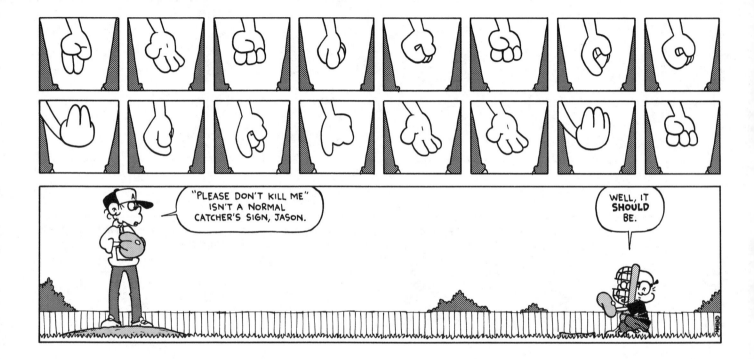

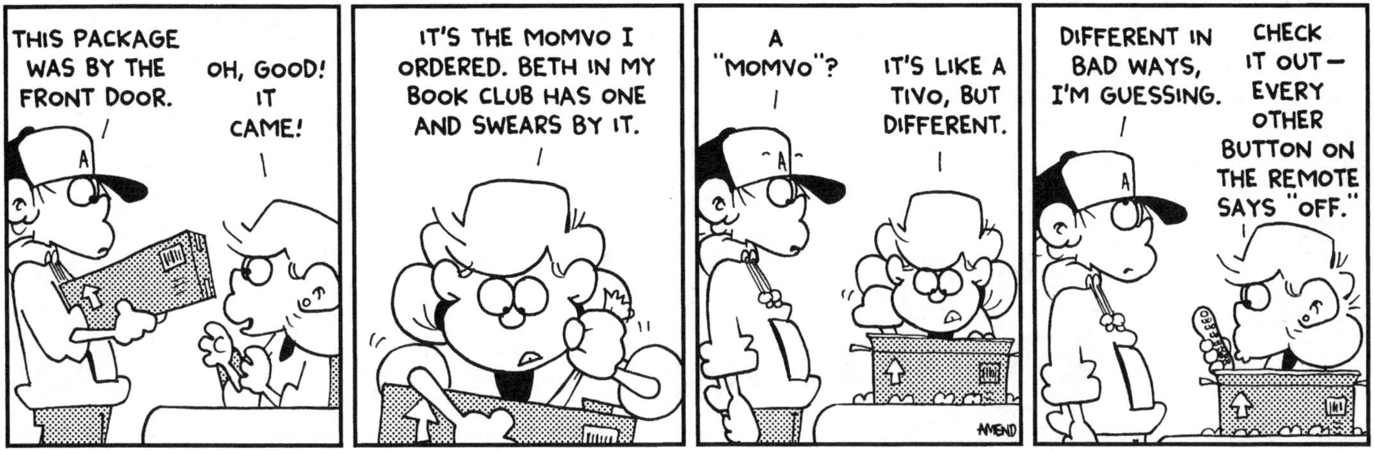
THIS PACKAGE WAS BY THE FRONT DOOR.
OH, GOOD! IT CAME!
IT'S THE MOMVO I ORDERED. BETH IN MY BOOK CLUB HAS ONE AND SWEARS BY IT.
A "MOMVO"?
IT'S LIKE A TIVO, BUT DIFFERENT.
AMEND
DIFFERENT IN BAD WAYS, I'M GUESSING.
CHECK IT OUT— EVERY OTHER BUTTON ON THE REMOTE SAYS "OFF."

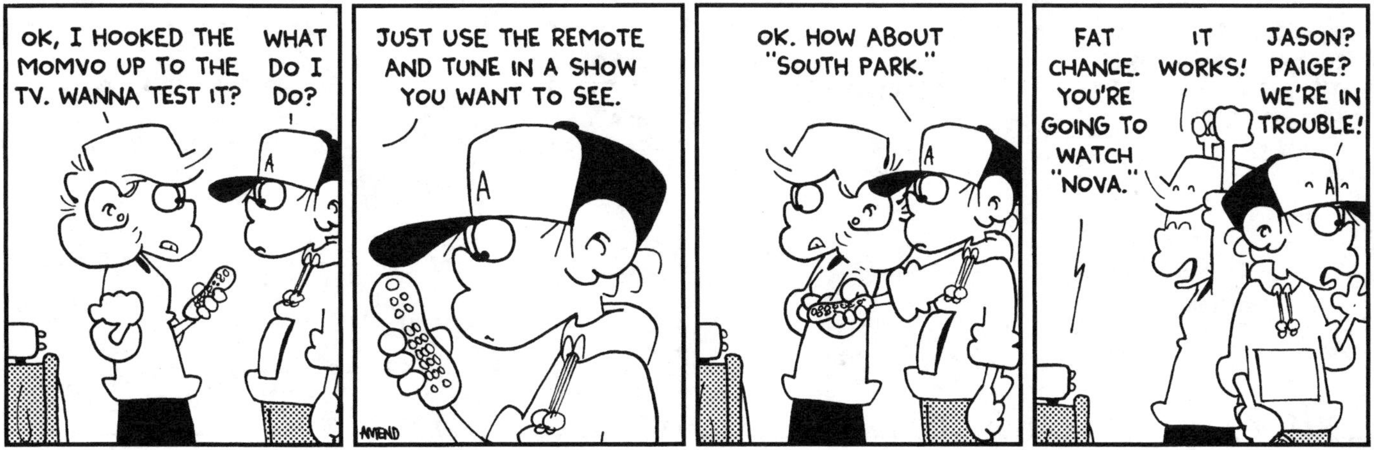
OK, I HOOKED THE MOMVO UP TO THE TV. WANNA TEST IT?
WHAT DO I DO?
JUST USE THE REMOTE AND TUNE IN A SHOW YOU WANT TO SEE.
AMEND
OK. HOW ABOUT "SOUTH PARK."
FAT CHANCE. YOU'RE GOING TO WATCH "NOVA."
IT WORKS!
JASON? PAIGE? WE'RE IN TROUBLE!

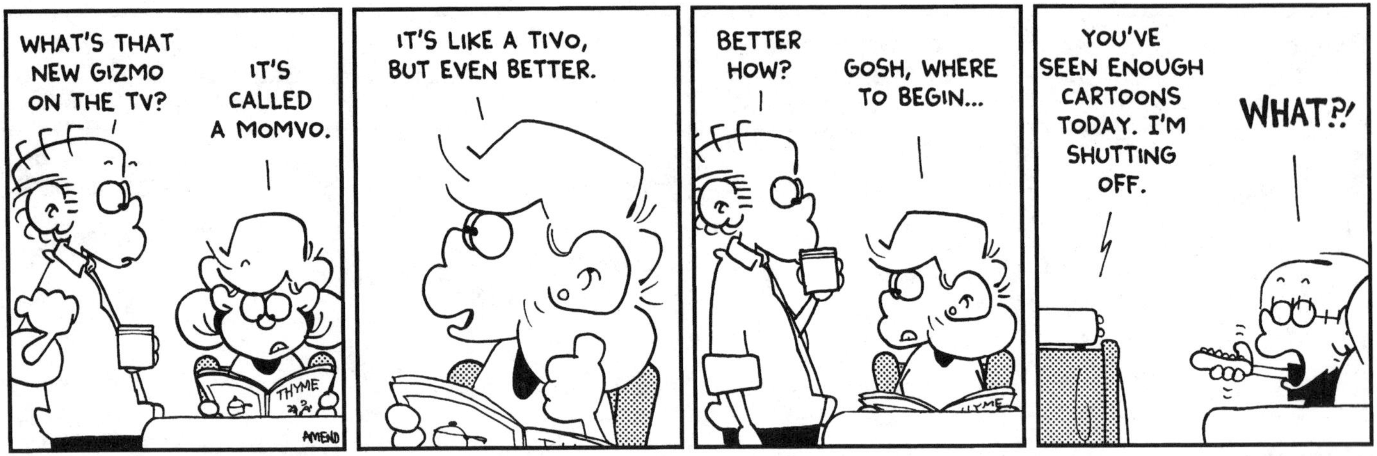
WHAT'S THAT NEW GIZMO ON THE TV?
IT'S CALLED A MOMVO.
THYME
AMEND
IT'S LIKE A TIVO, BUT EVEN BETTER.
BETTER HOW?
GOSH, WHERE TO BEGIN...
YOU'VE SEEN ENOUGH CARTOONS TODAY. I'M SHUTTING OFF.
WHAT?!

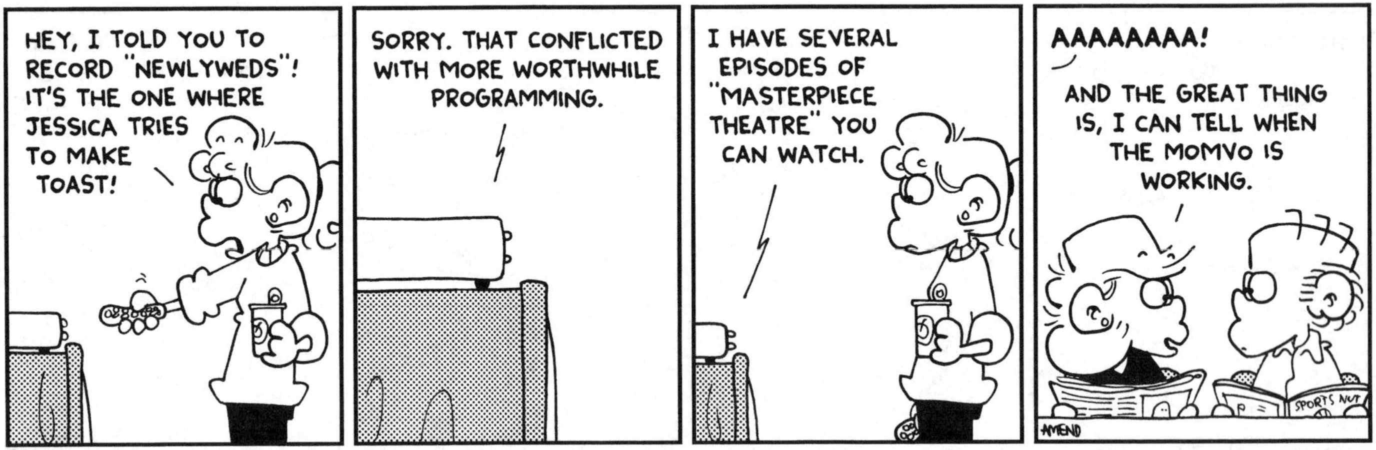
HEY, I TOLD YOU TO RECORD "NEWLYWEDS"! IT'S THE ONE WHERE JESSICA TRIES TO MAKE TOAST!
SORRY. THAT CONFLICTED WITH MORE WORTHWHILE PROGRAMMING.
I HAVE SEVERAL EPISODES OF "MASTERPIECE THEATRE" YOU CAN WATCH.
AAAAAAAA!
AND THE GREAT THING IS, I CAN TELL WHEN THE MOMVO IS WORKING.
SPORTS NUT
AMEND

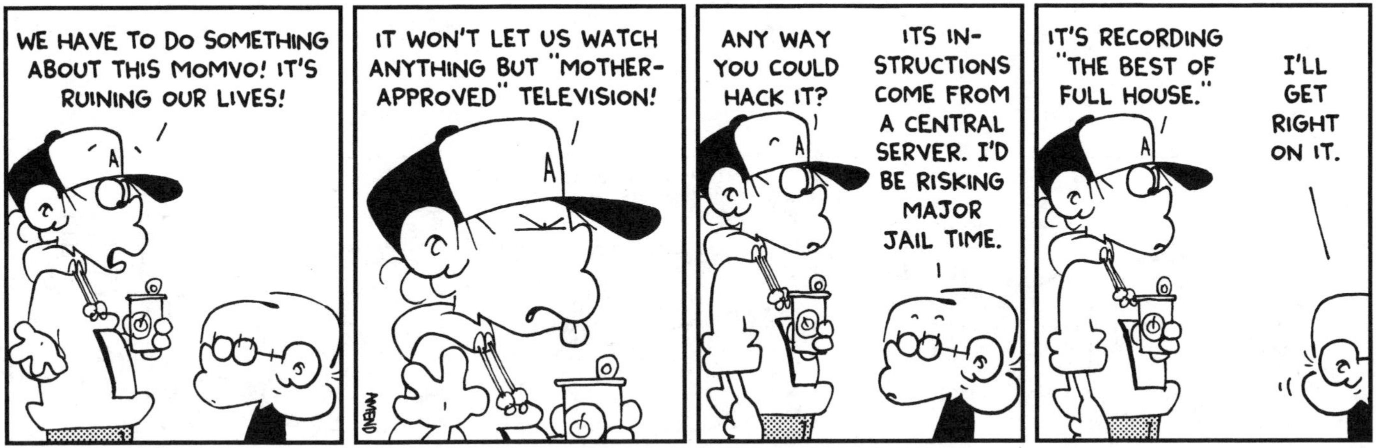
WE HAVE TO DO SOMETHING ABOUT THIS MOMVO! IT'S RUINING OUR LIVES!
IT WON'T LET US WATCH ANYTHING BUT "MOTHER-APPROVED" TELEVISION!
AMEND
ANY WAY YOU COULD HACK IT?
ITS IN-STRUCTIONS COME FROM A CENTRAL SERVER. I'D BE RISKING MAJOR JAIL TIME.
IT'S RECORDING "THE BEST OF FULL HOUSE."
I'LL GET RIGHT ON IT.

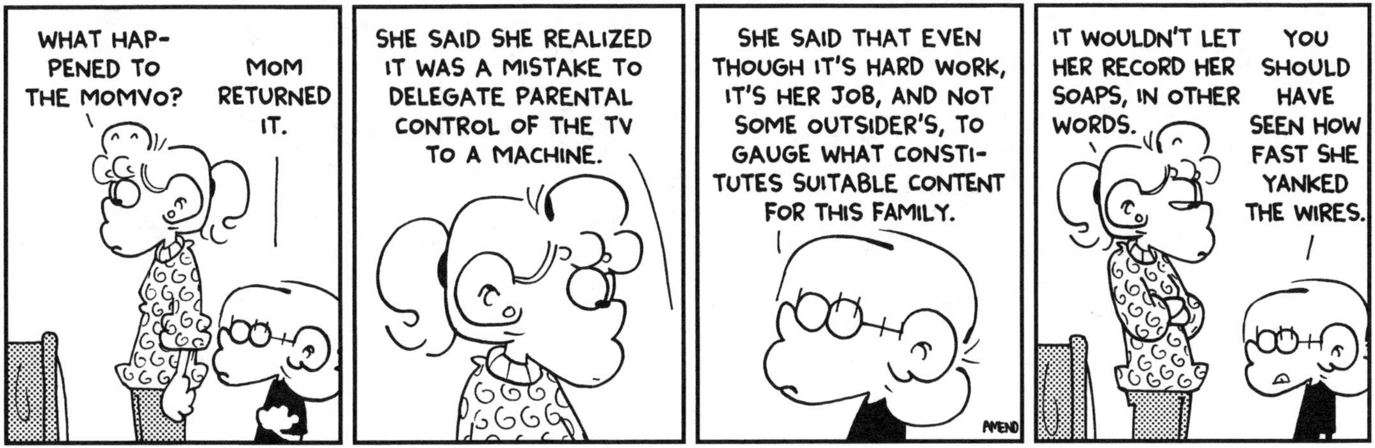
WHAT HAP-PENED TO THE MOMVO?
MOM RETURNED IT.
SHE SAID SHE REALIZED IT WAS A MISTAKE TO DELEGATE PARENTAL CONTROL OF THE TV TO A MACHINE.
SHE SAID THAT EVEN THOUGH IT'S HARD WORK, IT'S HER JOB, AND NOT SOME OUTSIDER'S, TO GAUGE WHAT CONSTI-TUTES SUITABLE CONTENT FOR THIS FAMILY.
AMEND
IT WOULDN'T LET HER RECORD HER SOAPS, IN OTHER WORDS.
YOU SHOULD HAVE SEEN HOW FAST SHE YANKED THE WIRES.

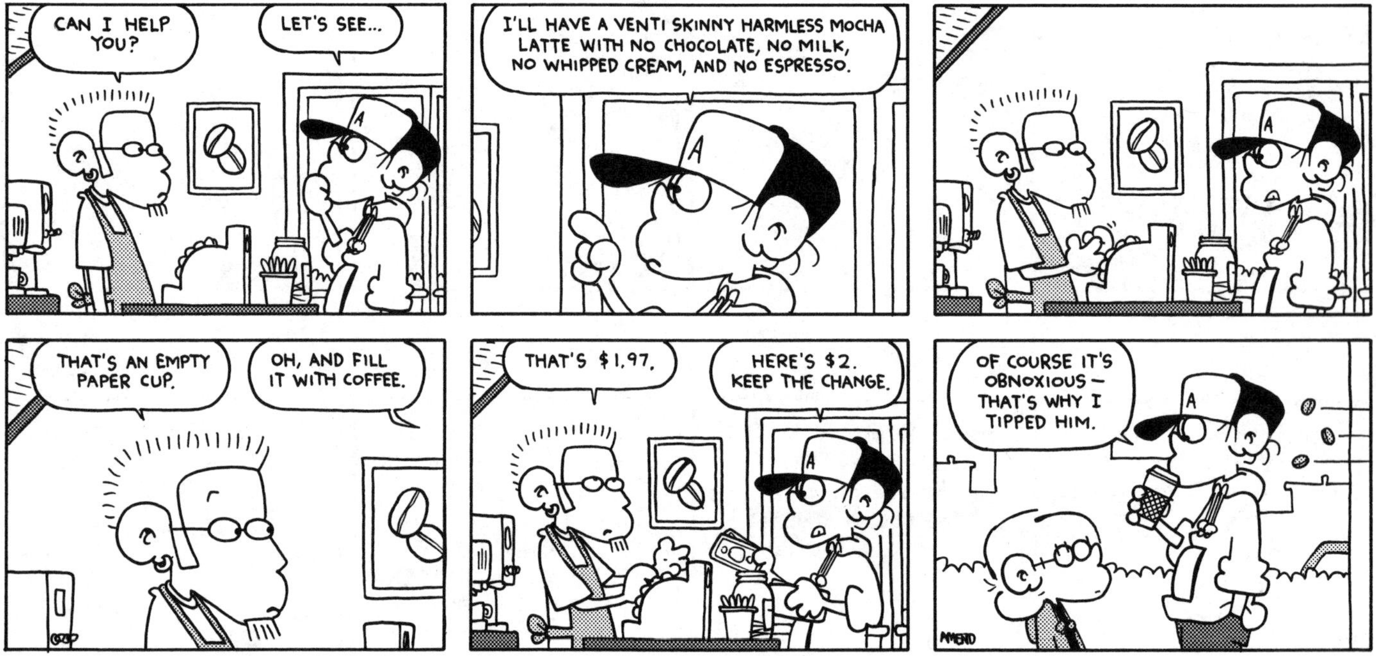
CAN I HELP YOU?
LET'S SEE...
I'LL HAVE A VENTI SKINNY HARMLESS MOCHA LATTE WITH NO CHOCOLATE, NO MILK, NO WHIPPED CREAM, AND NO ESPRESSO.
THAT'S AN EMPTY PAPER CUP.
OH, AND FILL IT WITH COFFEE.
THAT'S $1.97.
HERE'S $2. KEEP THE CHANGE.
OF COURSE IT'S OBNOXIOUS — THAT'S WHY I TIPPED HIM.
AMEND

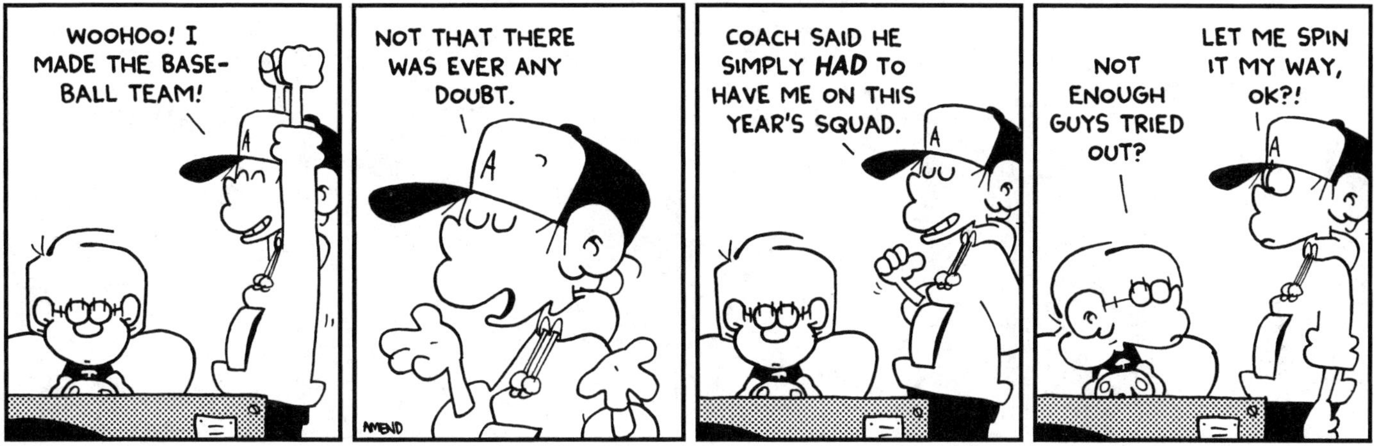
WOOHOO! I MADE THE BASE-BALL TEAM!
NOT THAT THERE WAS EVER ANY DOUBT.
AMEND
COACH SAID HE SIMPLY **HAD** TO HAVE ME ON THIS YEAR'S SQUAD.
NOT ENOUGH GUYS TRIED OUT?
LET ME SPIN IT MY WAY, OK?!

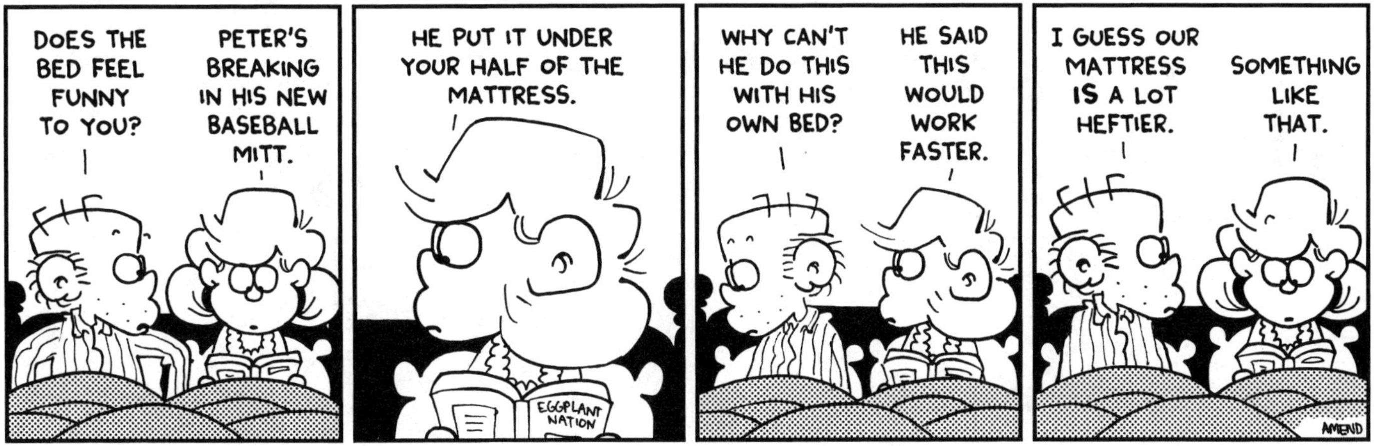
DOES THE BED FEEL FUNNY TO YOU?
PETER'S BREAKING IN HIS NEW BASEBALL MITT.
HE PUT IT UNDER YOUR HALF OF THE MATTRESS.
EGGPLANT NATION
WHY CAN'T HE DO THIS WITH HIS OWN BED?
HE SAID THIS WOULD WORK FASTER.
I GUESS OUR MATTRESS **IS** A LOT HEFTIER.
SOMETHING LIKE THAT.
AMEND

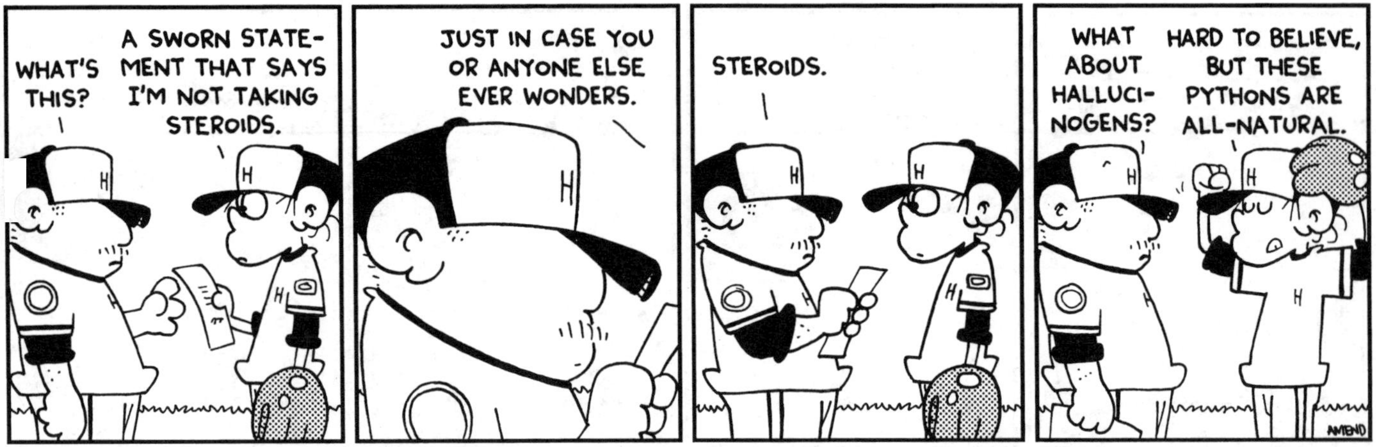
WHAT'S THIS?
A SWORN STATEMENT THAT SAYS I'M NOT TAKING STEROIDS.
JUST IN CASE YOU OR ANYONE ELSE EVER WONDERS.
STEROIDS.
WHAT ABOUT HALLUCINOGENS?
HARD TO BELIEVE, BUT THESE PYTHONS ARE ALL-NATURAL.
AMEND

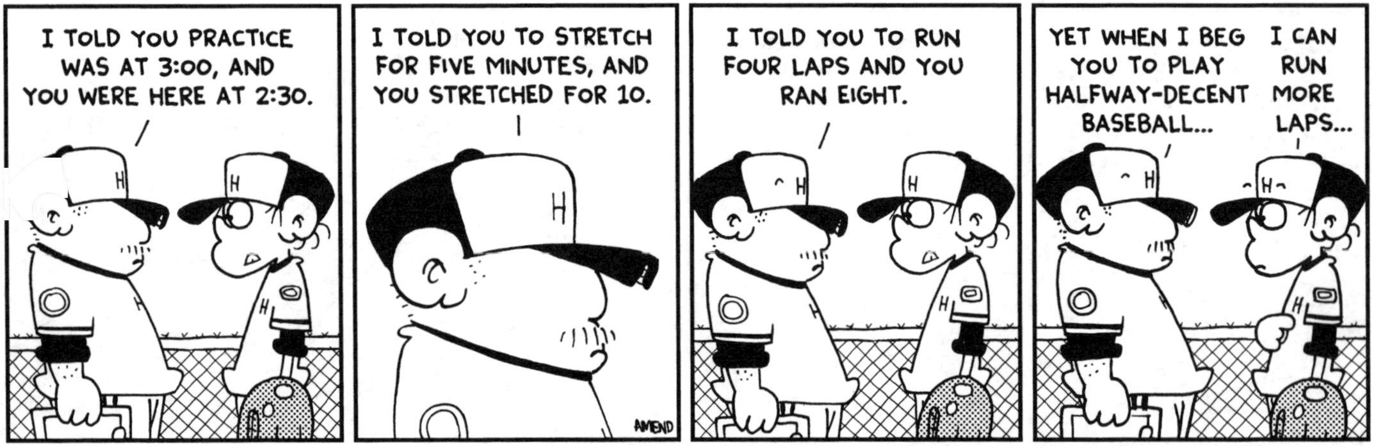
I TOLD YOU PRACTICE WAS AT 3:00, AND YOU WERE HERE AT 2:30.
I TOLD YOU TO STRETCH FOR FIVE MINUTES, AND YOU STRETCHED FOR 10.
I TOLD YOU TO RUN FOUR LAPS AND YOU RAN EIGHT.
YET WHEN I BEG YOU TO PLAY HALFWAY-DECENT BASEBALL...
I CAN RUN MORE LAPS...
AMEND

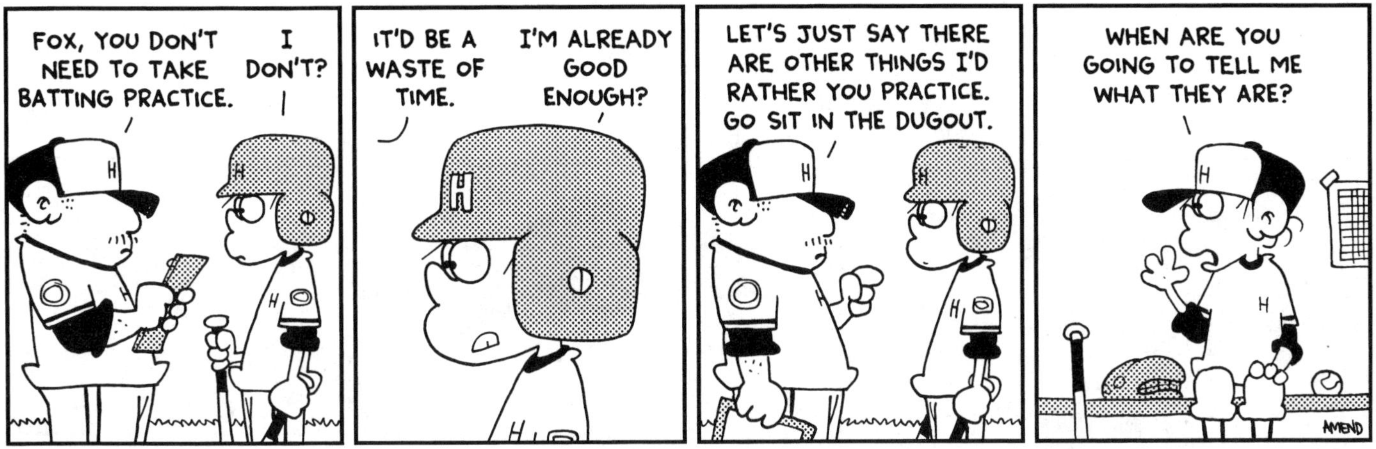
FOX, YOU DON'T NEED TO TAKE BATTING PRACTICE.
I DON'T?
IT'D BE A WASTE OF TIME.
I'M ALREADY GOOD ENOUGH?
LET'S JUST SAY THERE ARE OTHER THINGS I'D RATHER YOU PRACTICE. GO SIT IN THE DUGOUT.
WHEN ARE YOU GOING TO TELL ME WHAT THEY ARE?
AMEND

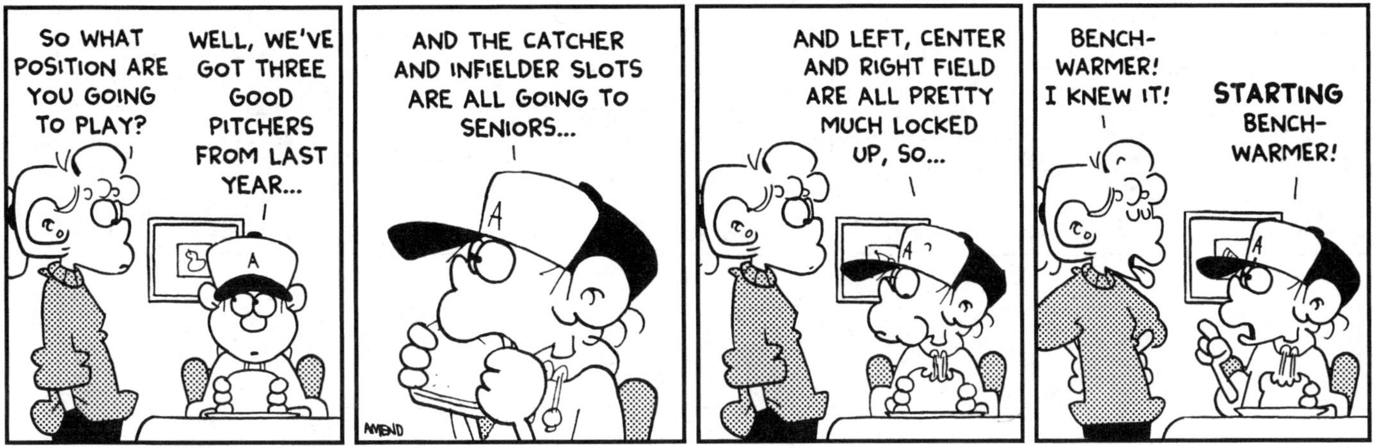
SO WHAT POSITION ARE YOU GOING TO PLAY?
WELL, WE'VE GOT THREE GOOD PITCHERS FROM LAST YEAR...
AND THE CATCHER AND INFIELDER SLOTS ARE ALL GOING TO SENIORS...
AMEND
AND LEFT, CENTER AND RIGHT FIELD ARE ALL PRETTY MUCH LOCKED UP, SO...
BENCH-WARMER! I KNEW IT!
STARTING BENCH-WARMER!

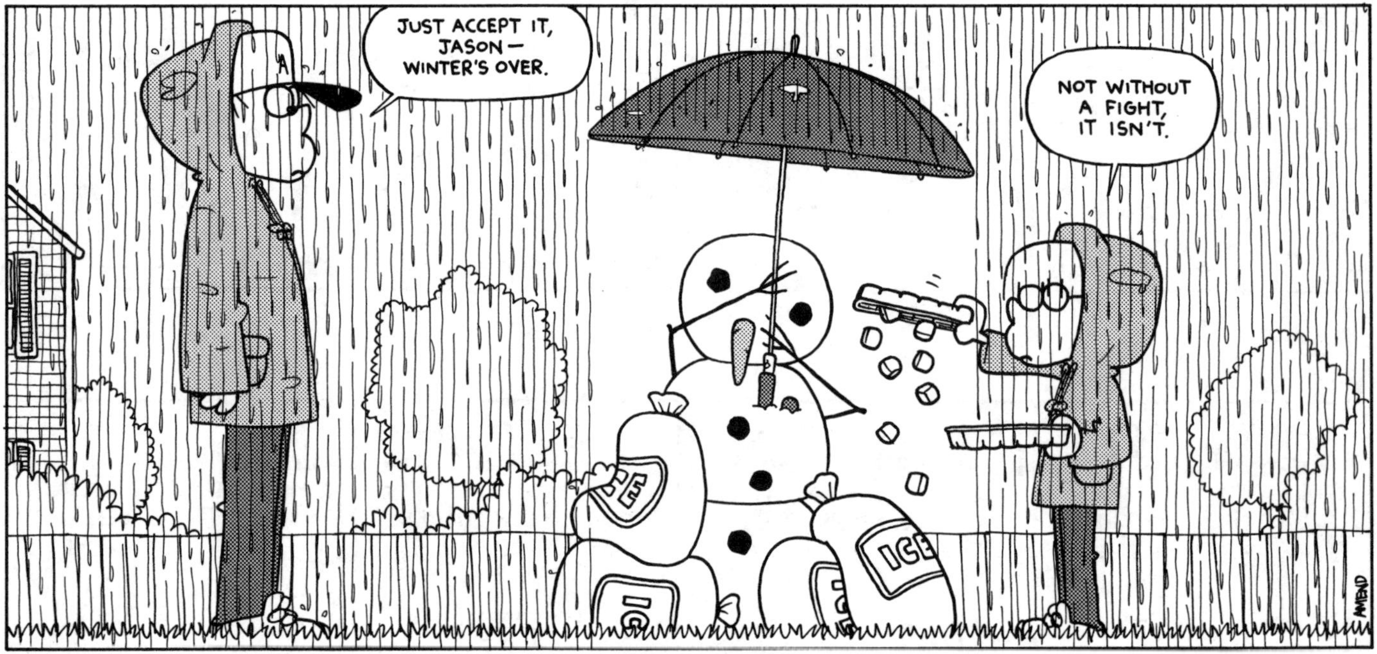
JUST ACCEPT IT, JASON— WINTER'S OVER.
NOT WITHOUT A FIGHT, IT ISN'T.
ICE
ICE
ICE
ICE
AMEND

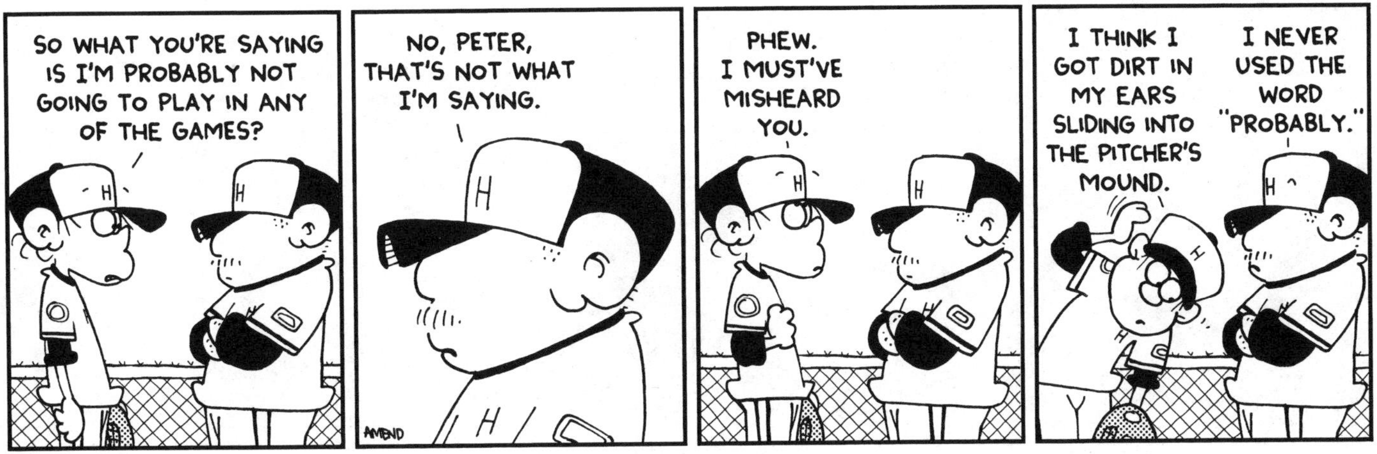
SO WHAT YOU'RE SAYING IS I'M PROBABLY NOT GOING TO PLAY IN ANY OF THE GAMES?
NO, PETER, THAT'S NOT WHAT I'M SAYING.
AMEND
PHEW. I MUST'VE MISHEARD YOU.
I THINK I GOT DIRT IN MY EARS SLIDING INTO THE PITCHER'S MOUND.
I NEVER USED THE WORD "PROBABLY."

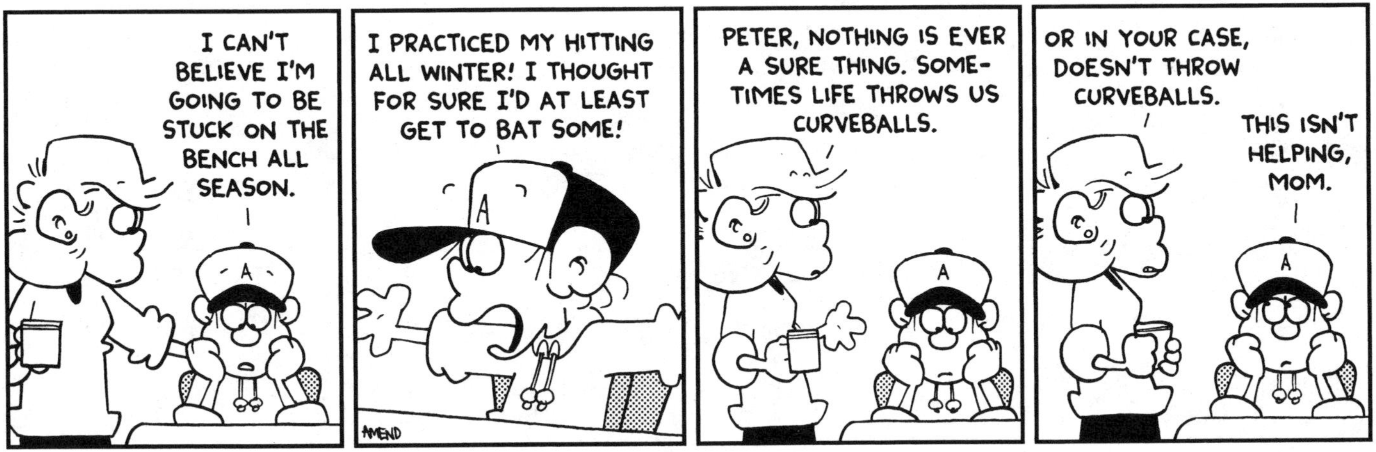
I CAN'T BELIEVE I'M GOING TO BE STUCK ON THE BENCH ALL SEASON.
I PRACTICED MY HITTING ALL WINTER! I THOUGHT FOR SURE I'D AT LEAST GET TO BAT SOME!
AMEND
PETER, NOTHING IS EVER A SURE THING. SOME-TIMES LIFE THROWS US CURVEBALLS.
OR IN YOUR CASE, DOESN'T THROW CURVEBALLS.
THIS ISN'T HELPING, MOM.

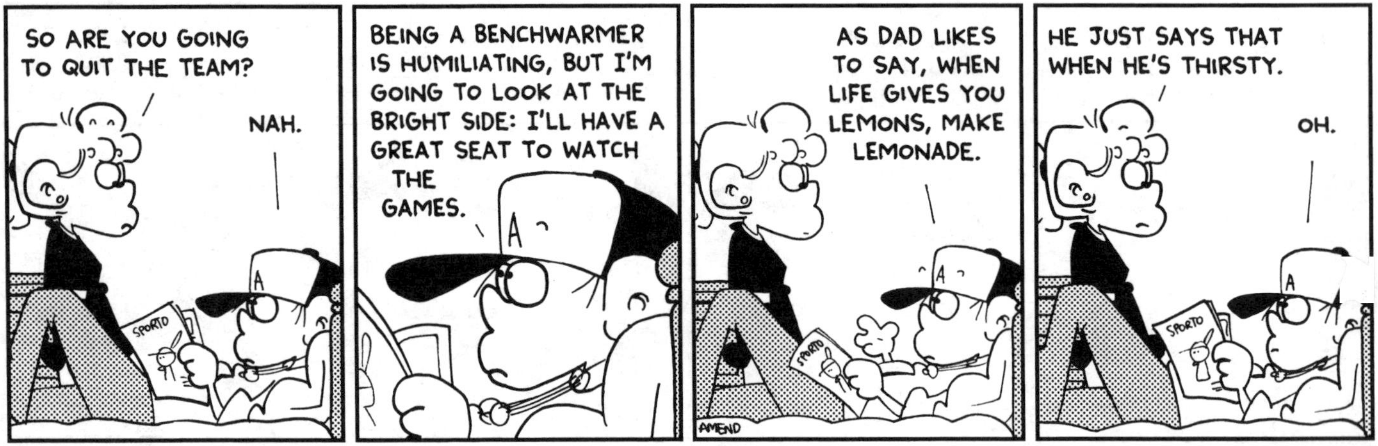
SO ARE YOU GOING TO QUIT THE TEAM?
NAH.
BEING A BENCHWARMER IS HUMILIATING, BUT I'M GOING TO LOOK AT THE BRIGHT SIDE: I'LL HAVE A GREAT SEAT TO WATCH THE GAMES.
AS DAD LIKES TO SAY, WHEN LIFE GIVES YOU LEMONS, MAKE LEMONADE.
HE JUST SAYS THAT WHEN HE'S THIRSTY.
OH.
SPORTO
AMEND

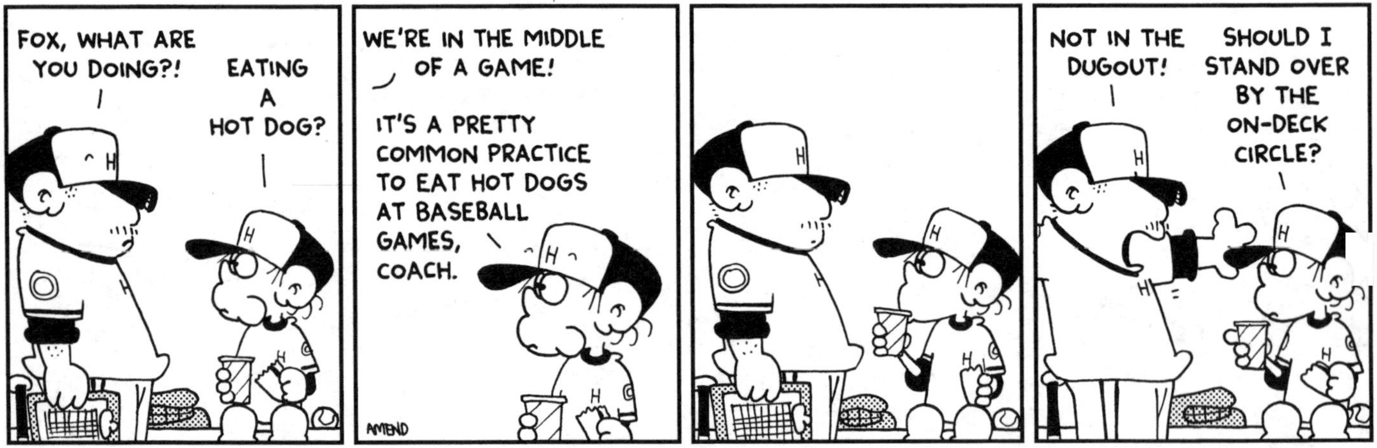
FOX, WHAT ARE YOU DOING?!
EATING A HOT DOG?
WE'RE IN THE MIDDLE OF A GAME!
IT'S A PRETTY COMMON PRACTICE TO EAT HOT DOGS AT BASEBALL GAMES, COACH.
NOT IN THE DUGOUT!
SHOULD I STAND OVER BY THE ON-DECK CIRCLE?
AMEND

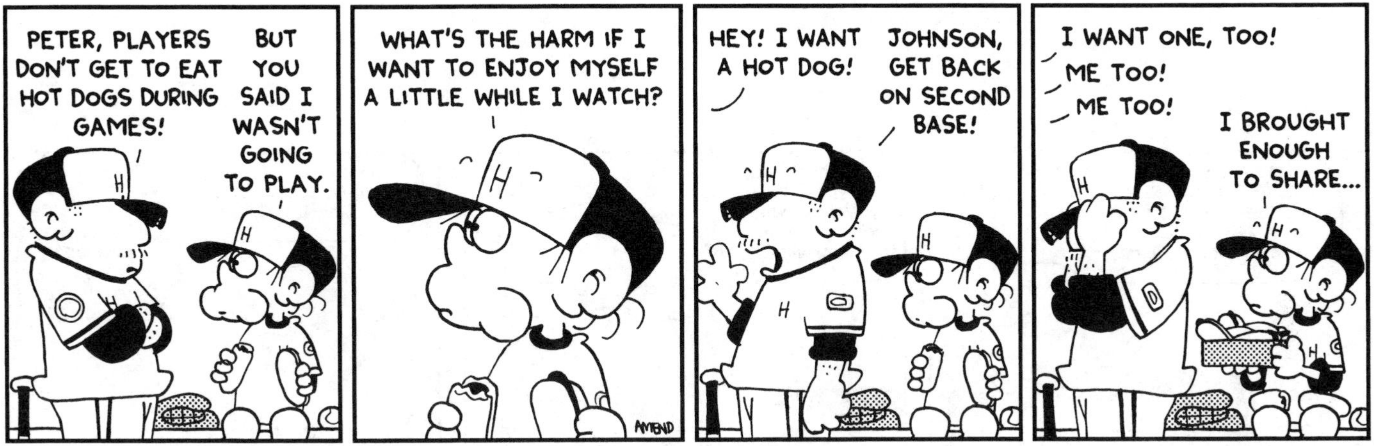
PETER, PLAYERS DON'T GET TO EAT HOT DOGS DURING GAMES!
BUT YOU SAID I WASN'T GOING TO PLAY.
WHAT'S THE HARM IF I WANT TO ENJOY MYSELF A LITTLE WHILE I WATCH?
AMEND
HEY! I WANT A HOT DOG!
JOHNSON, GET BACK ON SECOND BASE!
I WANT ONE, TOO!
ME TOO!
ME TOO!
I BROUGHT ENOUGH TO SHARE...

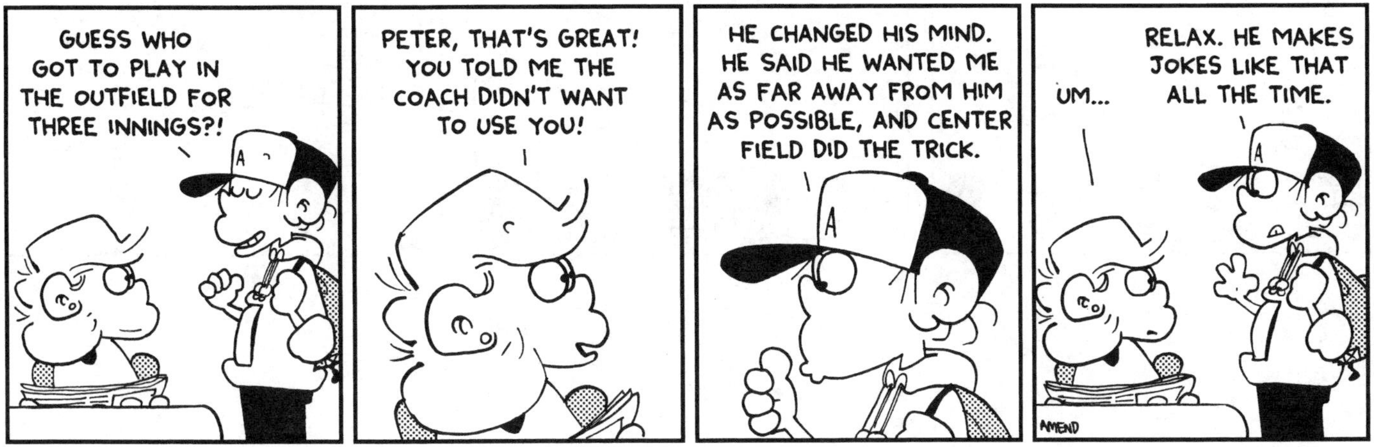
GUESS WHO GOT TO PLAY IN THE OUTFIELD FOR THREE INNINGS?!
PETER, THAT'S GREAT! YOU TOLD ME THE COACH DIDN'T WANT TO USE YOU!
HE CHANGED HIS MIND. HE SAID HE WANTED ME AS FAR AWAY FROM HIM AS POSSIBLE, AND CENTER FIELD DID THE TRICK.
UM...
RELAX. HE MAKES JOKES LIKE THAT ALL THE TIME.
AMEND

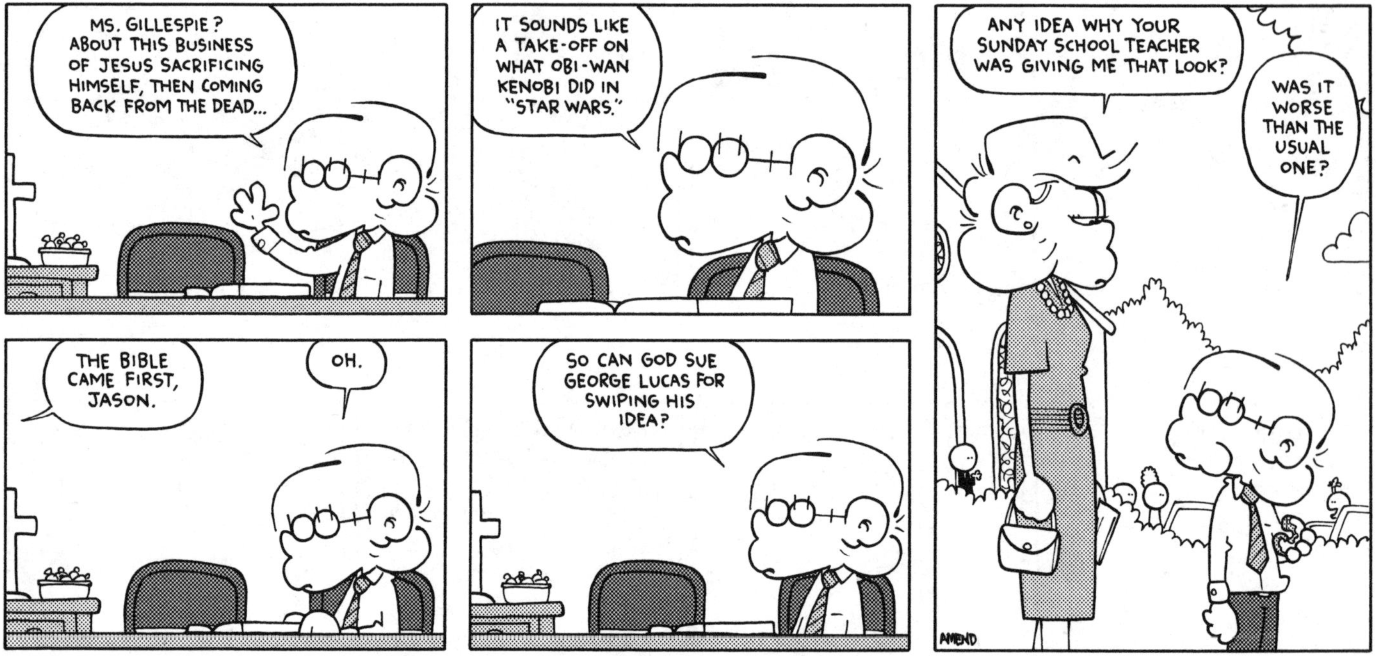
MS. GILLESPIE? ABOUT THIS BUSINESS OF JESUS SACRIFICING HIMSELF, THEN COMING BACK FROM THE DEAD...
IT SOUNDS LIKE A TAKE-OFF ON WHAT OBI-WAN KENOBI DID IN "STAR WARS."
THE BIBLE CAME FIRST, JASON.
OH.
SO CAN GOD SUE GEORGE LUCAS FOR SWIPING HIS IDEA?
ANY IDEA WHY YOUR SUNDAY SCHOOL TEACHER WAS GIVING ME THAT LOOK?
WAS IT WORSE THAN THE USUAL ONE?
AMEND

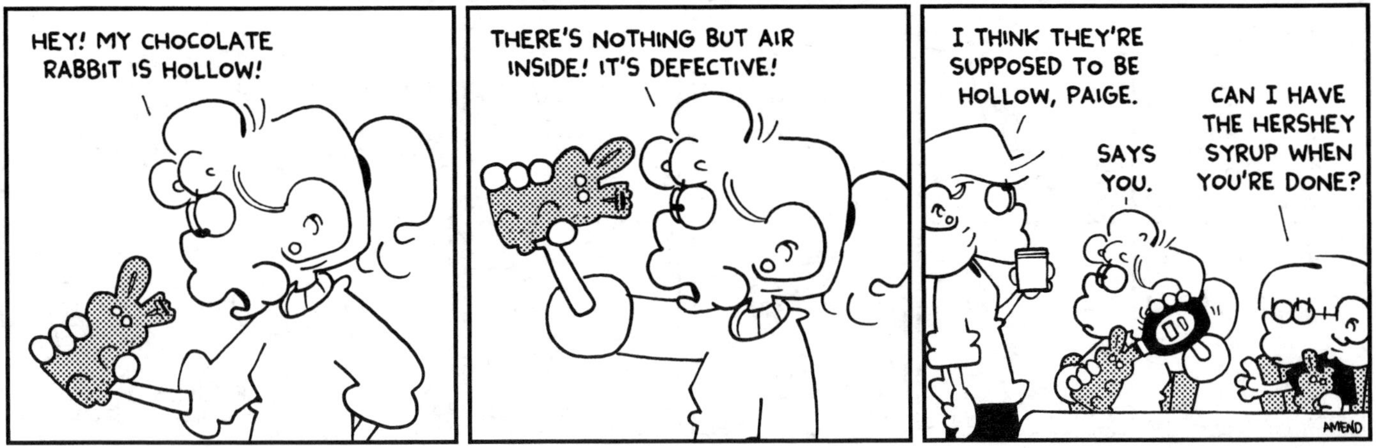
HEY! MY CHOCOLATE RABBIT IS HOLLOW!
THERE'S NOTHING BUT AIR INSIDE! IT'S DEFECTIVE!
I THINK THEY'RE SUPPOSED TO BE HOLLOW, PAIGE.
SAYS YOU.
CAN I HAVE THE HERSHEY SYRUP WHEN YOU'RE DONE?
AMEND

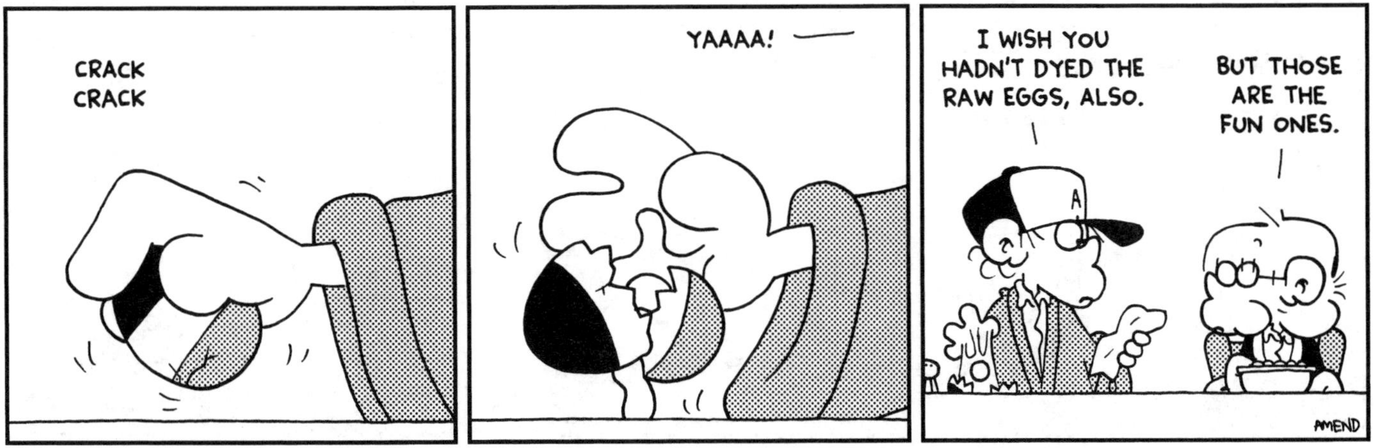
CRACK CRACK
YAAAA!
I WISH YOU HADN'T DYED THE RAW EGGS, ALSO.
BUT THOSE ARE THE FUN ONES.
AMEND

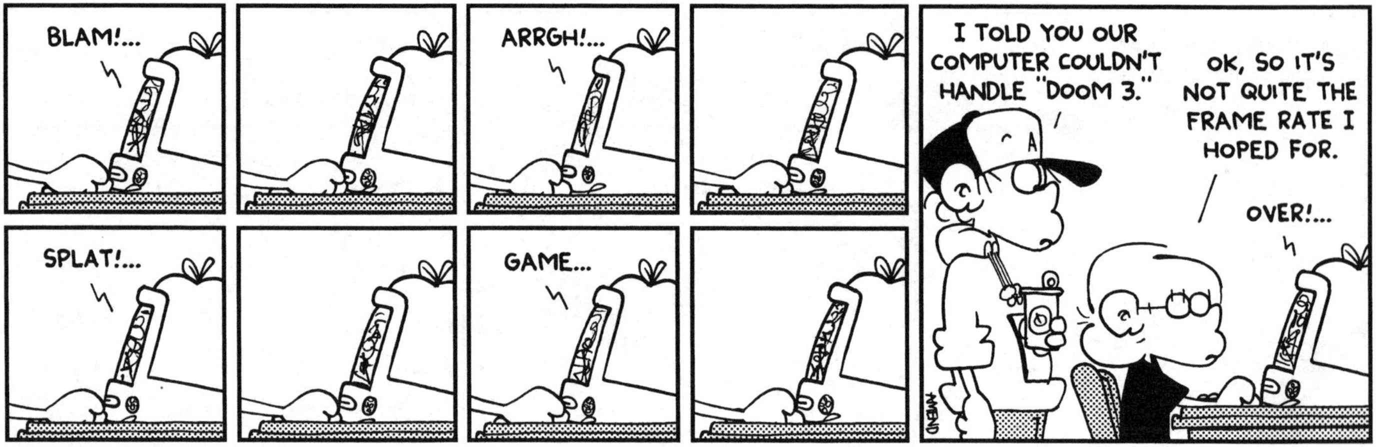
BLAM!...
ARRGH!...
SPLAT!...
GAME...
I TOLD YOU OUR COMPUTER COULDN'T HANDLE "DOOM 3."
OK, SO IT'S NOT QUITE THE FRAME RATE I HOPED FOR.
OVER!...
AMEND

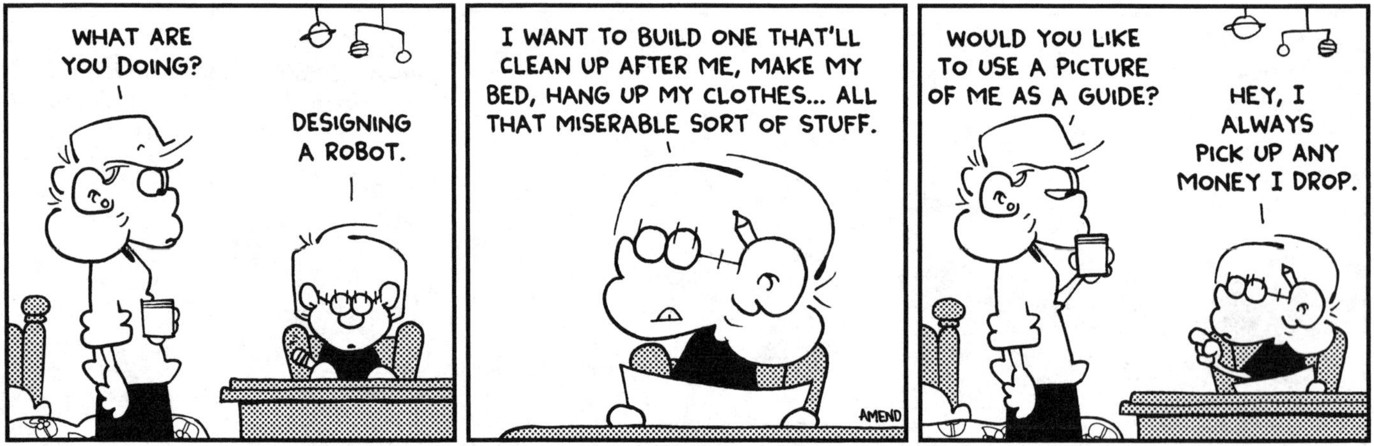
WHAT ARE YOU DOING?
DESIGNING A ROBOT.
I WANT TO BUILD ONE THAT'LL CLEAN UP AFTER ME, MAKE MY BED, HANG UP MY CLOTHES... ALL THAT MISERABLE SORT OF STUFF.
AMEND
WOULD YOU LIKE TO USE A PICTURE OF ME AS A GUIDE?
HEY, I ALWAYS PICK UP ANY MONEY I DROP.

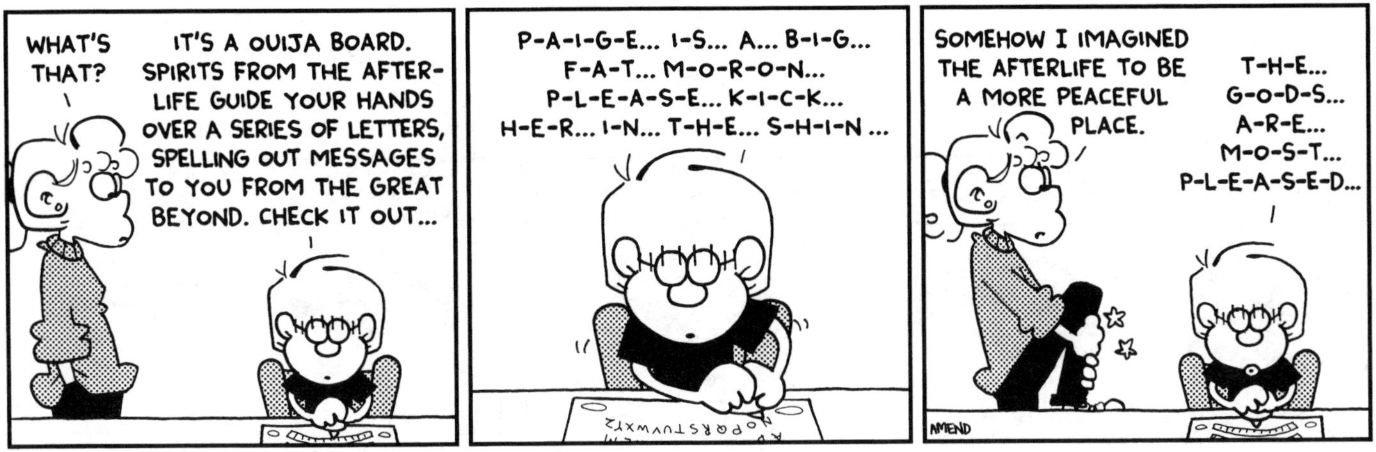
WHAT'S THAT?
IT'S A OUIJA BOARD. SPIRITS FROM THE AFTER-LIFE GUIDE YOUR HANDS OVER A SERIES OF LETTERS, SPELLING OUT MESSAGES TO YOU FROM THE GREAT BEYOND. CHECK IT OUT...
P-A-I-G-E... I-S... A... B-I-G... F-A-T... M-O-R-O-N... P-L-E-A-S-E... K-I-C-K... H-E-R... I-N... T-H-E... S-H-I-N ...
SOMEHOW I IMAGINED THE AFTERLIFE TO BE A MORE PEACEFUL PLACE.
T-H-E... G-O-D-S... A-R-E... M-O-S-T... P-L-E-A-S-E-D...
AMEND

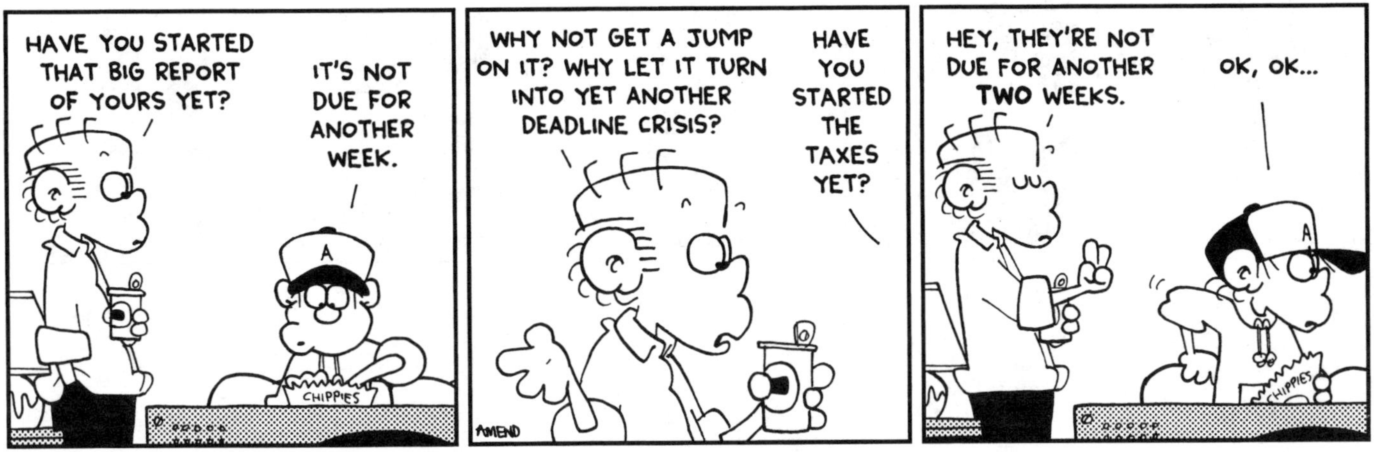
HAVE YOU STARTED THAT BIG REPORT OF YOURS YET?
IT'S NOT DUE FOR ANOTHER WEEK.
CHIPPIES
WHY NOT GET A JUMP ON IT? WHY LET IT TURN INTO YET ANOTHER DEADLINE CRISIS?
HAVE YOU STARTED THE TAXES YET?
AMEND
HEY, THEY'RE NOT DUE FOR ANOTHER **TWO** WEEKS.
OK, OK...
CHIPPIES

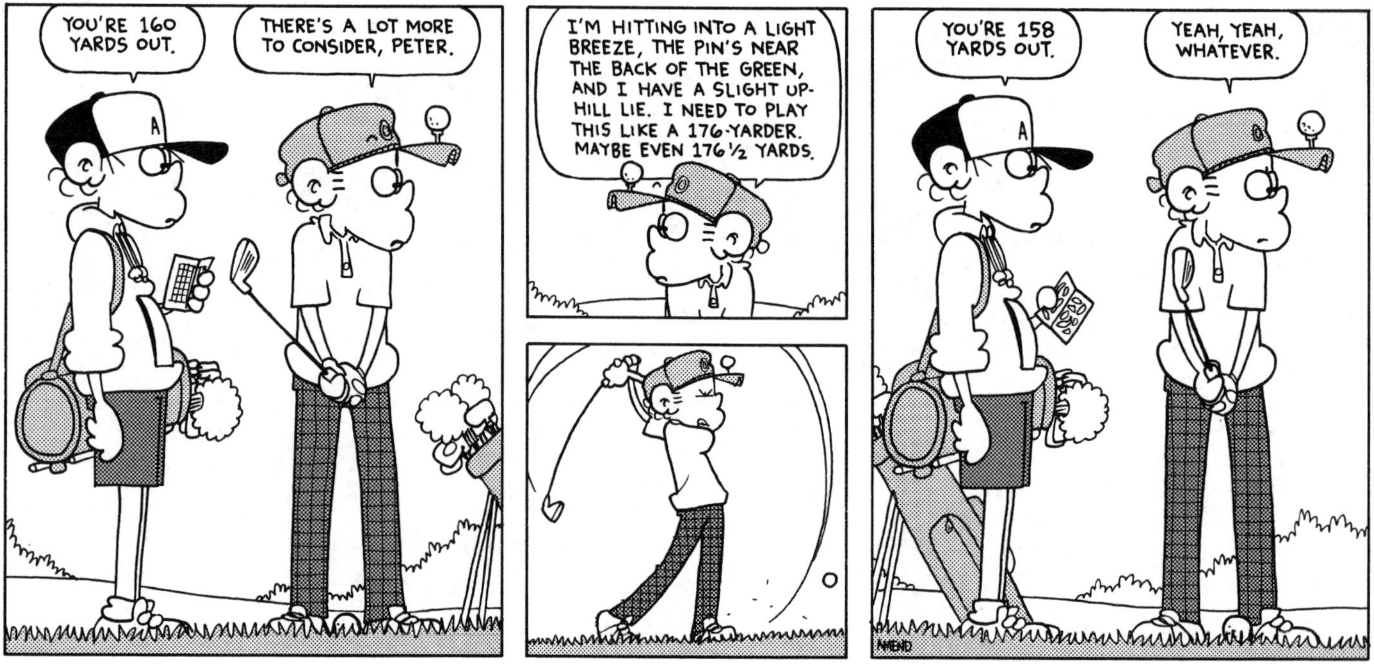
YOU'RE 160 YARDS OUT.
THERE'S A LOT MORE TO CONSIDER, PETER.
I'M HITTING INTO A LIGHT BREEZE, THE PIN'S NEAR THE BACK OF THE GREEN, AND I HAVE A SLIGHT UP-HILL LIE. I NEED TO PLAY THIS LIKE A 176-YARDER. MAYBE EVEN 176½ YARDS.
YOU'RE 158 YARDS OUT.
YEAH, YEAH, WHATEVER.

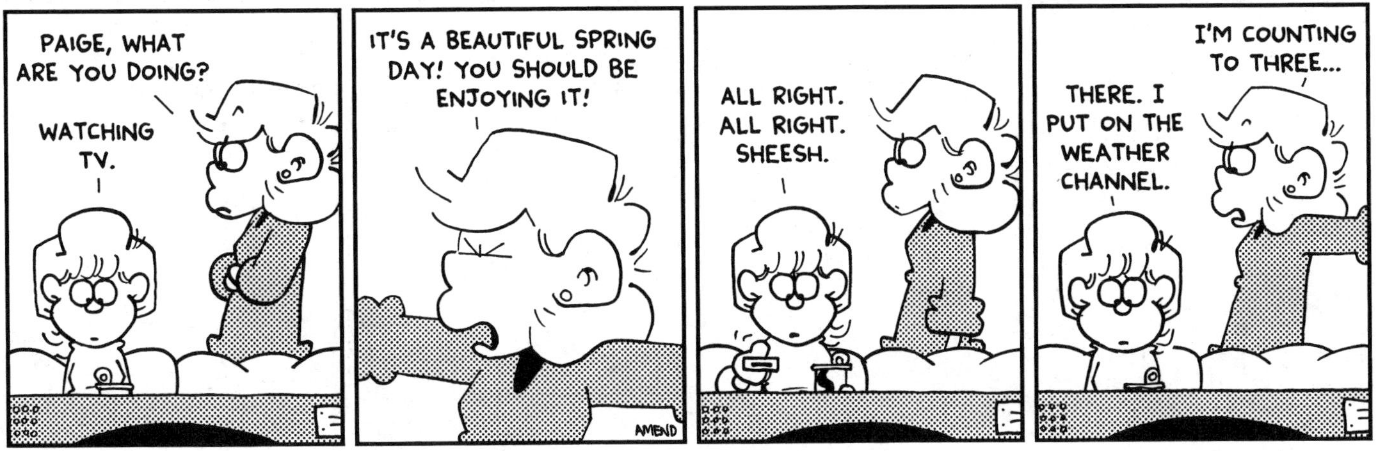
PAIGE, WHAT ARE YOU DOING?
WATCHING TV.
IT'S A BEAUTIFUL SPRING DAY! YOU SHOULD BE ENJOYING IT!
AMEND
ALL RIGHT. ALL RIGHT. SHEESH.
THERE. I PUT ON THE WEATHER CHANNEL.
I'M COUNTING TO THREE...

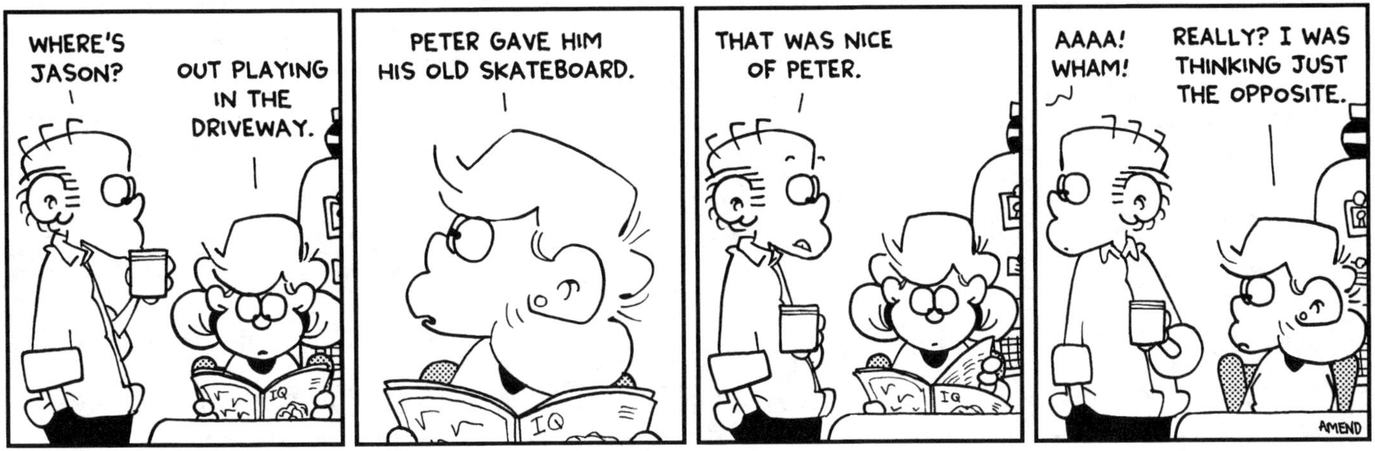
WHERE'S JASON?
OUT PLAYING IN THE DRIVEWAY.
PETER GAVE HIM HIS OLD SKATEBOARD.
THAT WAS NICE OF PETER.
AAAA! WHAM!
REALLY? I WAS THINKING JUST THE OPPOSITE.
AMEND

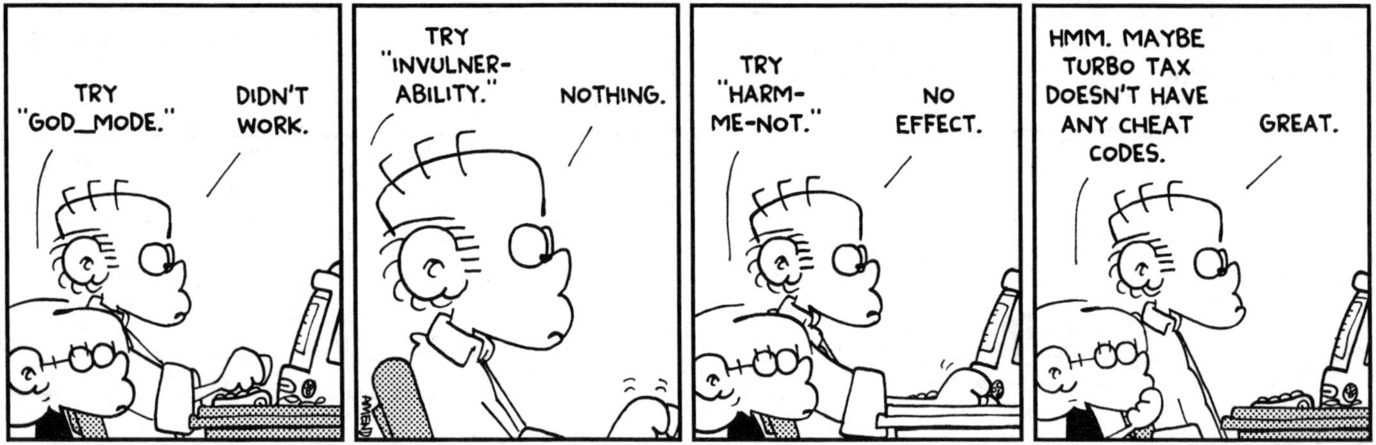
TRY "GOD_MODE."
DIDN'T WORK.
TRY "INVULNER-ABILITY."
NOTHING.
TRY "HARM-ME-NOT."
NO EFFECT.
HMM. MAYBE TURBO TAX DOESN'T HAVE ANY CHEAT CODES.
GREAT.
AMEND

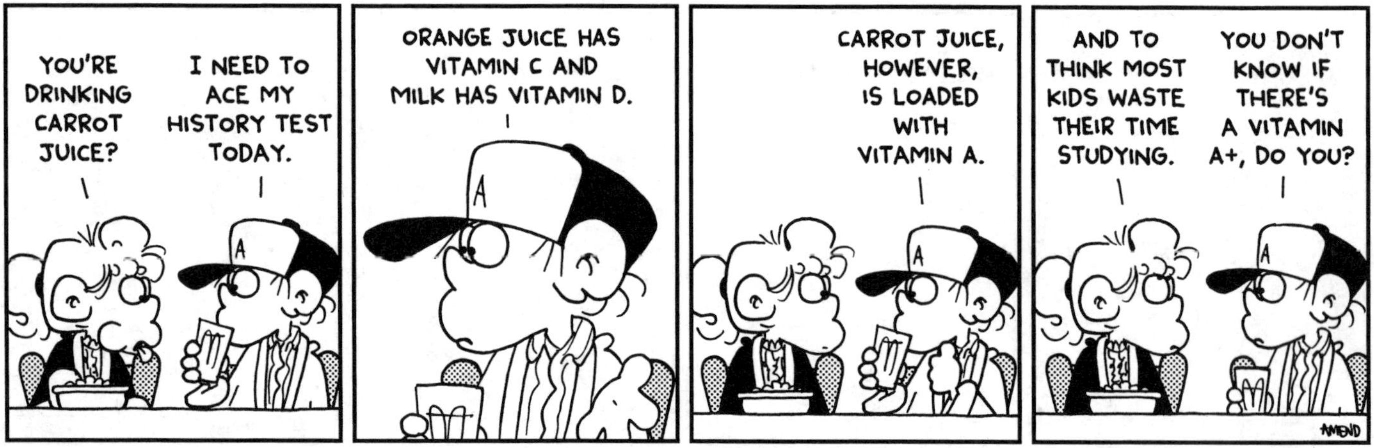
YOU'RE DRINKING CARROT JUICE?
I NEED TO ACE MY HISTORY TEST TODAY.
ORANGE JUICE HAS VITAMIN C AND MILK HAS VITAMIN D.
CARROT JUICE, HOWEVER, IS LOADED WITH VITAMIN A.
AND TO THINK MOST KIDS WASTE THEIR TIME STUDYING.
YOU DON'T KNOW IF THERE'S A VITAMIN A+, DO YOU?
AMEND

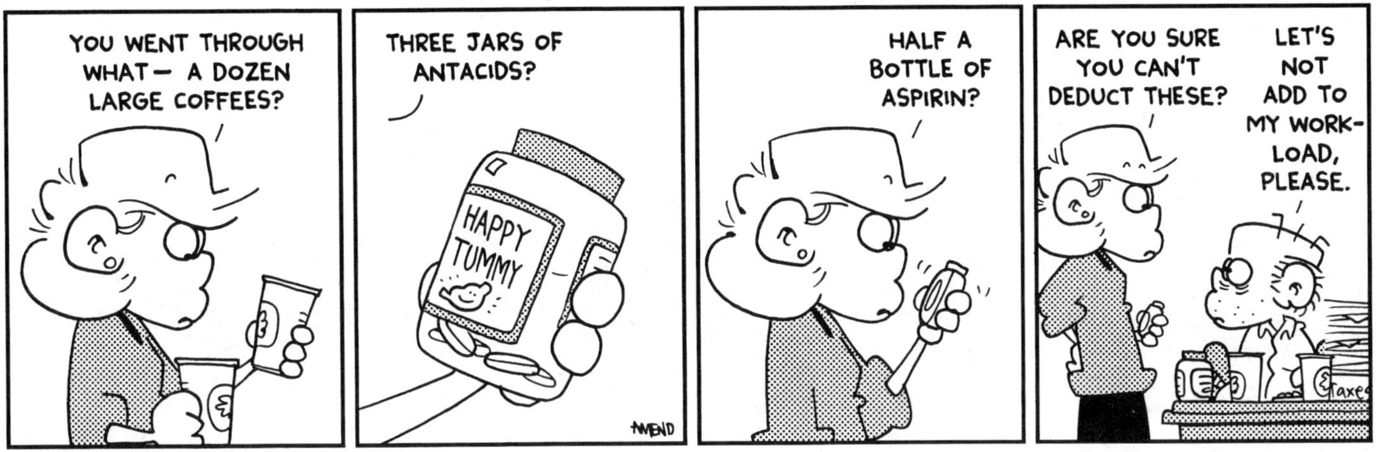
YOU WENT THROUGH WHAT— A DOZEN LARGE COFFEES?
THREE JARS OF ANTACIDS?
HAPPY TUMMY
HALF A BOTTLE OF ASPIRIN?
ARE YOU SURE YOU CAN'T DEDUCT THESE?
LET'S NOT ADD TO MY WORK-LOAD, PLEASE.
AMEND

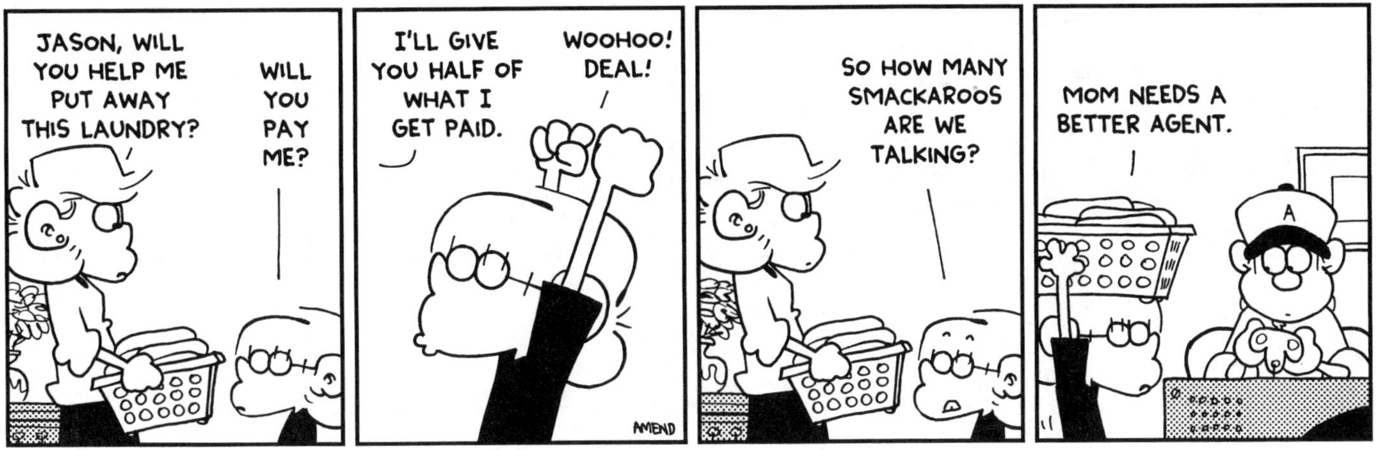
JASON, WILL YOU HELP ME PUT AWAY THIS LAUNDRY?
WILL YOU PAY ME?
I'LL GIVE YOU HALF OF WHAT I GET PAID.
WOOHOO! DEAL!
AMEND
SO HOW MANY SMACKAROOS ARE WE TALKING?
MOM NEEDS A BETTER AGENT.

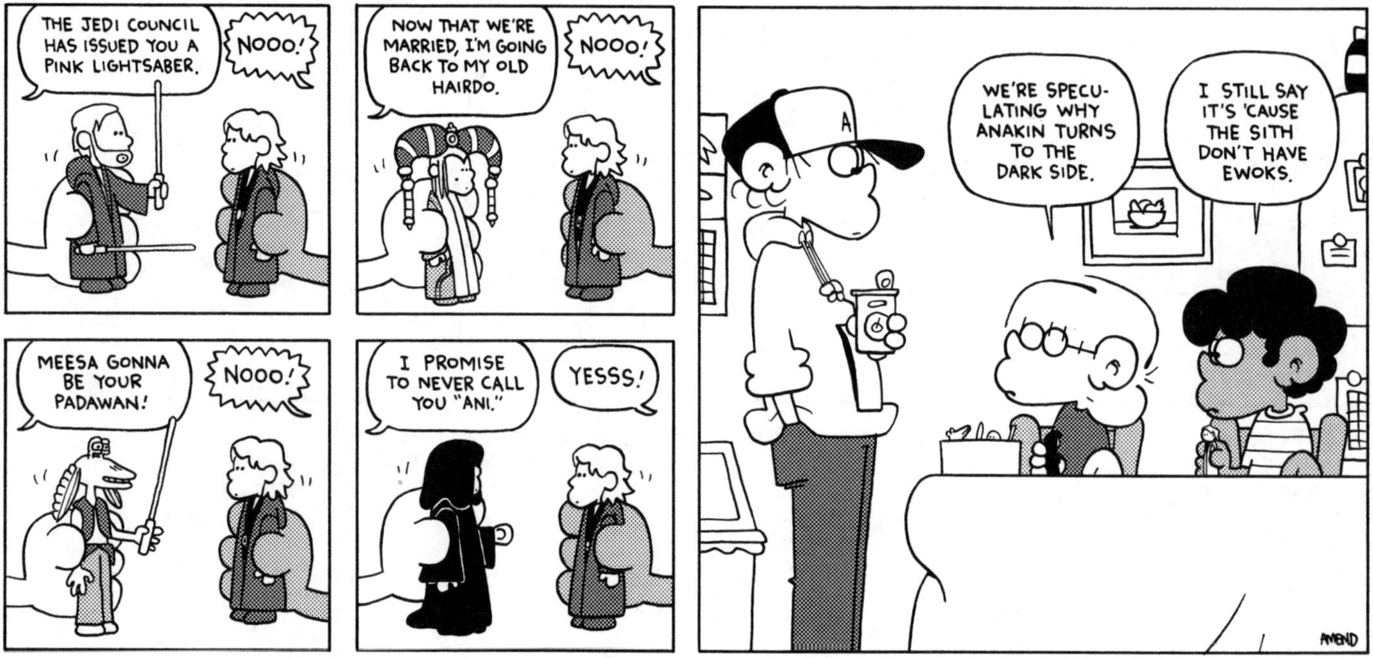
THE JEDI COUNCIL HAS ISSUED YOU A PINK LIGHTSABER.
NOOO!
NOW THAT WE'RE MARRIED, I'M GOING BACK TO MY OLD HAIRDO.
NOOO!
MEESA GONNA BE YOUR PADAWAN!
NOOO!
I PROMISE TO NEVER CALL YOU "ANI."
YESSS!
WE'RE SPECULATING WHY ANAKIN TURNS TO THE DARK SIDE.
I STILL SAY IT'S 'CAUSE THE SITH DON'T HAVE EWOKS.
AMEND

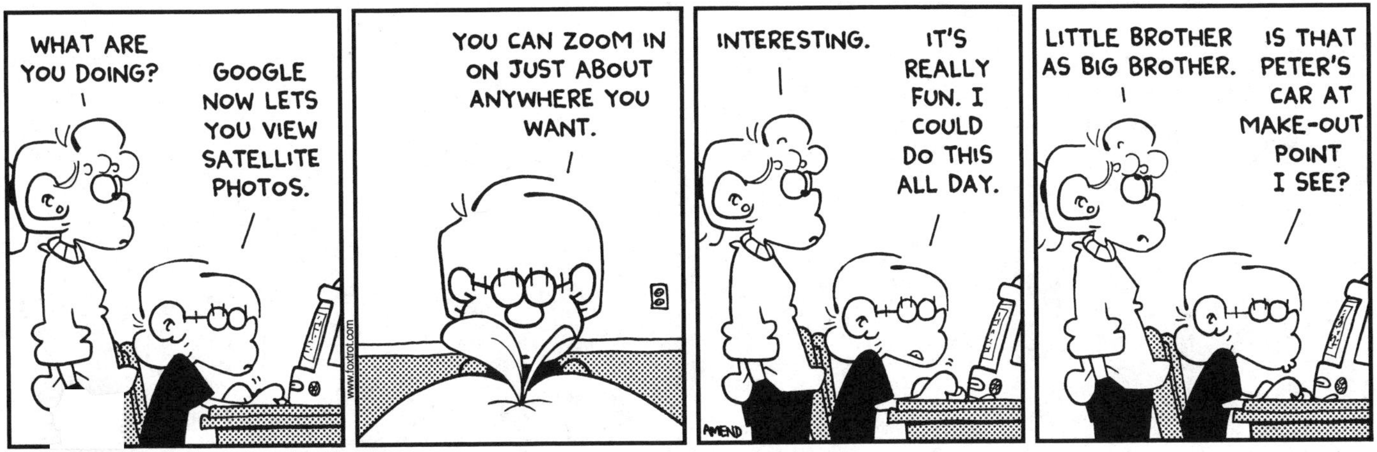
WHAT ARE YOU DOING?
GOOGLE NOW LETS YOU VIEW SATELLITE PHOTOS.
www.foxtrot.com
YOU CAN ZOOM IN ON JUST ABOUT ANYWHERE YOU WANT.
INTERESTING.
IT'S REALLY FUN. I COULD DO THIS ALL DAY.
AMEND
LITTLE BROTHER AS BIG BROTHER.
IS THAT PETER'S CAR AT MAKE-OUT POINT I SEE?

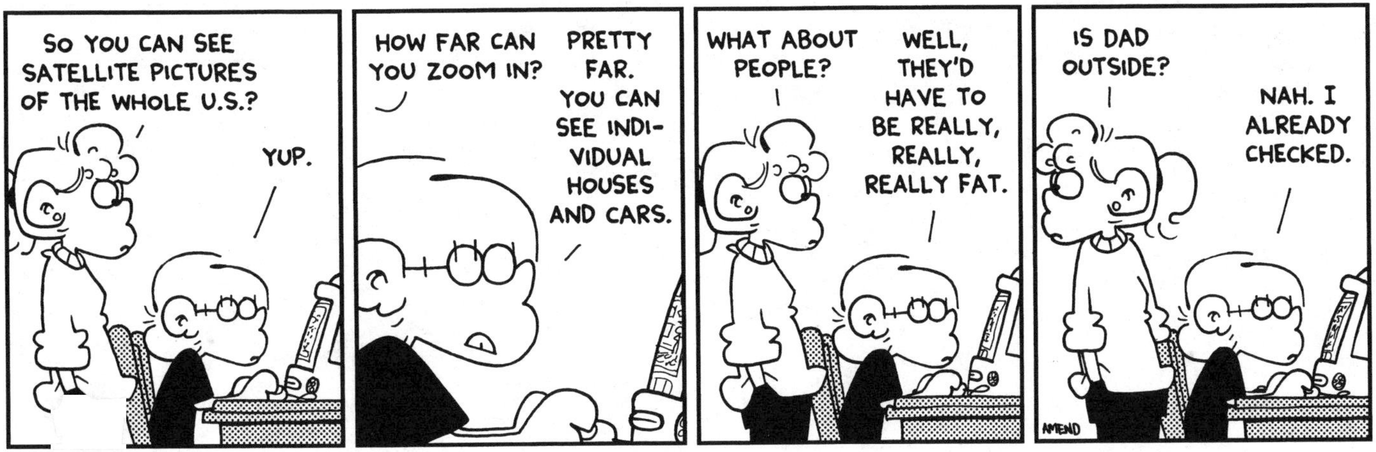
SO YOU CAN SEE SATELLITE PICTURES OF THE WHOLE U.S.?
YUP.
HOW FAR CAN YOU ZOOM IN?
PRETTY FAR. YOU CAN SEE INDI-VIDUAL HOUSES AND CARS.
WHAT ABOUT PEOPLE?
WELL, THEY'D HAVE TO BE REALLY, REALLY, REALLY FAT.
IS DAD OUTSIDE?
NAH. I ALREADY CHECKED.
AMEND

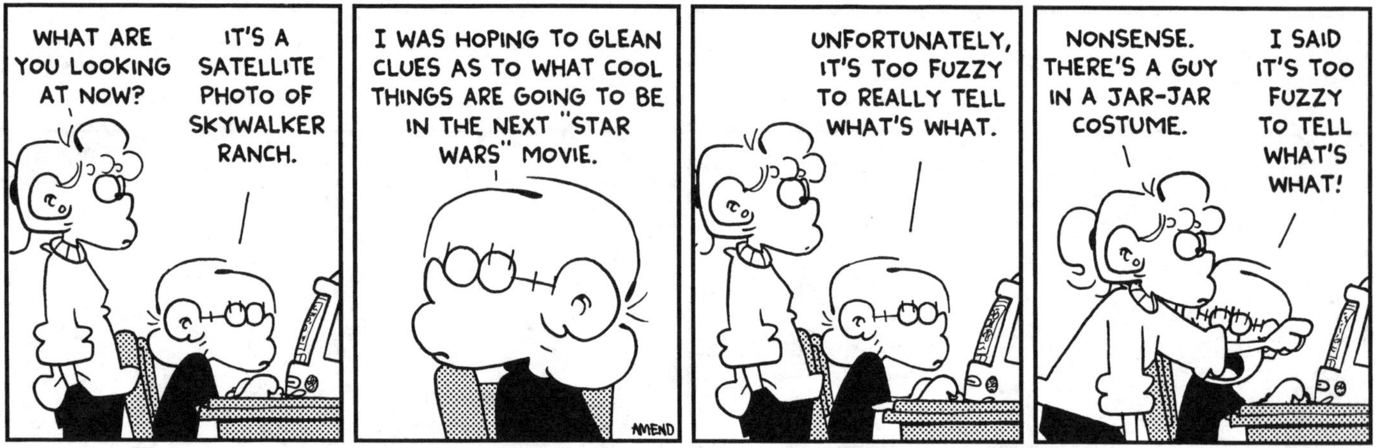
WHAT ARE YOU LOOKING AT NOW?
IT'S A SATELLITE PHOTO OF SKYWALKER RANCH.
I WAS HOPING TO GLEAN CLUES AS TO WHAT COOL THINGS ARE GOING TO BE IN THE NEXT "STAR WARS" MOVIE.
AMEND
UNFORTUNATELY, IT'S TOO FUZZY TO REALLY TELL WHAT'S WHAT.
NONSENSE. THERE'S A GUY IN A JAR-JAR COSTUME.
I SAID IT'S TOO FUZZY TO TELL WHAT'S WHAT!

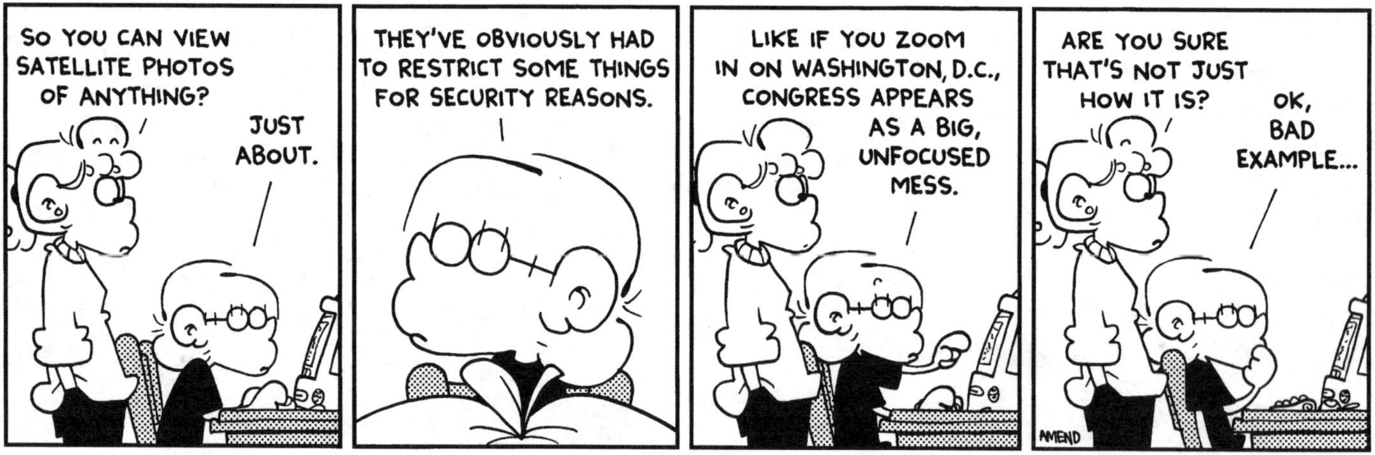
SO YOU CAN VIEW SATELLITE PHOTOS OF ANYTHING?
JUST ABOUT.
THEY'VE OBVIOUSLY HAD TO RESTRICT SOME THINGS FOR SECURITY REASONS.
LIKE IF YOU ZOOM IN ON WASHINGTON, D.C., CONGRESS APPEARS AS A BIG, UNFOCUSED MESS.
ARE YOU SURE THAT'S NOT JUST HOW IT IS?
OK, BAD EXAMPLE...
AMEND

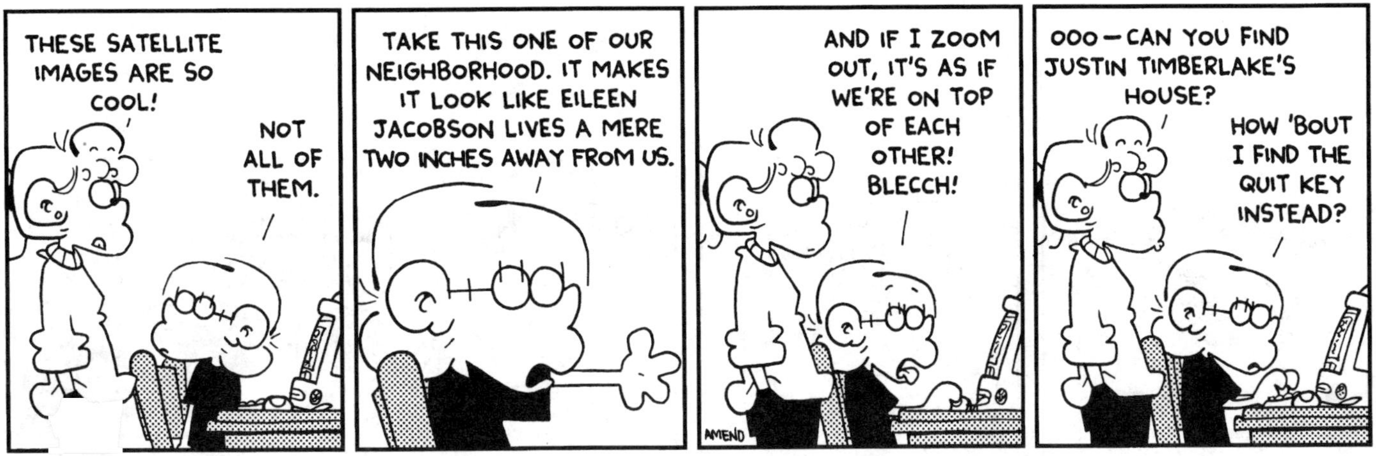
THESE SATELLITE IMAGES ARE SO COOL!
NOT ALL OF THEM.
TAKE THIS ONE OF OUR NEIGHBORHOOD. IT MAKES IT LOOK LIKE EILEEN JACOBSON LIVES A MERE TWO INCHES AWAY FROM US.
AND IF I ZOOM OUT, IT'S AS IF WE'RE ON TOP OF EACH OTHER! BLECCH!
AMEND
OOO—CAN YOU FIND JUSTIN TIMBERLAKE'S HOUSE?
HOW 'BOUT I FIND THE QUIT KEY INSTEAD?

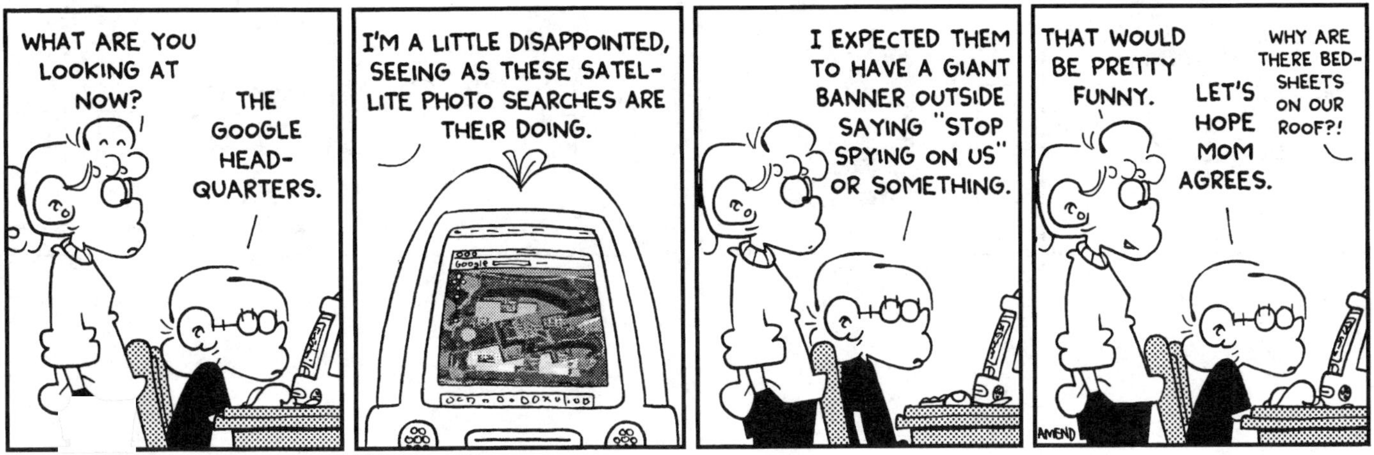
WHAT ARE YOU LOOKING AT NOW?
THE GOOGLE HEAD-QUARTERS.
I'M A LITTLE DISAPPOINTED, SEEING AS THESE SATEL-LITE PHOTO SEARCHES ARE THEIR DOING.
I EXPECTED THEM TO HAVE A GIANT BANNER OUTSIDE SAYING "STOP SPYING ON US" OR SOMETHING.
THAT WOULD BE PRETTY FUNNY.
LET'S HOPE MOM AGREES.
WHY ARE THERE BED-SHEETS ON OUR ROOF?!
AMEND

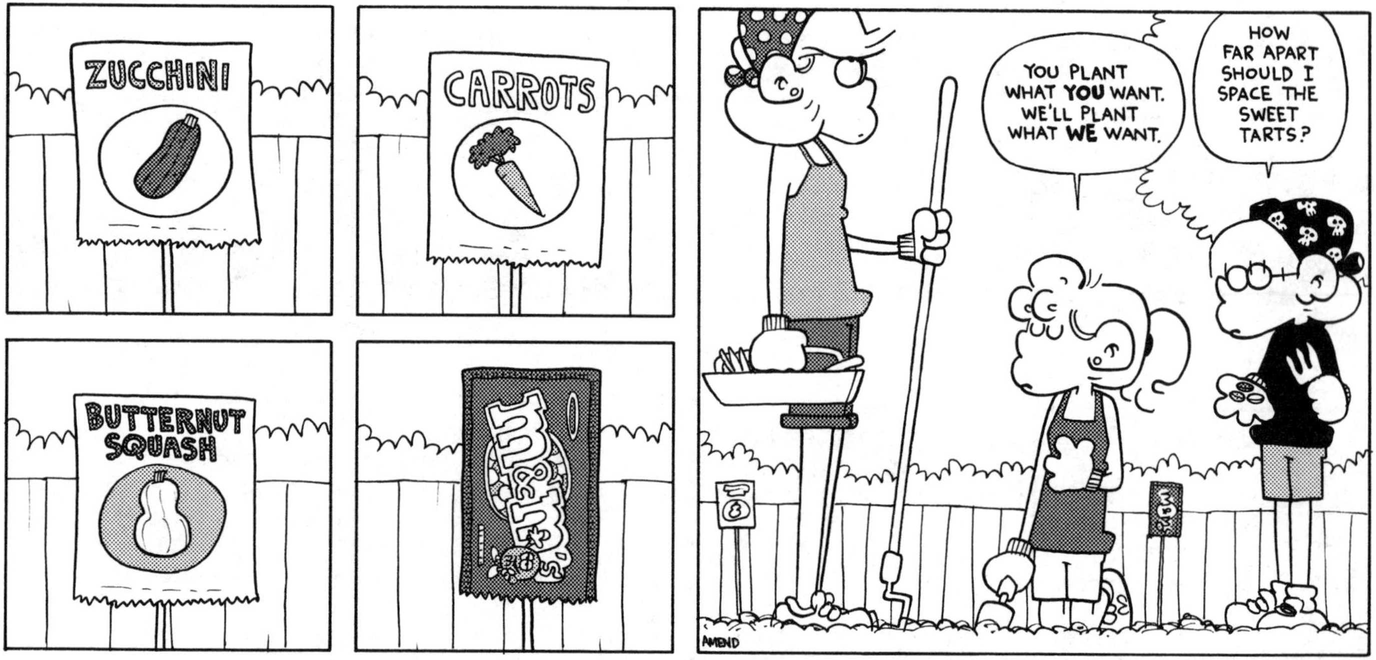
ZUCCHINI
CARROTS
BUTTERNUT SQUASH
m&m's
YOU PLANT WHAT YOU WANT. WE'LL PLANT WHAT WE WANT.
HOW FAR APART SHOULD I SPACE THE SWEET TARTS?
AMEND

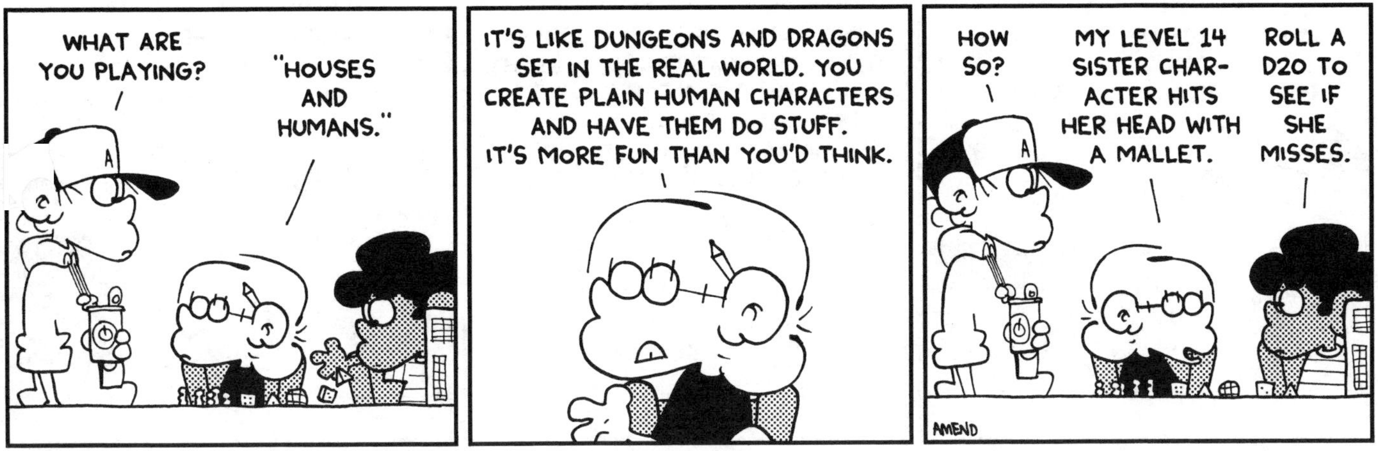
WHAT ARE YOU PLAYING?
"HOUSES AND HUMANS."
IT'S LIKE DUNGEONS AND DRAGONS SET IN THE REAL WORLD. YOU CREATE PLAIN HUMAN CHARACTERS AND HAVE THEM DO STUFF. IT'S MORE FUN THAN YOU'D THINK.
HOW SO?
MY LEVEL 14 SISTER CHARACTER HITS HER HEAD WITH A MALLET.
ROLL A D20 TO SEE IF SHE MISSES.
AMEND

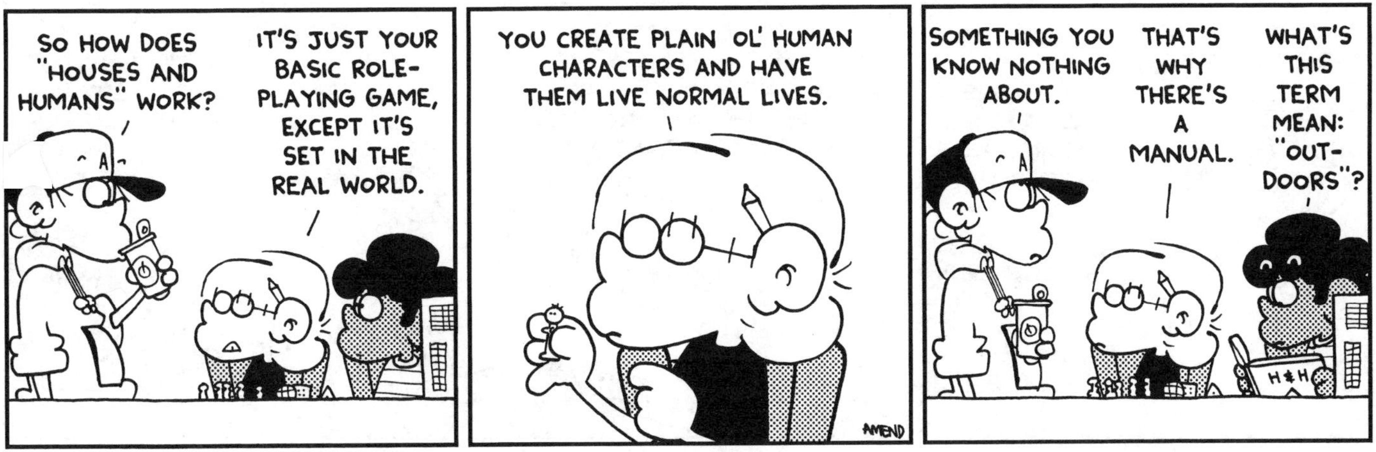
SO HOW DOES "HOUSES AND HUMANS" WORK?
IT'S JUST YOUR BASIC ROLE-PLAYING GAME, EXCEPT IT'S SET IN THE REAL WORLD.
YOU CREATE PLAIN OL' HUMAN CHARACTERS AND HAVE THEM LIVE NORMAL LIVES.
AMEND
SOMETHING YOU KNOW NOTHING ABOUT.
THAT'S WHY THERE'S A MANUAL.
WHAT'S THIS TERM MEAN: "OUTDOORS"?
H&H

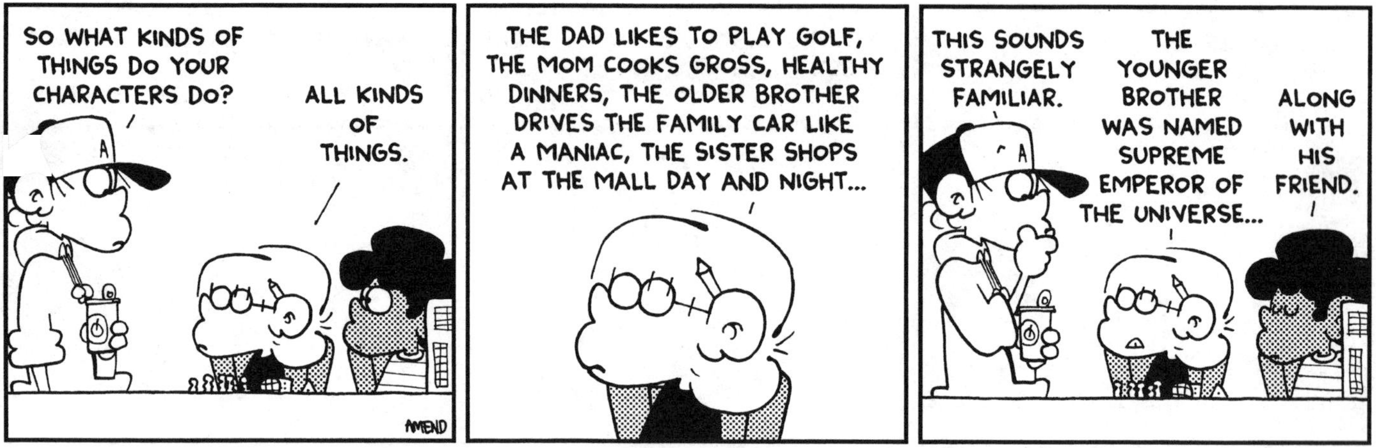
SO WHAT KINDS OF THINGS DO YOUR CHARACTERS DO?
ALL KINDS OF THINGS.
AMEND
THE DAD LIKES TO PLAY GOLF, THE MOM COOKS GROSS, HEALTHY DINNERS, THE OLDER BROTHER DRIVES THE FAMILY CAR LIKE A MANIAC, THE SISTER SHOPS AT THE MALL DAY AND NIGHT...
THIS SOUNDS STRANGELY FAMILIAR.
THE YOUNGER BROTHER WAS NAMED SUPREME EMPEROR OF THE UNIVERSE...
ALONG WITH HIS FRIEND.

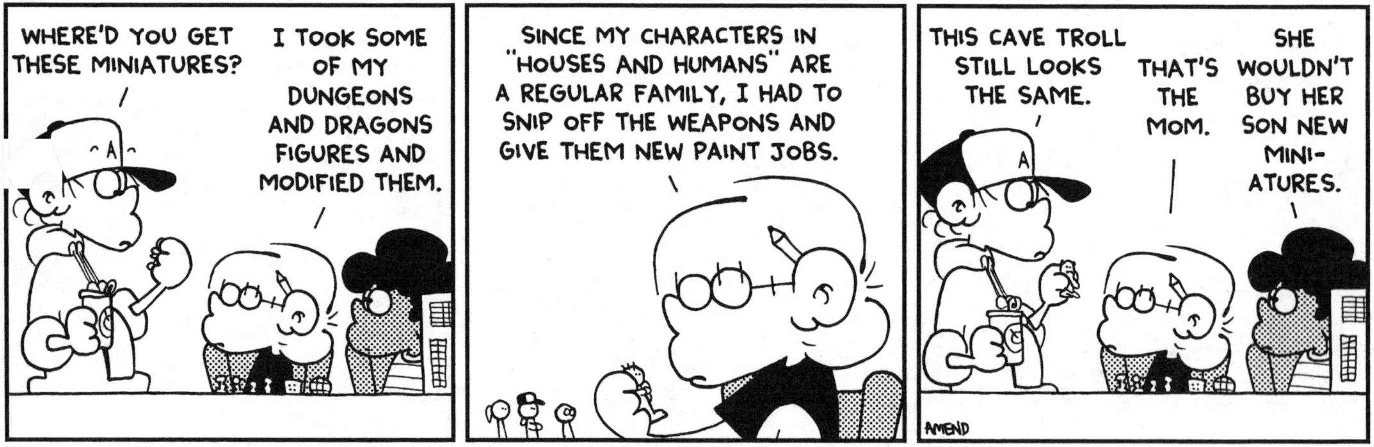
WHERE'D YOU GET THESE MINIATURES?
I TOOK SOME OF MY DUNGEONS AND DRAGONS FIGURES AND MODIFIED THEM.
SINCE MY CHARACTERS IN "HOUSES AND HUMANS" ARE A REGULAR FAMILY, I HAD TO SNIP OFF THE WEAPONS AND GIVE THEM NEW PAINT JOBS.
THIS CAVE TROLL STILL LOOKS THE SAME.
THAT'S THE MOM.
SHE WOULDN'T BUY HER SON NEW MINI-ATURES.
AMEND

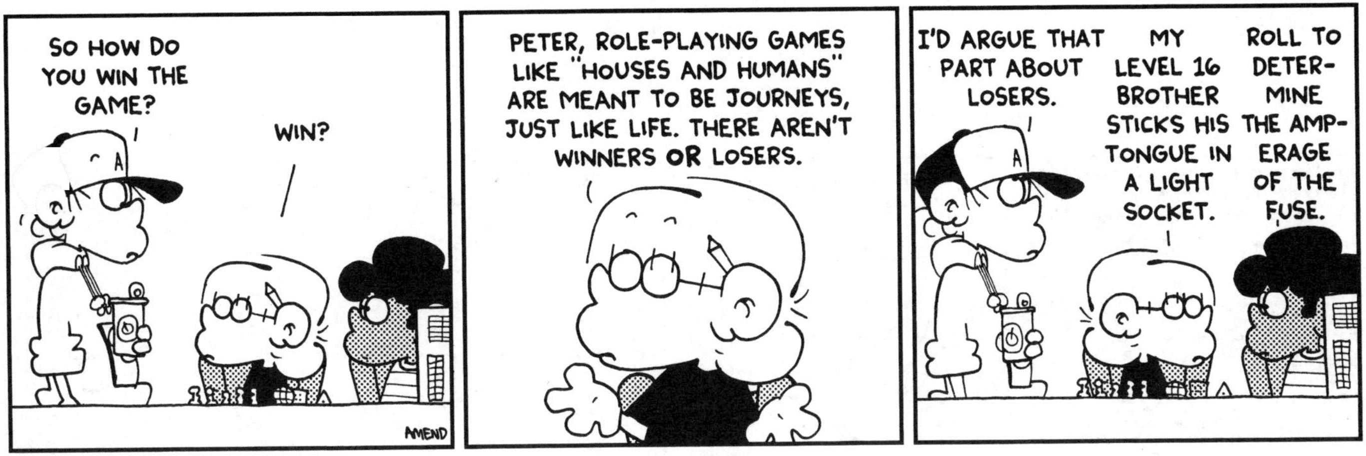
SO HOW DO YOU WIN THE GAME?
WIN?
AMEND
PETER, ROLE-PLAYING GAMES LIKE "HOUSES AND HUMANS" ARE MEANT TO BE JOURNEYS, JUST LIKE LIFE. THERE AREN'T WINNERS OR LOSERS.
I'D ARGUE THAT PART ABOUT LOSERS.
MY LEVEL 16 BROTHER STICKS HIS TONGUE IN A LIGHT SOCKET.
ROLL TO DETERMINE THE AMPERAGE OF THE FUSE.

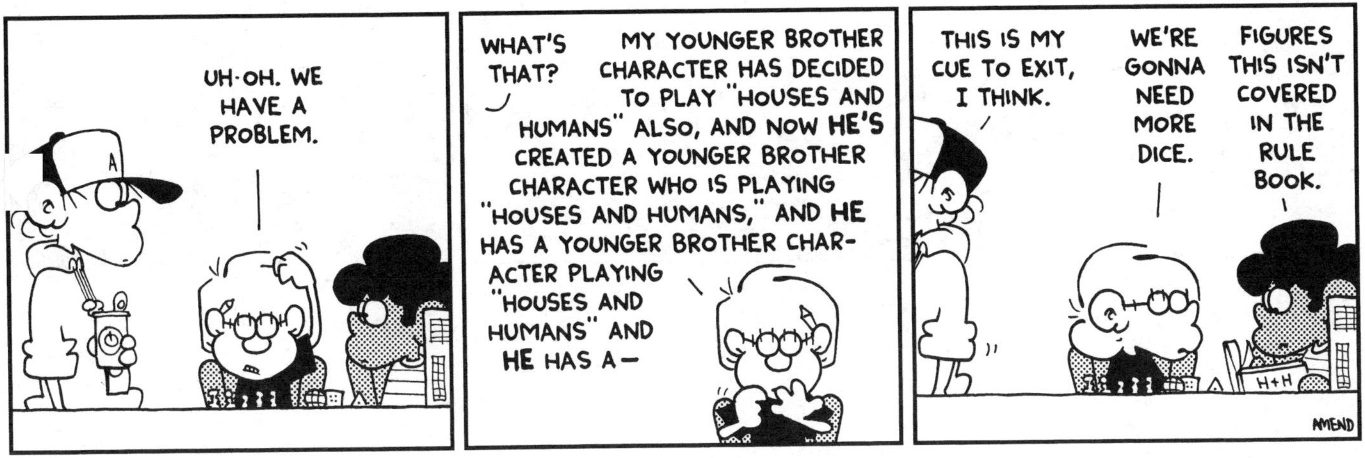
UH-OH. WE HAVE A PROBLEM.
WHAT'S THAT?
MY YOUNGER BROTHER CHARACTER HAS DECIDED TO PLAY "HOUSES AND HUMANS" ALSO, AND NOW HE'S CREATED A YOUNGER BROTHER CHARACTER WHO IS PLAYING "HOUSES AND HUMANS," AND HE HAS A YOUNGER BROTHER CHARACTER PLAYING "HOUSES AND HUMANS" AND HE HAS A—
THIS IS MY CUE TO EXIT, I THINK.
WE'RE GONNA NEED MORE DICE.
FIGURES THIS ISN'T COVERED IN THE RULE BOOK.
H+H
AMEND

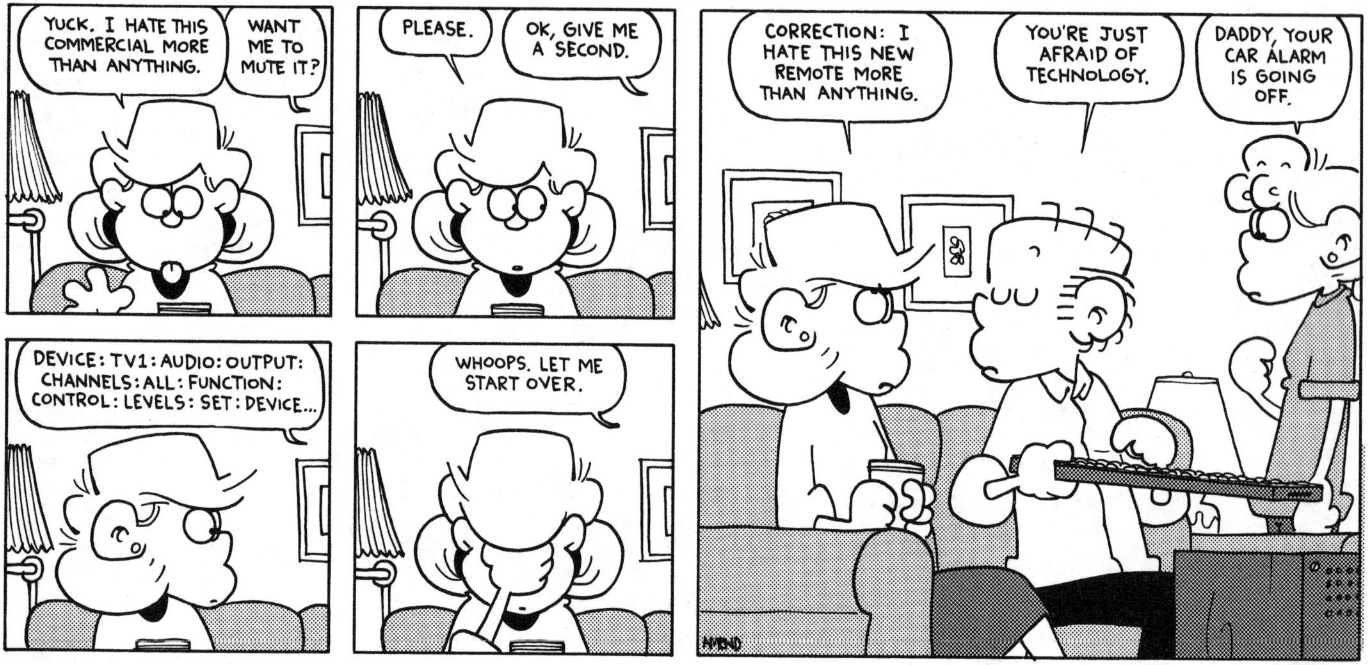
YUCK. I HATE THIS COMMERCIAL MORE THAN ANYTHING.
WANT ME TO MUTE IT?
PLEASE.
OK, GIVE ME A SECOND.
DEVICE: TV1: AUDIO: OUTPUT: CHANNELS: ALL: FUNCTION: CONTROL: LEVELS: SET: DEVICE...
WHOOPS. LET ME START OVER.
CORRECTION: I HATE THIS NEW REMOTE MORE THAN ANYTHING.
YOU'RE JUST AFRAID OF TECHNOLOGY.
DADDY, YOUR CAR ALARM IS GOING OFF.
AMEND

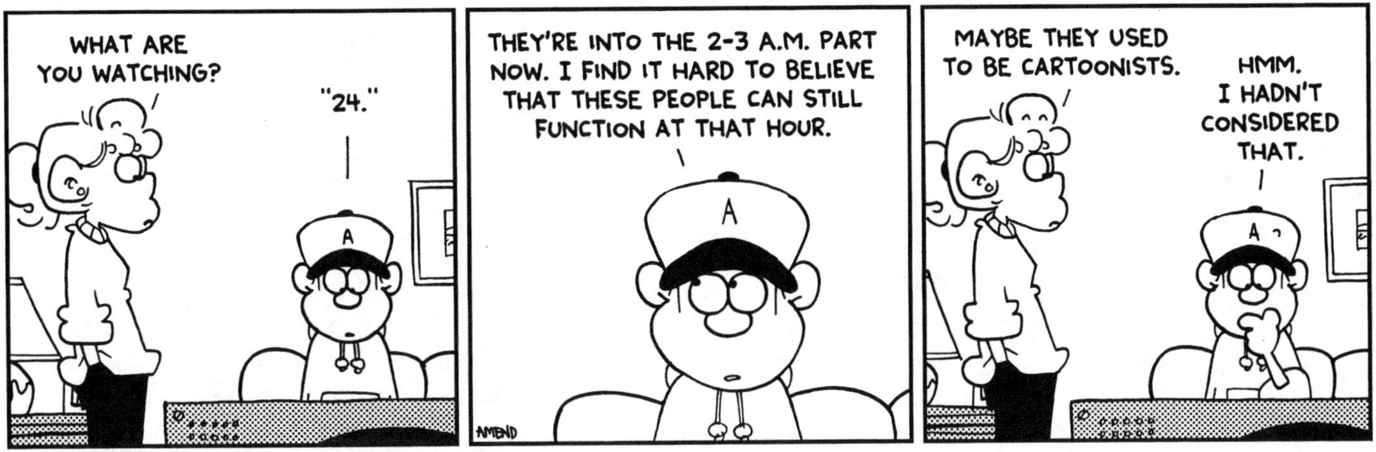
WHAT ARE YOU WATCHING?
"24."
THEY'RE INTO THE 2-3 A.M. PART NOW. I FIND IT HARD TO BELIEVE THAT THESE PEOPLE CAN STILL FUNCTION AT THAT HOUR.
MAYBE THEY USED TO BE CARTOONISTS.
HMM. I HADN'T CONSIDERED THAT.
AMEND

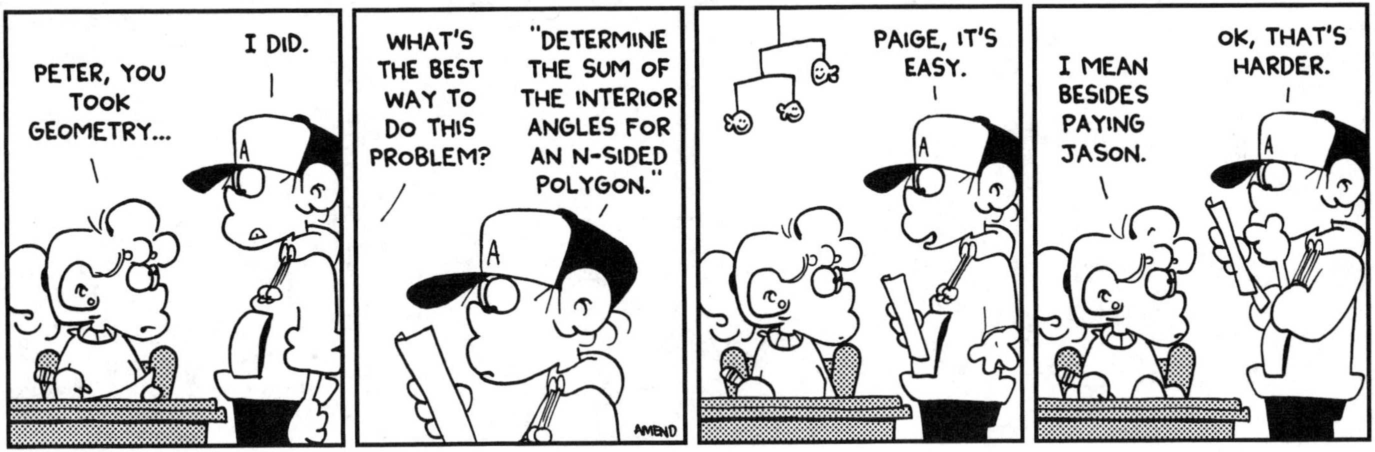
PETER, YOU TOOK GEOMETRY...
I DID.
WHAT'S THE BEST WAY TO DO THIS PROBLEM?
"DETERMINE THE SUM OF THE INTERIOR ANGLES FOR AN N-SIDED POLYGON."
PAIGE, IT'S EASY.
I MEAN BESIDES PAYING JASON.
OK, THAT'S HARDER.
AMEND

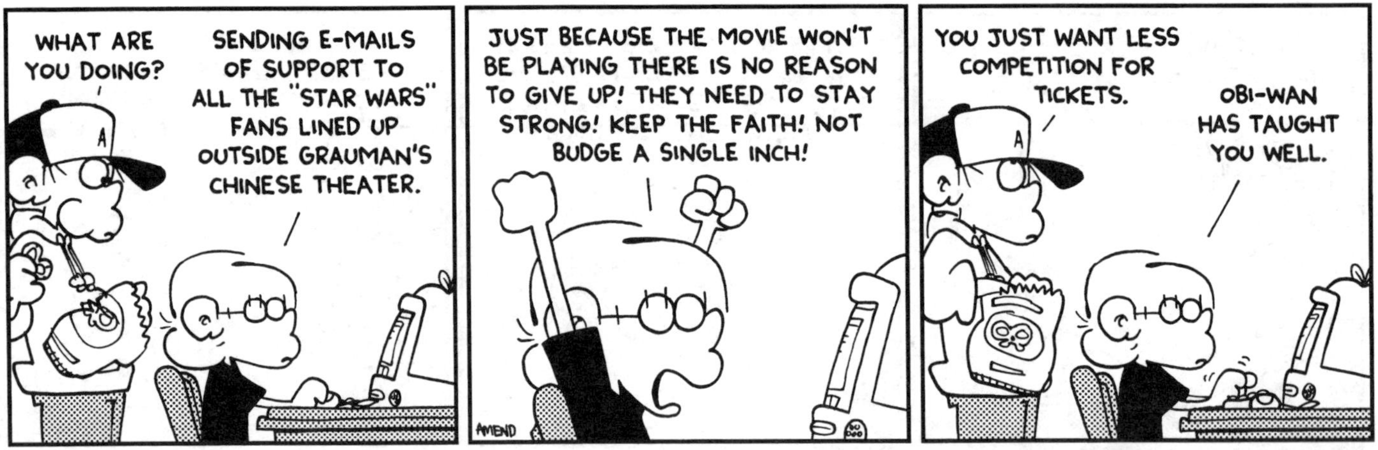
WHAT ARE YOU DOING?
SENDING E-MAILS OF SUPPORT TO ALL THE "STAR WARS" FANS LINED UP OUTSIDE GRAUMAN'S CHINESE THEATER.
JUST BECAUSE THE MOVIE WON'T BE PLAYING THERE IS NO REASON TO GIVE UP! THEY NEED TO STAY STRONG! KEEP THE FAITH! NOT BUDGE A SINGLE INCH!
AMEND
YOU JUST WANT LESS COMPETITION FOR TICKETS.
OBI-WAN HAS TAUGHT YOU WELL.

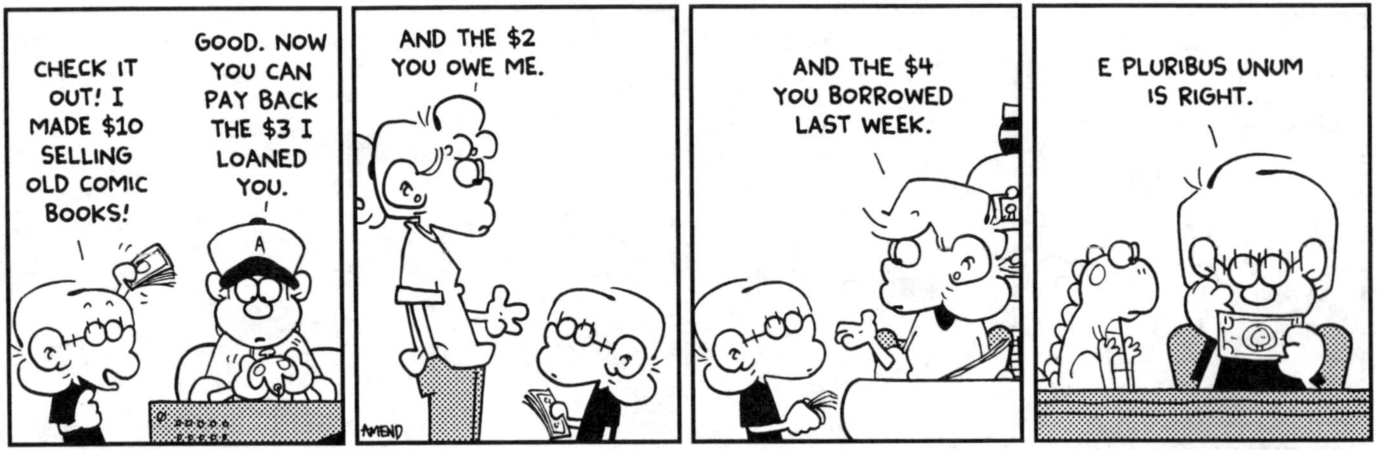
CHECK IT OUT! I MADE $10 SELLING OLD COMIC BOOKS!
GOOD. NOW YOU CAN PAY BACK THE $3 I LOANED YOU.
AND THE $2 YOU OWE ME.
AMEND
AND THE $4 YOU BORROWED LAST WEEK.
E PLURIBUS UNUM IS RIGHT.

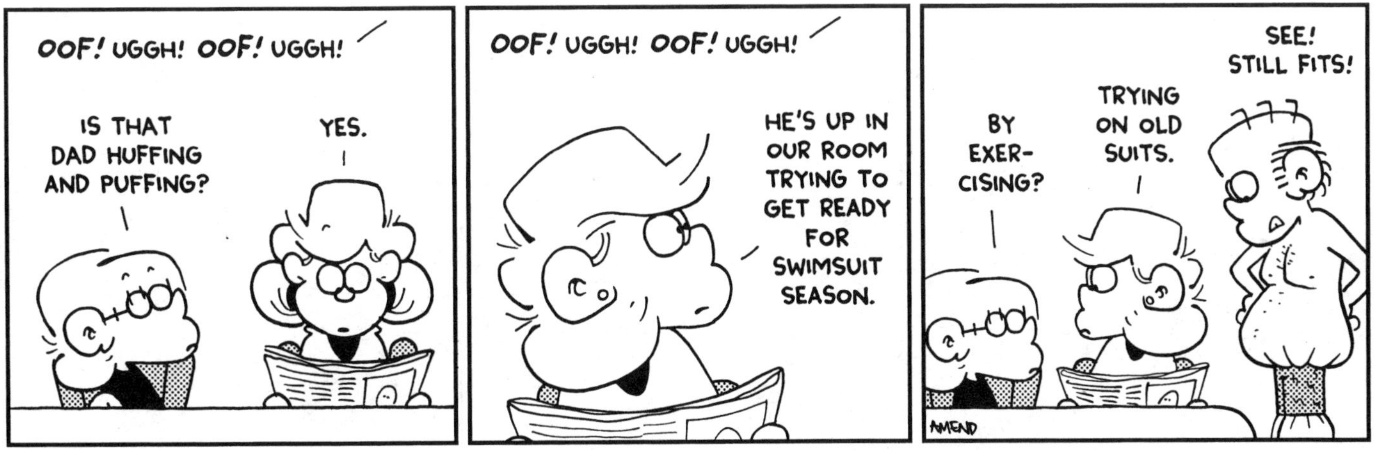
OOF! UGGH! OOF! UGGH!
IS THAT DAD HUFFING AND PUFFING?
YES.
OOF! UGGH! OOF! UGGH!
HE'S UP IN OUR ROOM TRYING TO GET READY FOR SWIMSUIT SEASON.
BY EXER-CISING?
TRYING ON OLD SUITS.
SEE! STILL FITS!
AMEND

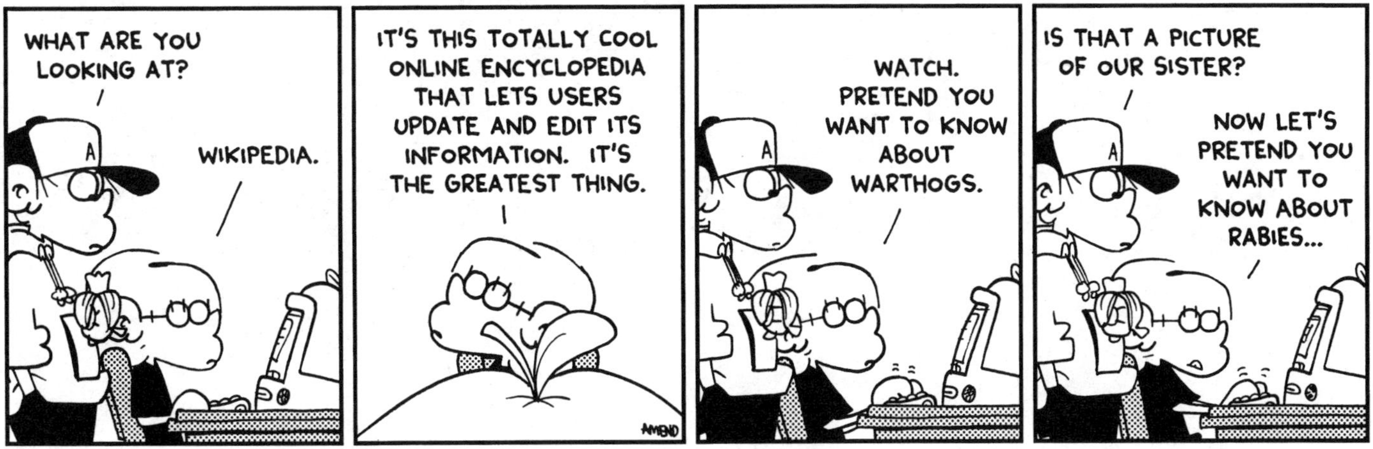
WHAT ARE YOU LOOKING AT?
WIKIPEDIA.
IT'S THIS TOTALLY COOL ONLINE ENCYCLOPEDIA THAT LETS USERS UPDATE AND EDIT ITS INFORMATION. IT'S THE GREATEST THING.
AMEND
WATCH. PRETEND YOU WANT TO KNOW ABOUT WARTHOGS.
IS THAT A PICTURE OF OUR SISTER?
NOW LET'S PRETEND YOU WANT TO KNOW ABOUT RABIES...

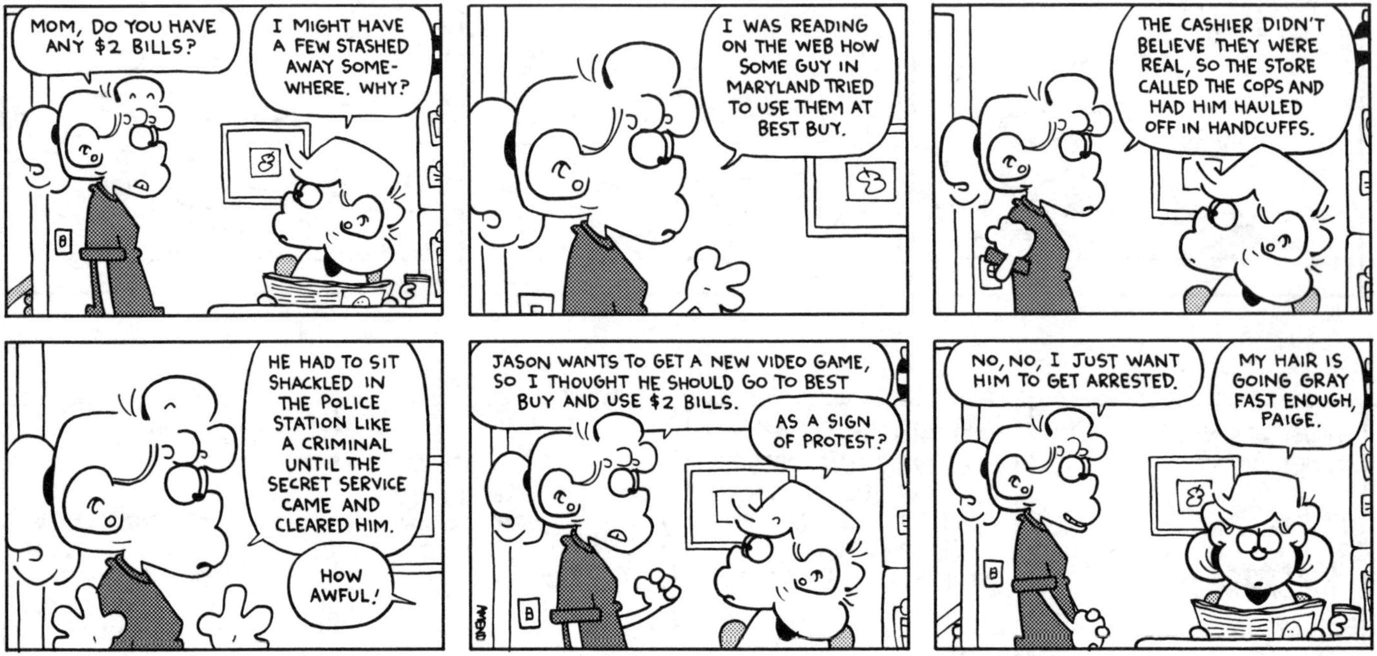
MOM, DO YOU HAVE ANY $2 BILLS?
I MIGHT HAVE A FEW STASHED AWAY SOMEWHERE. WHY?
I WAS READING ON THE WEB HOW SOME GUY IN MARYLAND TRIED TO USE THEM AT BEST BUY.
THE CASHIER DIDN'T BELIEVE THEY WERE REAL, SO THE STORE CALLED THE COPS AND HAD HIM HAULED OFF IN HANDCUFFS.
HE HAD TO SIT SHACKLED IN THE POLICE STATION LIKE A CRIMINAL UNTIL THE SECRET SERVICE CAME AND CLEARED HIM.
HOW AWFUL!
JASON WANTS TO GET A NEW VIDEO GAME, SO I THOUGHT HE SHOULD GO TO BEST BUY AND USE $2 BILLS.
AS A SIGN OF PROTEST?
NO, NO, I JUST WANT HIM TO GET ARRESTED.
MY HAIR IS GOING GRAY FAST ENOUGH, PAIGE.

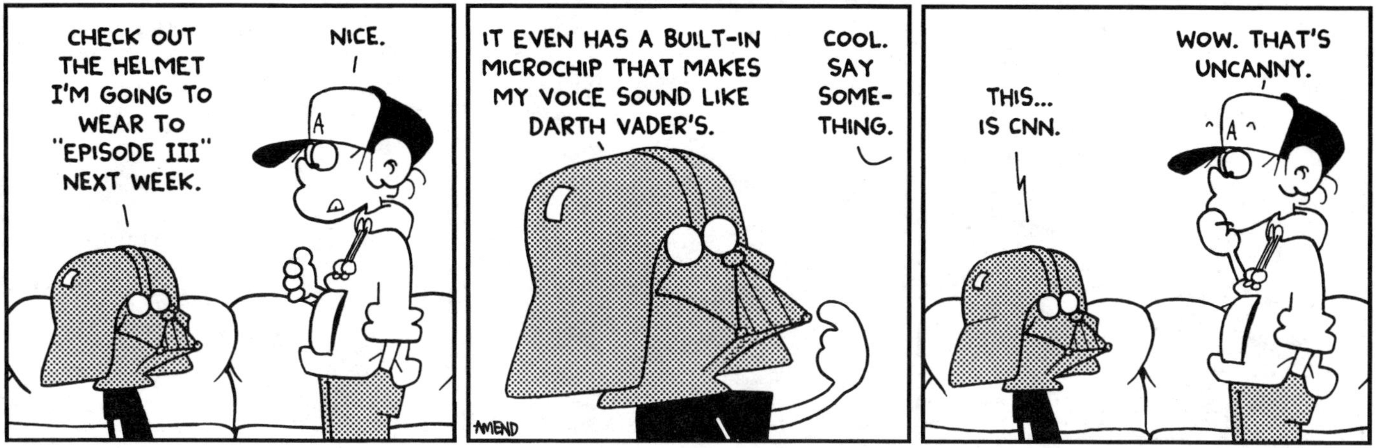
CHECK OUT THE HELMET I'M GOING TO WEAR TO "EPISODE III" NEXT WEEK.
NICE.
IT EVEN HAS A BUILT-IN MICROCHIP THAT MAKES MY VOICE SOUND LIKE DARTH VADER'S.
COOL. SAY SOME-THING.
AMEND
THIS... IS CNN.
WOW. THAT'S UNCANNY.

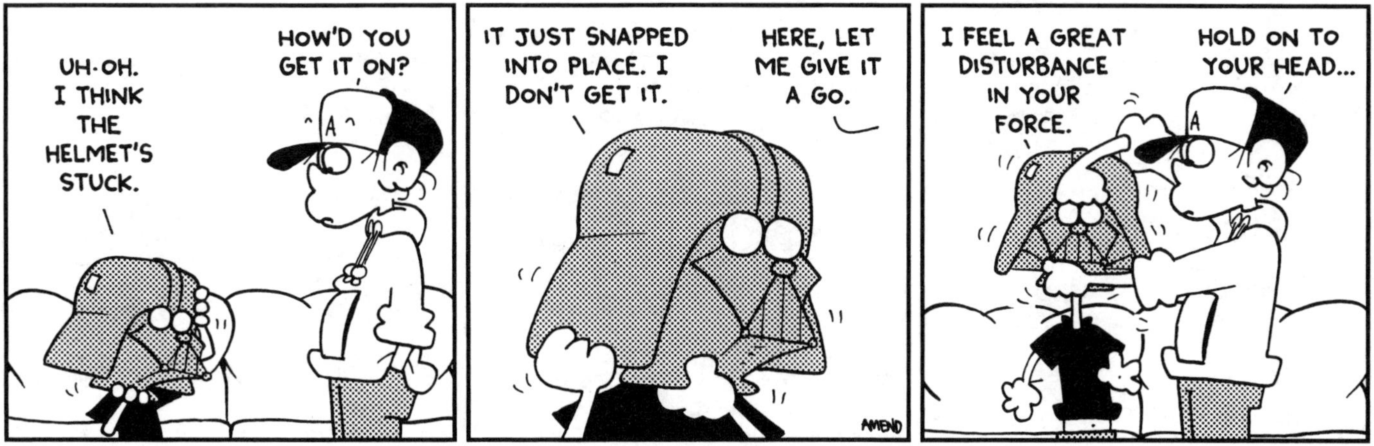
UH-OH. I THINK THE HELMET'S STUCK.
HOW'D YOU GET IT ON?
IT JUST SNAPPED INTO PLACE. I DON'T GET IT.
HERE, LET ME GIVE IT A GO.
AMEND
I FEEL A GREAT DISTURBANCE IN YOUR FORCE.
HOLD ON TO YOUR HEAD...

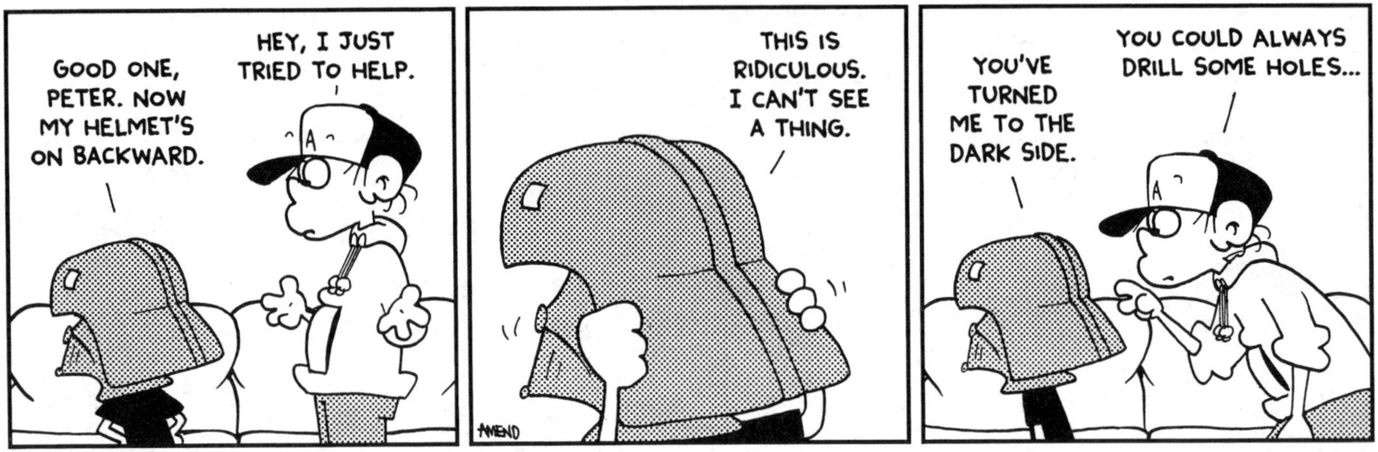
GOOD ONE, PETER. NOW MY HELMET'S ON BACKWARD.
HEY, I JUST TRIED TO HELP.
THIS IS RIDICULOUS. I CAN'T SEE A THING.
AMEND
YOU'VE TURNED ME TO THE DARK SIDE.
YOU COULD ALWAYS DRILL SOME HOLES...

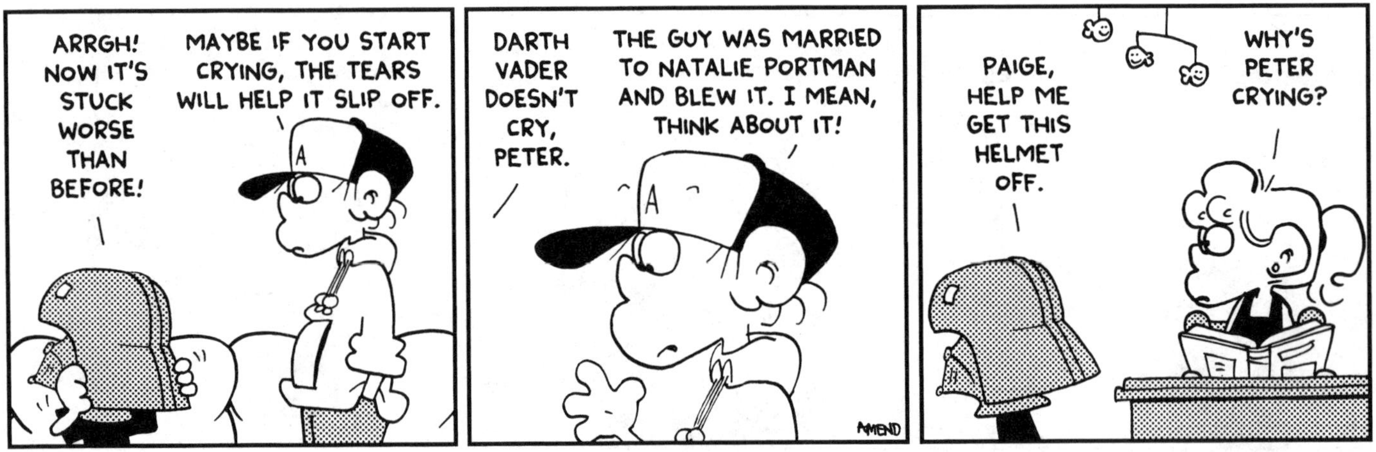
ARRGH! NOW IT'S STUCK WORSE THAN BEFORE!
MAYBE IF YOU START CRYING, THE TEARS WILL HELP IT SLIP OFF.
DARTH VADER DOESN'T CRY, PETER.
THE GUY WAS MARRIED TO NATALIE PORTMAN AND BLEW IT. I MEAN, THINK ABOUT IT!
AMEND
PAIGE, HELP ME GET THIS HELMET OFF.
WHY'S PETER CRYING?

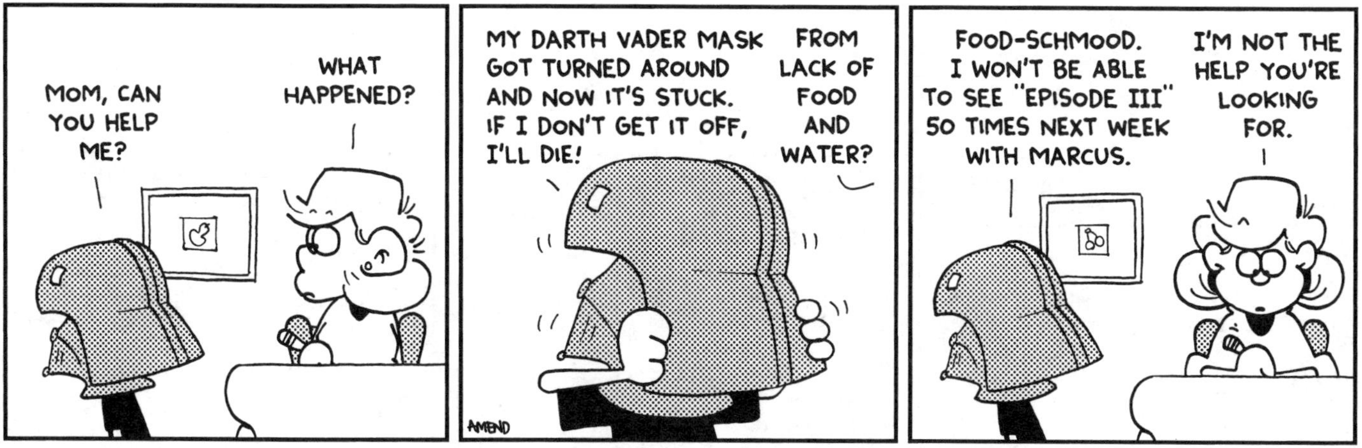
MOM, CAN YOU HELP ME?
WHAT HAPPENED?
MY DARTH VADER MASK GOT TURNED AROUND AND NOW IT'S STUCK. IF I DON'T GET IT OFF, I'LL DIE!
FROM LACK OF FOOD AND WATER?
AMEND
FOOD-SCHMOOD. I WON'T BE ABLE TO SEE "EPISODE III" 50 TIMES NEXT WEEK WITH MARCUS.
I'M NOT THE HELP YOU'RE LOOKING FOR.

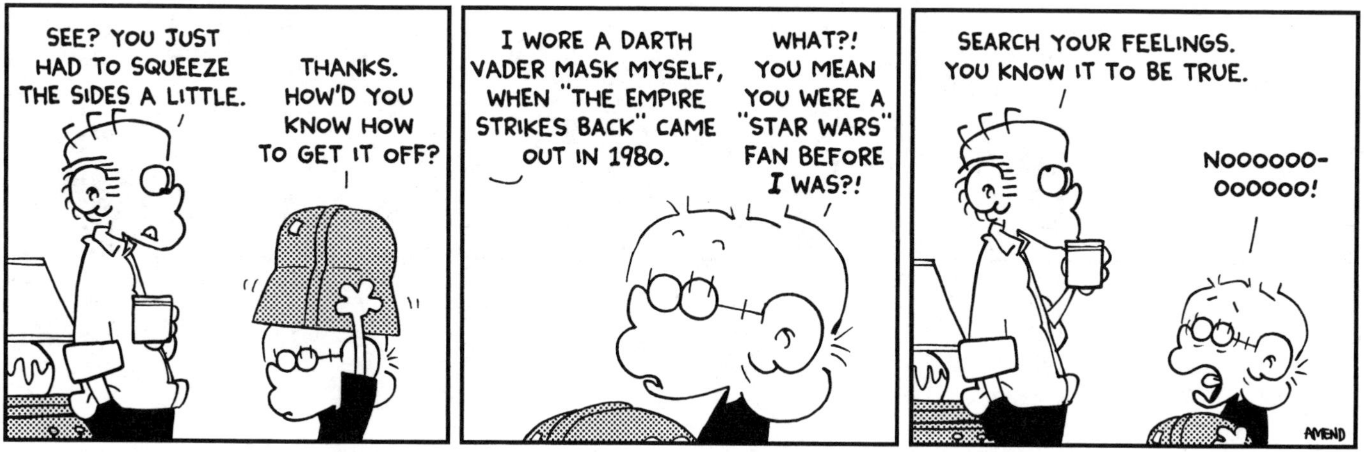
SEE? YOU JUST HAD TO SQUEEZE THE SIDES A LITTLE.
THANKS. HOW'D YOU KNOW HOW TO GET IT OFF?
I WORE A DARTH VADER MASK MYSELF, WHEN "THE EMPIRE STRIKES BACK" CAME OUT IN 1980.
WHAT?! YOU MEAN YOU WERE A "STAR WARS" FAN BEFORE I WAS?!
SEARCH YOUR FEELINGS. YOU KNOW IT TO BE TRUE.
NOOOOOO-OOOOOO!
AMEND

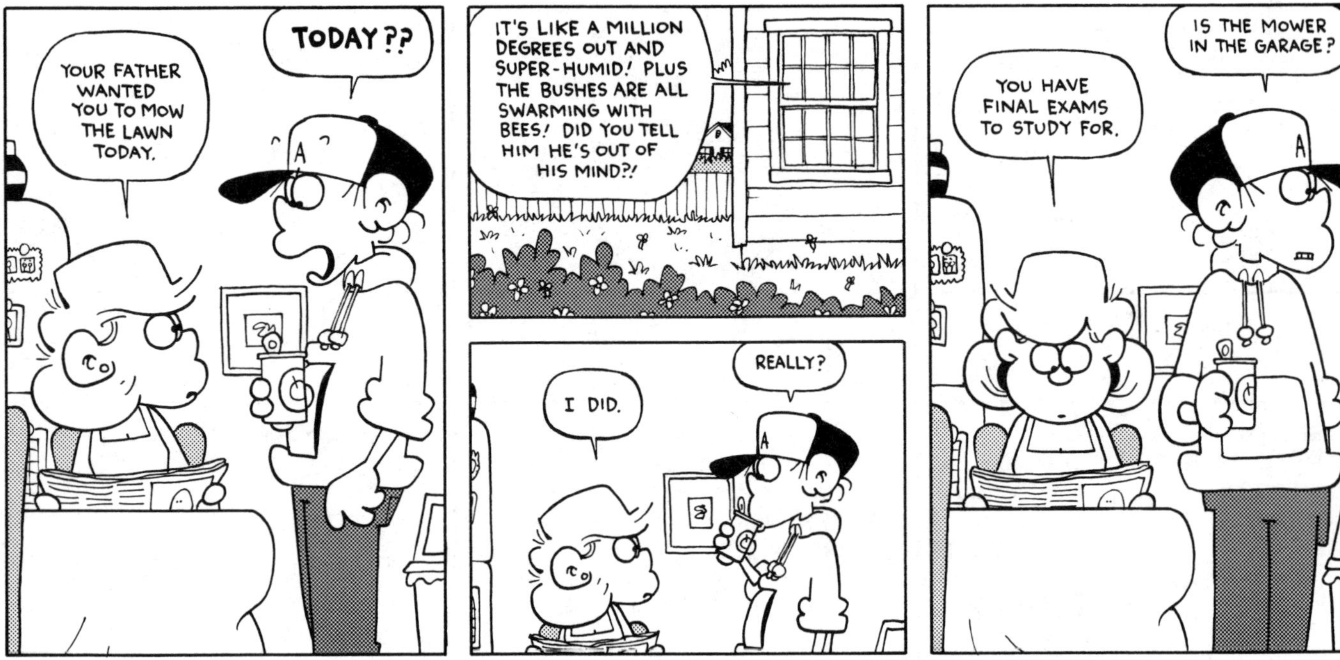
YOUR FATHER WANTED YOU TO MOW THE LAWN TODAY.
TODAY??
IT'S LIKE A MILLION DEGREES OUT AND SUPER-HUMID! PLUS THE BUSHES ARE ALL SWARMING WITH BEES! DID YOU TELL HIM HE'S OUT OF HIS MIND?!
I DID.
REALLY?
YOU HAVE FINAL EXAMS TO STUDY FOR.
IS THE MOWER IN THE GARAGE?
AMEND

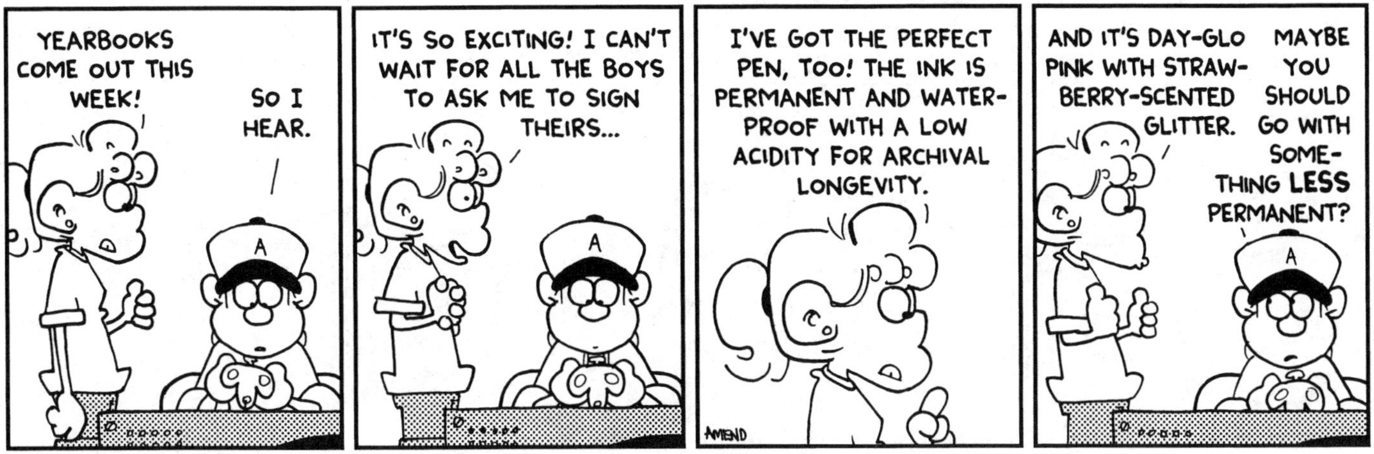
YEARBOOKS COME OUT THIS WEEK!
SO I HEAR.
IT'S SO EXCITING! I CAN'T WAIT FOR ALL THE BOYS TO ASK ME TO SIGN THEIRS...
I'VE GOT THE PERFECT PEN, TOO! THE INK IS PERMANENT AND WATER-PROOF WITH A LOW ACIDITY FOR ARCHIVAL LONGEVITY.
AMEND
AND IT'S DAY-GLO PINK WITH STRAW-BERRY-SCENTED GLITTER.
MAYBE YOU SHOULD GO WITH SOME-THING **LESS** PERMANENT?

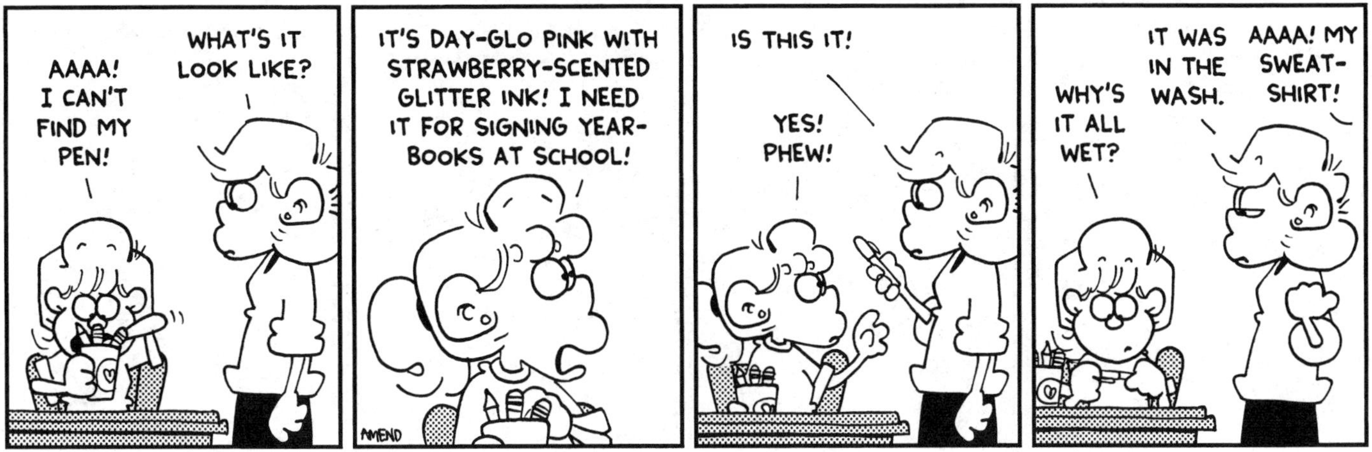
AAAA! I CAN'T FIND MY PEN!
WHAT'S IT LOOK LIKE?
IT'S DAY-GLO PINK WITH STRAWBERRY-SCENTED GLITTER INK! I NEED IT FOR SIGNING YEAR-BOOKS AT SCHOOL!
AMEND
IS THIS IT!
YES! PHEW!
WHY'S IT ALL WET?
IT WAS IN THE WASH.
AAAA! MY SWEAT-SHIRT!

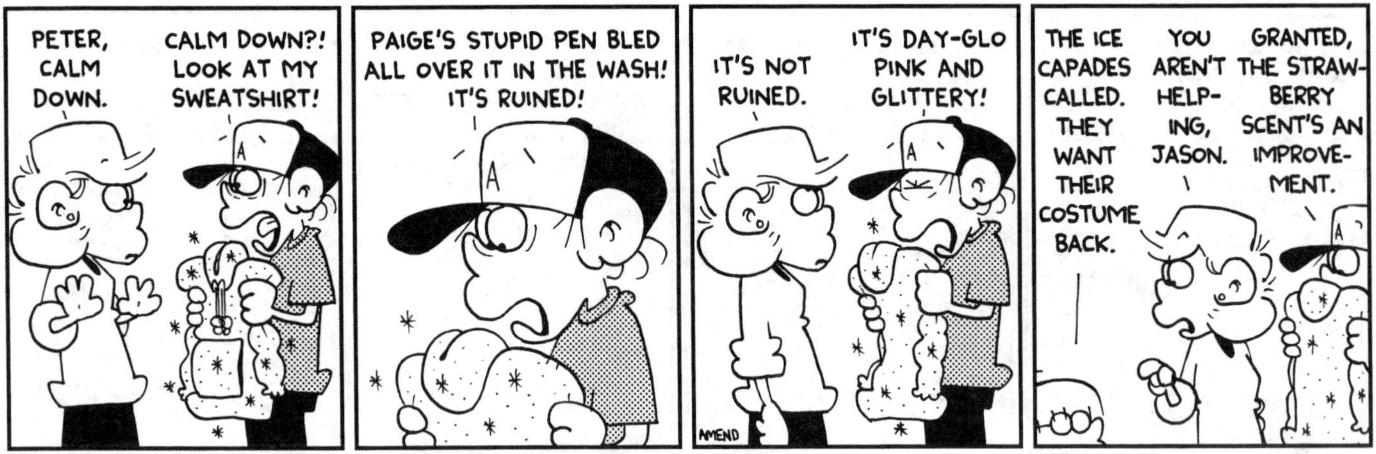
PETER, CALM DOWN.
CALM DOWN?! LOOK AT MY SWEATSHIRT!
PAIGE'S STUPID PEN BLED ALL OVER IT IN THE WASH! IT'S RUINED!
IT'S NOT RUINED.
IT'S DAY-GLO PINK AND GLITTERY!
AMEND
THE ICE CAPADES CALLED. THEY WANT THEIR COSTUME BACK.
YOU AREN'T HELP-ING, JASON.
GRANTED, THE STRAW-BERRY SCENT'S AN IMPROVE-MENT.

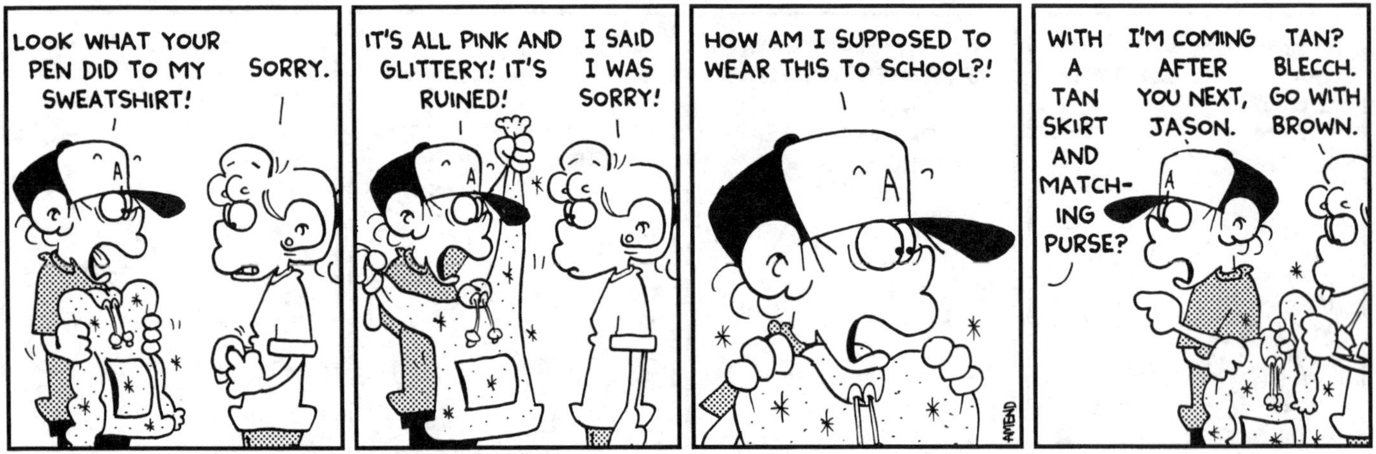
LOOK WHAT YOUR PEN DID TO MY SWEATSHIRT!
SORRY.
IT'S ALL PINK AND GLITTERY! IT'S RUINED!
I SAID I WAS SORRY!
HOW AM I SUPPOSED TO WEAR THIS TO SCHOOL?!
AMEND
WITH A TAN SKIRT AND MATCH-ING PURSE?
I'M COMING AFTER YOU NEXT, JASON.
TAN? BLECCH. GO WITH BROWN.

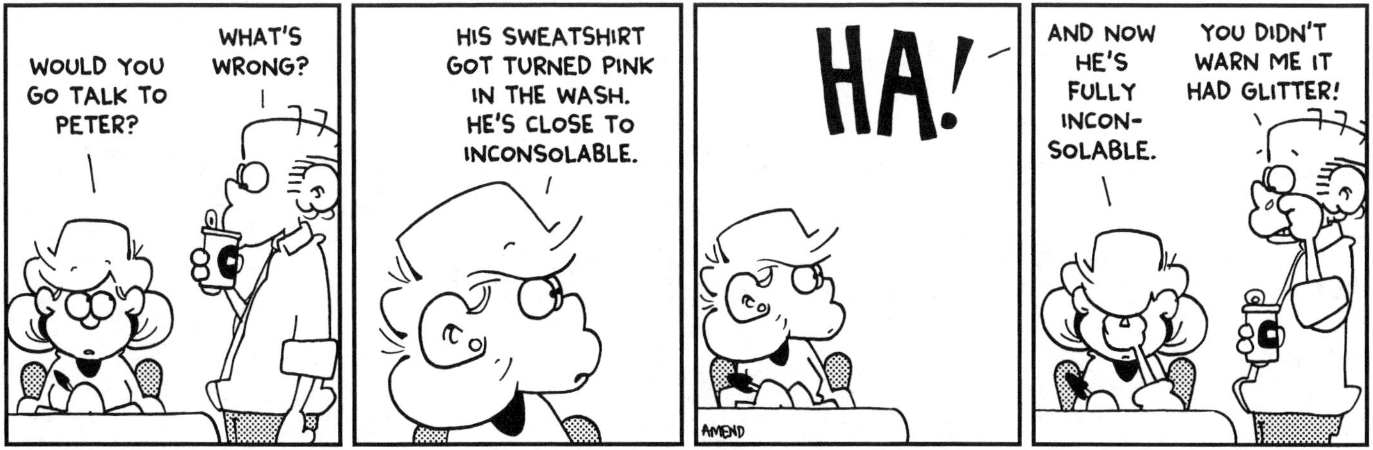
WOULD YOU GO TALK TO PETER?
WHAT'S WRONG?
HIS SWEATSHIRT GOT TURNED PINK IN THE WASH. HE'S CLOSE TO INCONSOLABLE.
HA!
AND NOW HE'S FULLY INCON-SOLABLE.
YOU DIDN'T WARN ME IT HAD GLITTER!
AMEND

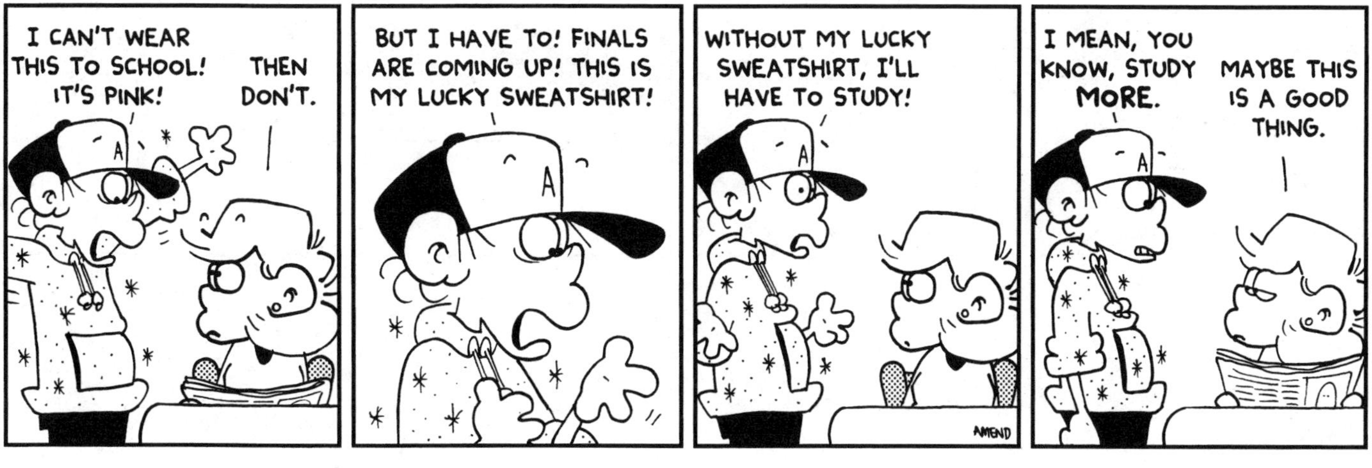
I CAN'T WEAR THIS TO SCHOOL! IT'S PINK!
THEN DON'T.
BUT I HAVE TO! FINALS ARE COMING UP! THIS IS MY LUCKY SWEATSHIRT!
WITHOUT MY LUCKY SWEATSHIRT, I'LL HAVE TO STUDY!
I MEAN, YOU KNOW, STUDY MORE.
MAYBE THIS IS A GOOD THING.
AMEND

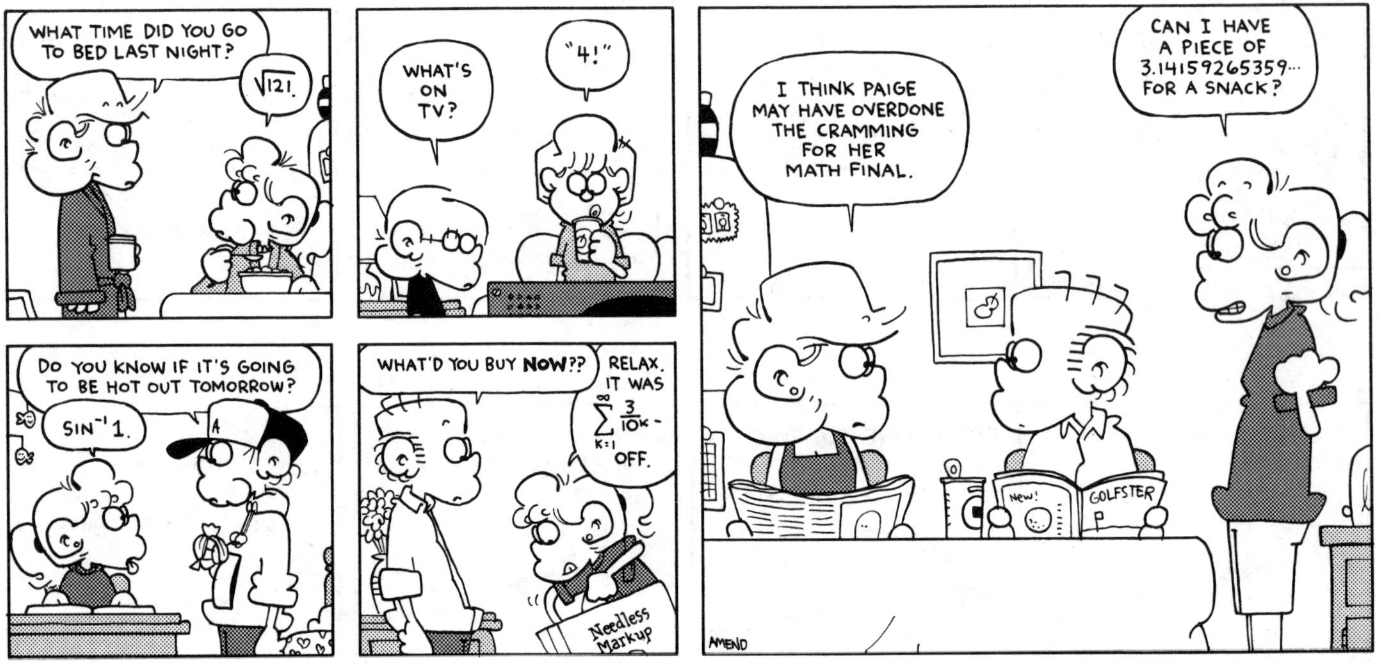
WHAT TIME DID YOU GO TO BED LAST NIGHT?
$\sqrt{121}$.
WHAT'S ON TV?
"4!"
DO YOU KNOW IF IT'S GOING TO BE HOT OUT TOMORROW?
$\sin^{-1} 1$.
WHAT'D YOU BUY **NOW**??
RELAX. IT WAS $\sum_{k=1}^{\infty} \frac{3}{10^k}$ - OFF.
Needless Markup
I THINK PAIGE MAY HAVE OVERDONE THE CRAMMING FOR HER MATH FINAL.
CAN I HAVE A PIECE OF 3.14159265359... FOR A SNACK?
New!
GOLFSTER
AMEND

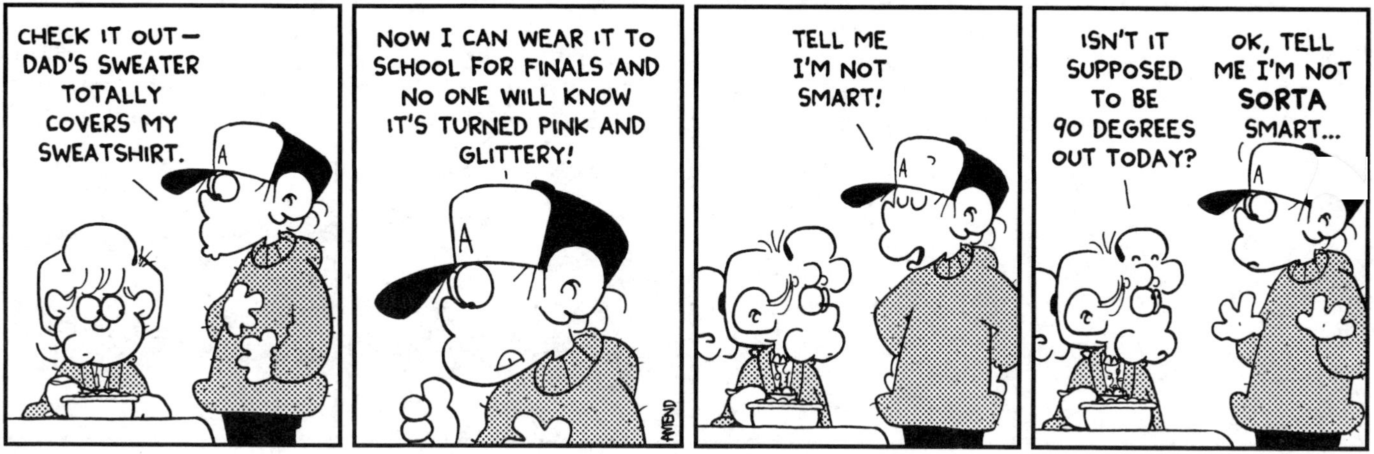
CHECK IT OUT— DAD'S SWEATER TOTALLY COVERS MY SWEATSHIRT.
NOW I CAN WEAR IT TO SCHOOL FOR FINALS AND NO ONE WILL KNOW IT'S TURNED PINK AND GLITTERY!
TELL ME I'M NOT SMART!
ISN'T IT SUPPOSED TO BE 90 DEGREES OUT TODAY?
OK, TELL ME I'M NOT SORTA SMART...
AMEND

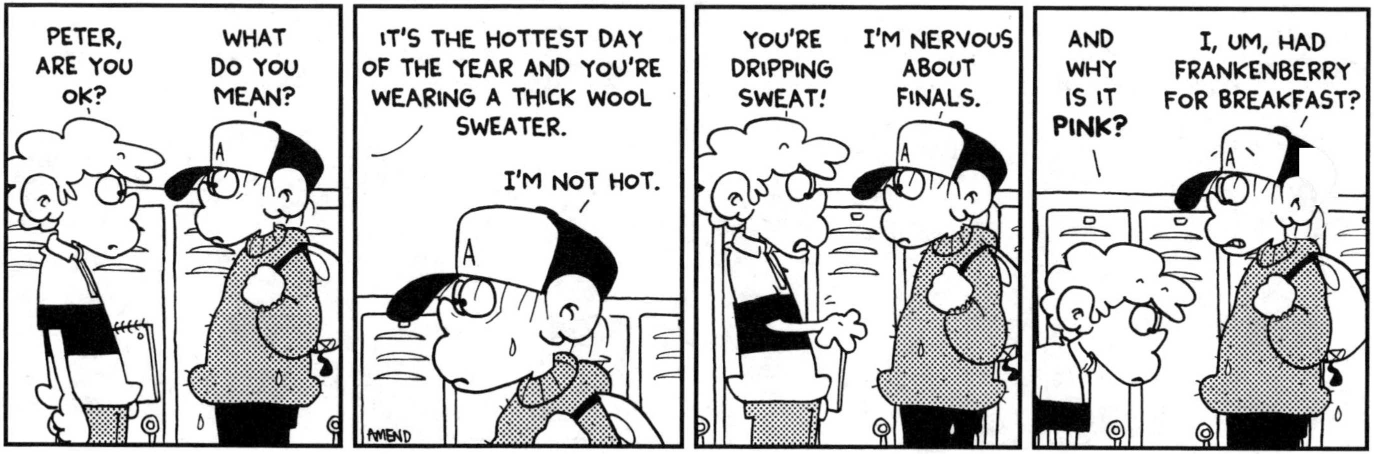
PETER, ARE YOU OK?
WHAT DO YOU MEAN?
IT'S THE HOTTEST DAY OF THE YEAR AND YOU'RE WEARING A THICK WOOL SWEATER.
I'M NOT HOT.
AMEND
YOU'RE DRIPPING SWEAT!
I'M NERVOUS ABOUT FINALS.
AND WHY IS IT PINK?
I, UM, HAD FRANKENBERRY FOR BREAKFAST?

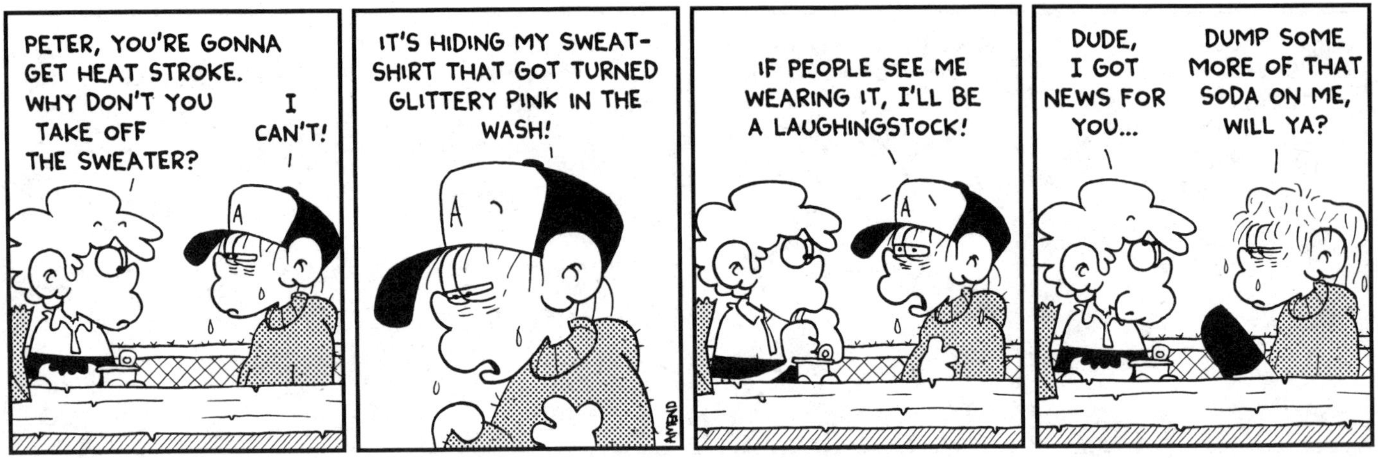
PETER, YOU'RE GONNA GET HEAT STROKE. WHY DON'T YOU TAKE OFF THE SWEATER?
I CAN'T!
IT'S HIDING MY SWEAT-SHIRT THAT GOT TURNED GLITTERY PINK IN THE WASH!
AMEND
IF PEOPLE SEE ME WEARING IT, I'LL BE A LAUGHINGSTOCK!
DUDE, I GOT NEWS FOR YOU...
DUMP SOME MORE OF THAT SODA ON ME, WILL YA?

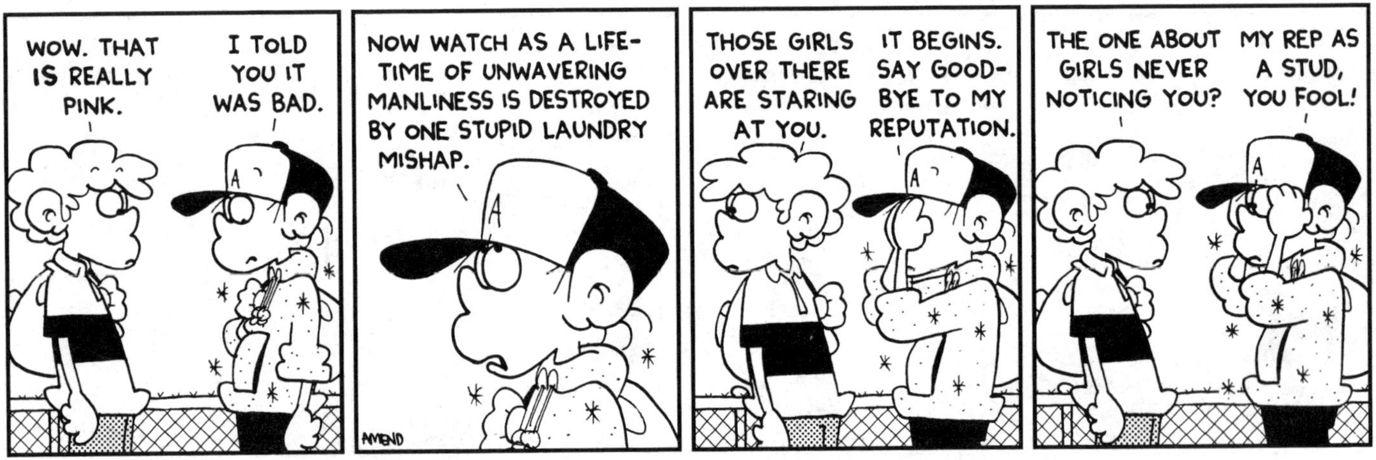
WOW. THAT IS REALLY PINK.
I TOLD YOU IT WAS BAD.
NOW WATCH AS A LIFE-TIME OF UNWAVERING MANLINESS IS DESTROYED BY ONE STUPID LAUNDRY MISHAP.
AMEND
THOSE GIRLS OVER THERE ARE STARING AT YOU.
IT BEGINS. SAY GOOD-BYE TO MY REPUTATION.
THE ONE ABOUT GIRLS NEVER NOTICING YOU?
MY REP AS A STUD, YOU FOOL!

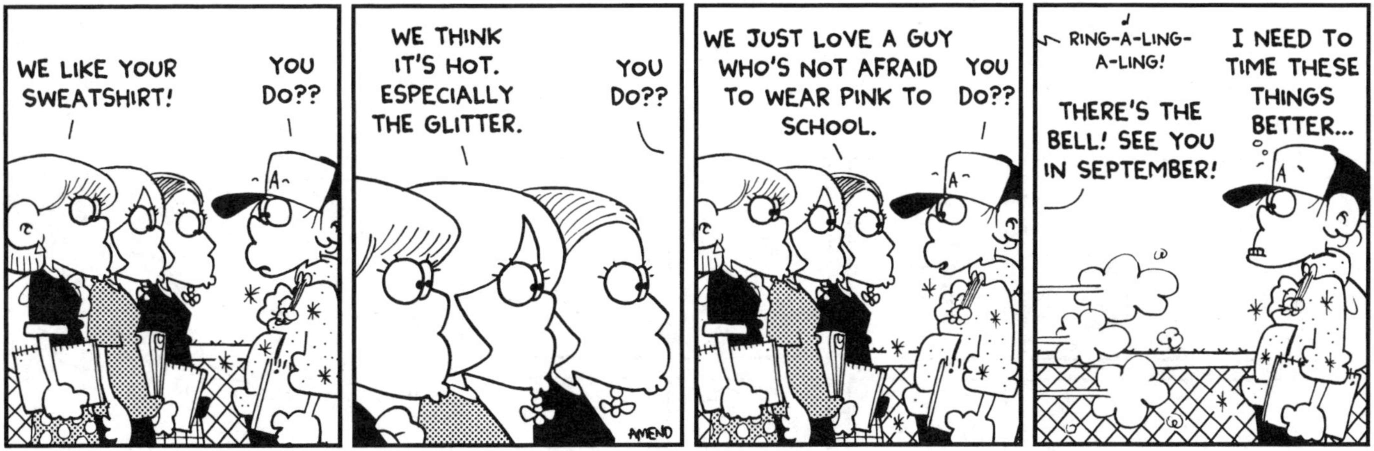
WE LIKE YOUR SWEATSHIRT!
YOU DO??
WE THINK IT'S HOT. ESPECIALLY THE GLITTER.
YOU DO??
AMEND
WE JUST LOVE A GUY WHO'S NOT AFRAID TO WEAR PINK TO SCHOOL.
YOU DO??
RING-A-LING-A-LING!
THERE'S THE BELL! SEE YOU IN SEPTEMBER!
I NEED TO TIME THESE THINGS BETTER...

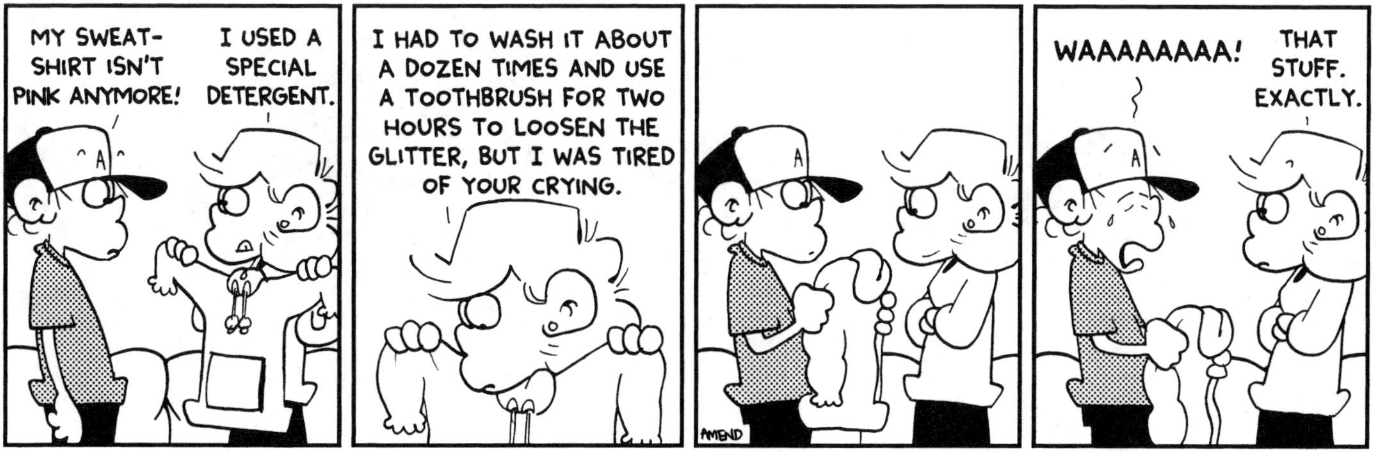
MY SWEAT-SHIRT ISN'T PINK ANYMORE!
I USED A SPECIAL DETERGENT.
I HAD TO WASH IT ABOUT A DOZEN TIMES AND USE A TOOTHBRUSH FOR TWO HOURS TO LOOSEN THE GLITTER, BUT I WAS TIRED OF YOUR CRYING.
AMEND
WAAAAAAAA!
THAT STUFF. EXACTLY.

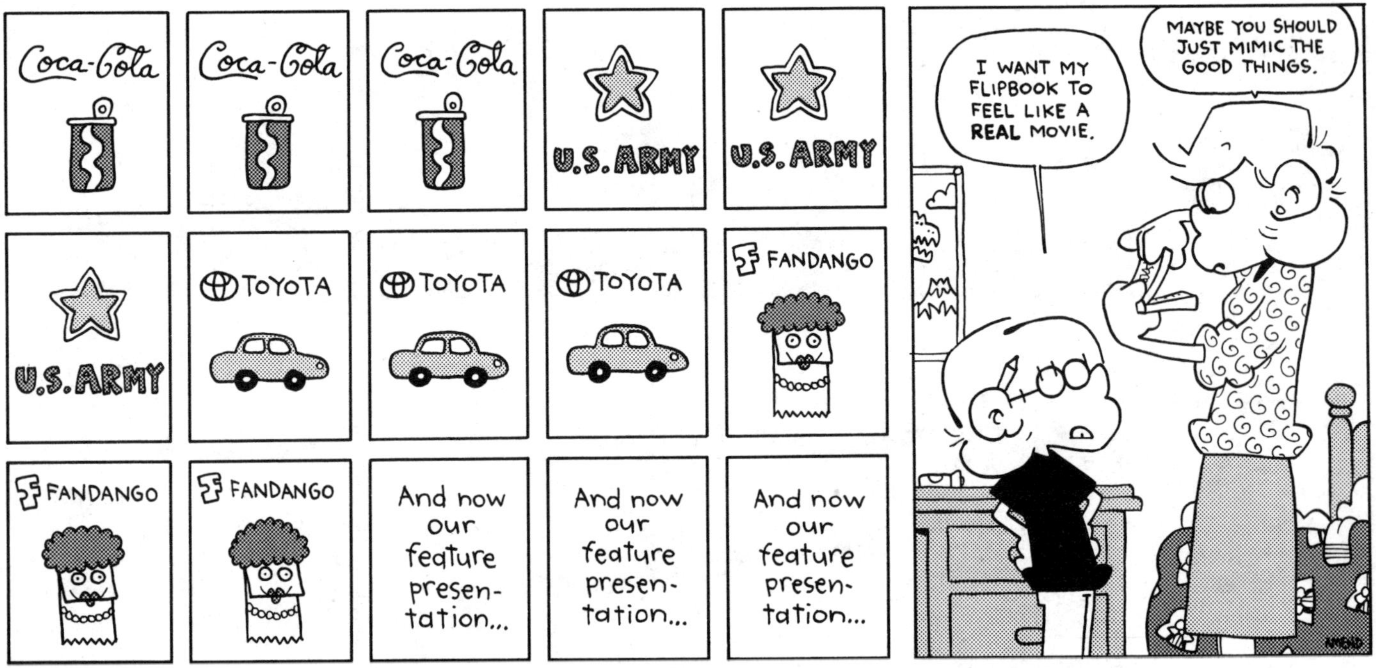

Coca-Cola
Coca-Cola
Coca-Cola
U.S. ARMY
U.S. ARMY
U.S. ARMY
TOYOTA
TOYOTA
TOYOTA
FANDANGO
FANDANGO
FANDANGO
And now our feature presen-tation...
And now our feature presen-tation...
And now our feature presen-tation...
I WANT MY FLIPBOOK TO FEEL LIKE A **REAL** MOVIE.
MAYBE YOU SHOULD JUST MIMIC THE GOOD THINGS.

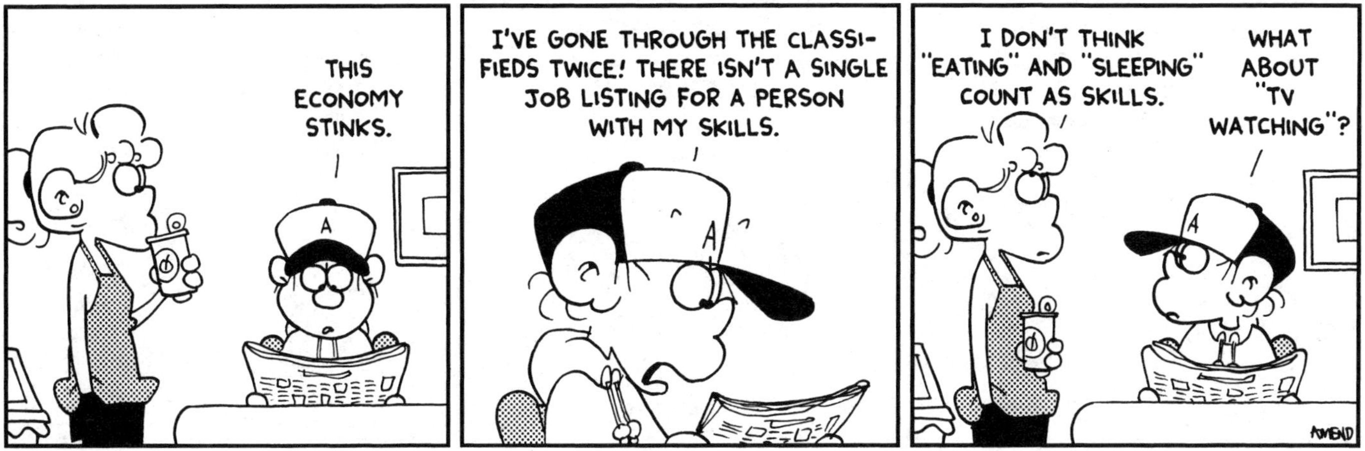
THIS ECONOMY STINKS.
I'VE GONE THROUGH THE CLASSIFIEDS TWICE! THERE ISN'T A SINGLE JOB LISTING FOR A PERSON WITH MY SKILLS.
I DON'T THINK "EATING" AND "SLEEPING" COUNT AS SKILLS.
WHAT ABOUT "TV WATCHING"?
AMEND

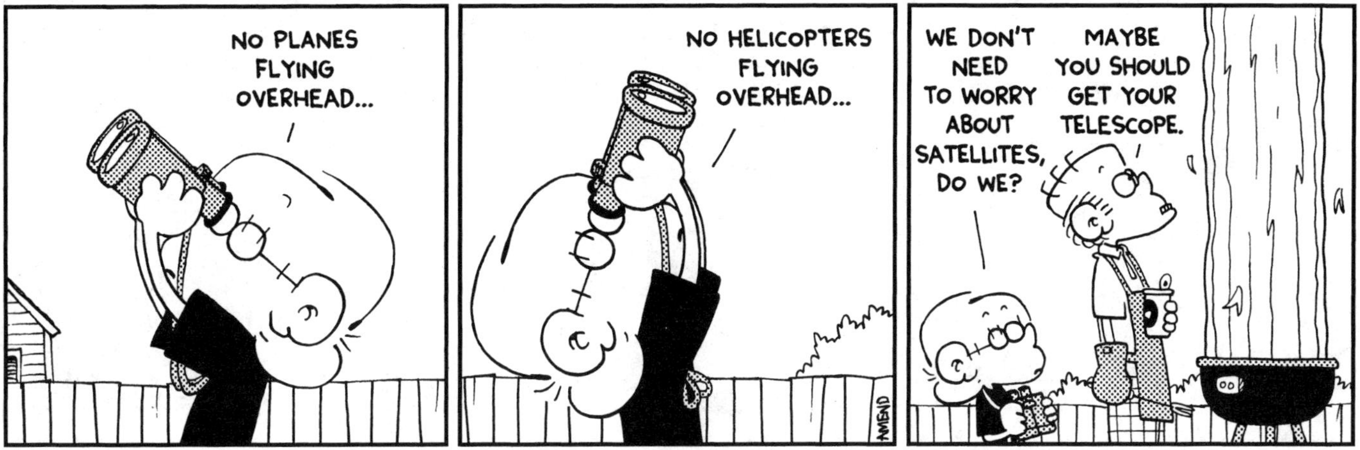
NO PLANES FLYING OVERHEAD...
NO HELICOPTERS FLYING OVERHEAD...
AMEND
WE DON'T NEED TO WORRY ABOUT SATELLITES, DO WE?
MAYBE YOU SHOULD GET YOUR TELESCOPE.

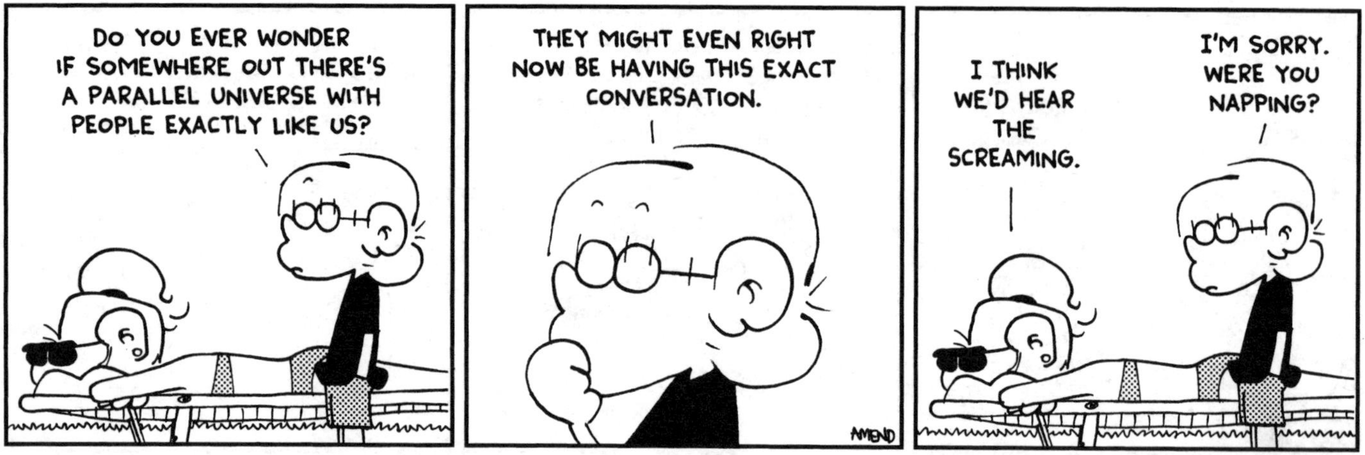
DO YOU EVER WONDER IF SOMEWHERE OUT THERE'S A PARALLEL UNIVERSE WITH PEOPLE EXACTLY LIKE US?
THEY MIGHT EVEN RIGHT NOW BE HAVING THIS EXACT EXACT CONVERSATION.
AMEND
I THINK WE'D HEAR THE SCREAMING.
I'M SORRY. WERE YOU NAPPING?

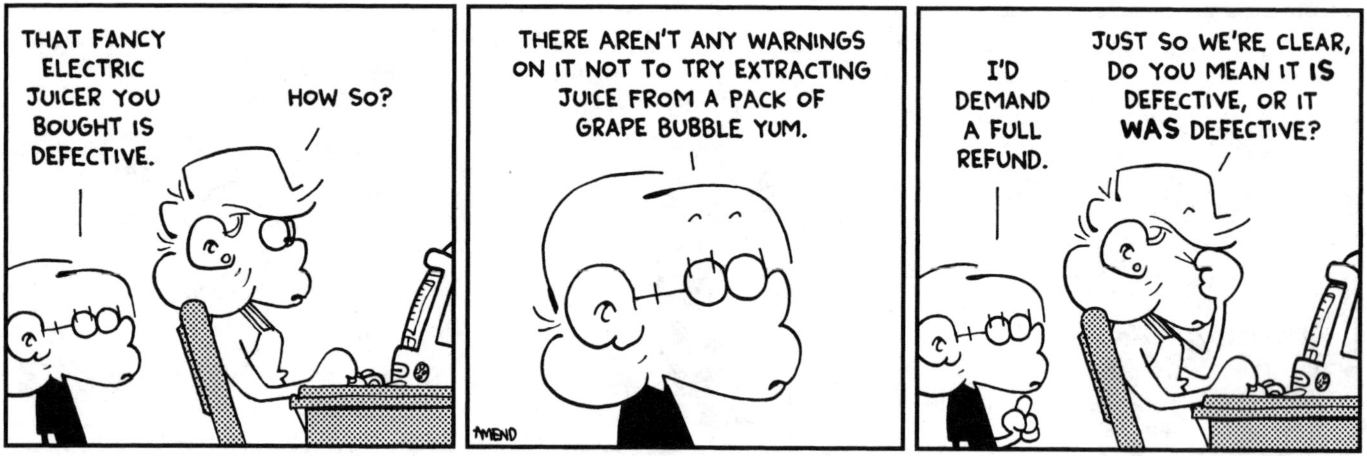
THAT FANCY ELECTRIC JUICER YOU BOUGHT IS DEFECTIVE.
HOW SO?
THERE AREN'T ANY WARNINGS ON IT NOT TO TRY EXTRACTING JUICE FROM A PACK OF GRAPE BUBBLE YUM.
AMEND
I'D DEMAND A FULL REFUND.
JUST SO WE'RE CLEAR, DO YOU MEAN IT **IS** DEFECTIVE, OR IT **WAS** DEFECTIVE?

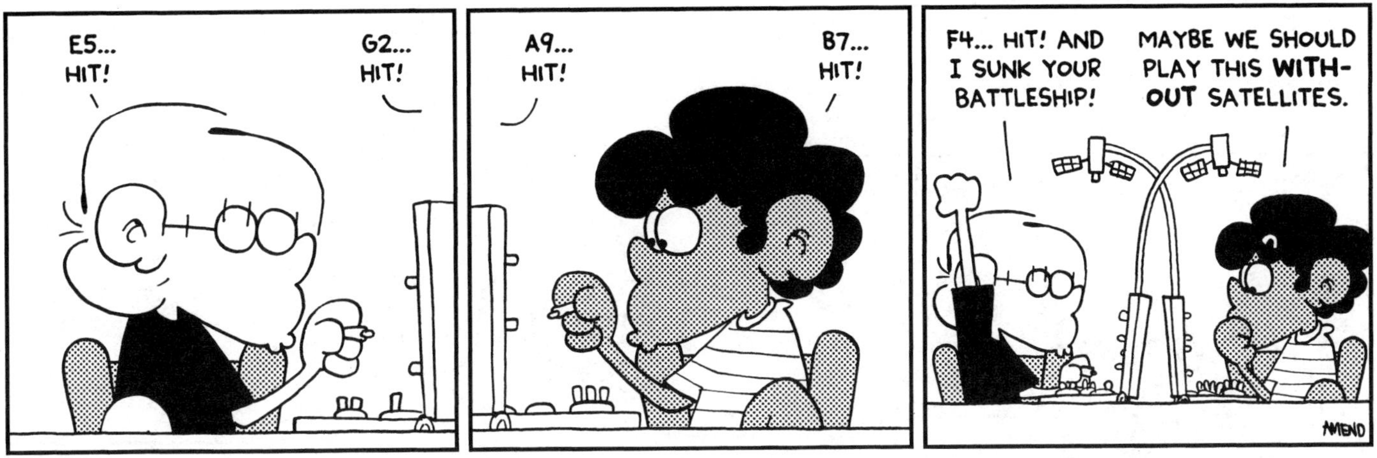
E5... HIT!
G2... HIT!
A9... HIT!
B7... HIT!
F4... HIT! AND I SUNK YOUR BATTLESHIP!
MAYBE WE SHOULD PLAY THIS **WITH-OUT** SATELLITES.
AMEND

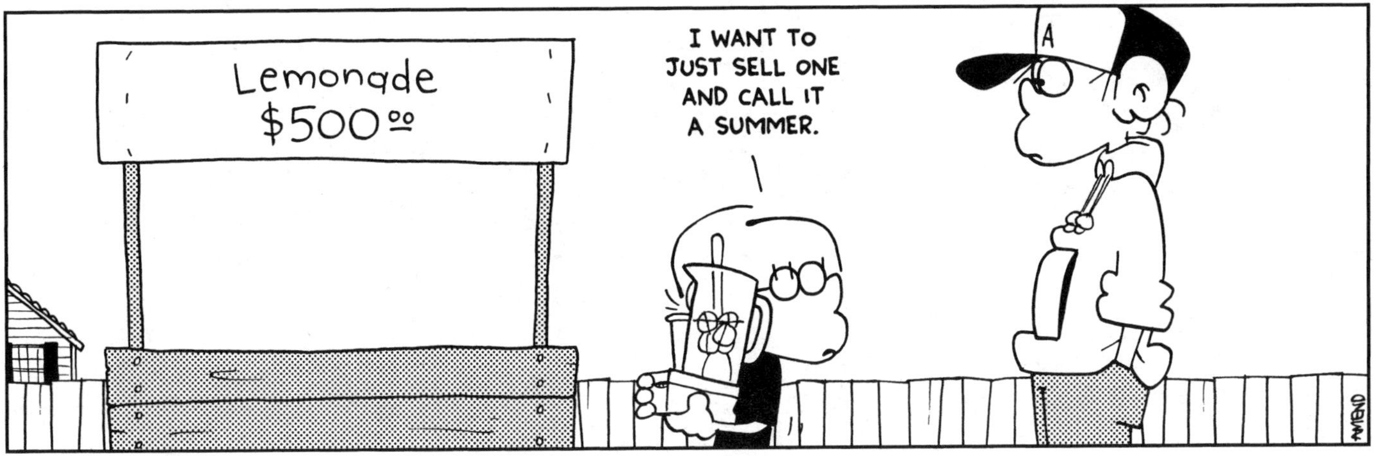
Lemonade $500.00
I WANT TO JUST SELL ONE AND CALL IT A SUMMER.
A
AMEND

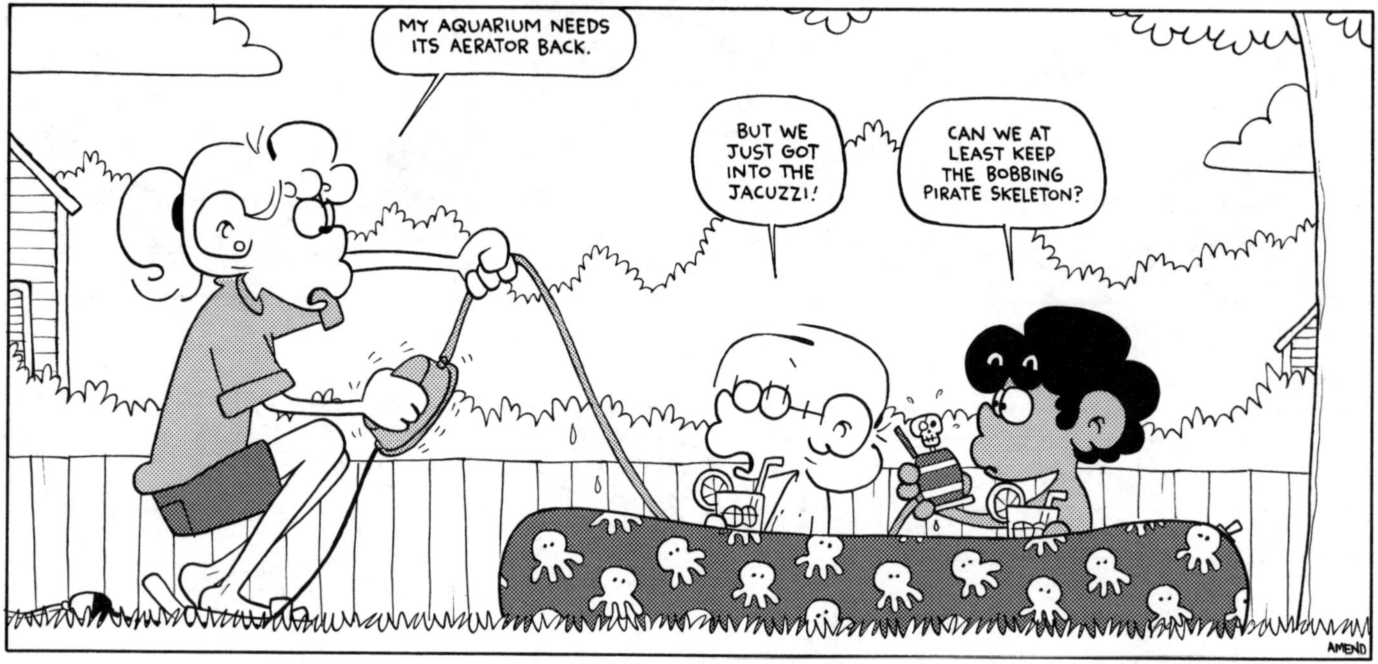
MY AQUARIUM NEEDS ITS AERATOR BACK.
BUT WE JUST GOT INTO THE JACUZZI!
CAN WE AT LEAST KEEP THE BOBBING PIRATE SKELETON?
AMEND

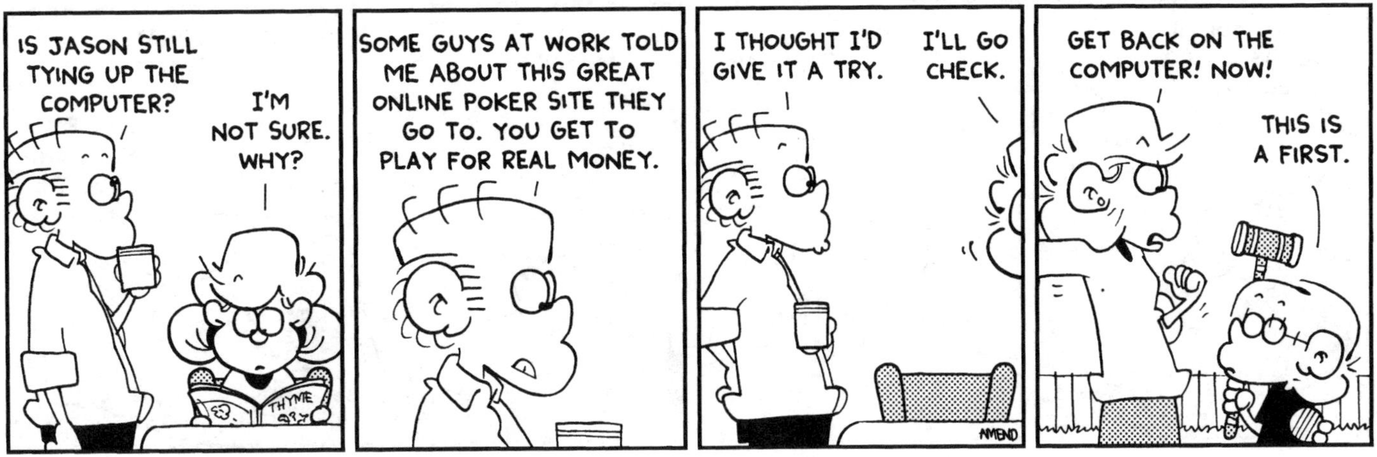
IS JASON STILL TYING UP THE COMPUTER?
I'M NOT SURE. WHY?
THYME
SOME GUYS AT WORK TOLD ME ABOUT THIS GREAT ONLINE POKER SITE THEY GO TO. YOU GET TO PLAY FOR REAL MONEY.
I THOUGHT I'D GIVE IT A TRY.
I'LL GO CHECK.
AMEND
GET BACK ON THE COMPUTER! NOW!
THIS IS A FIRST.

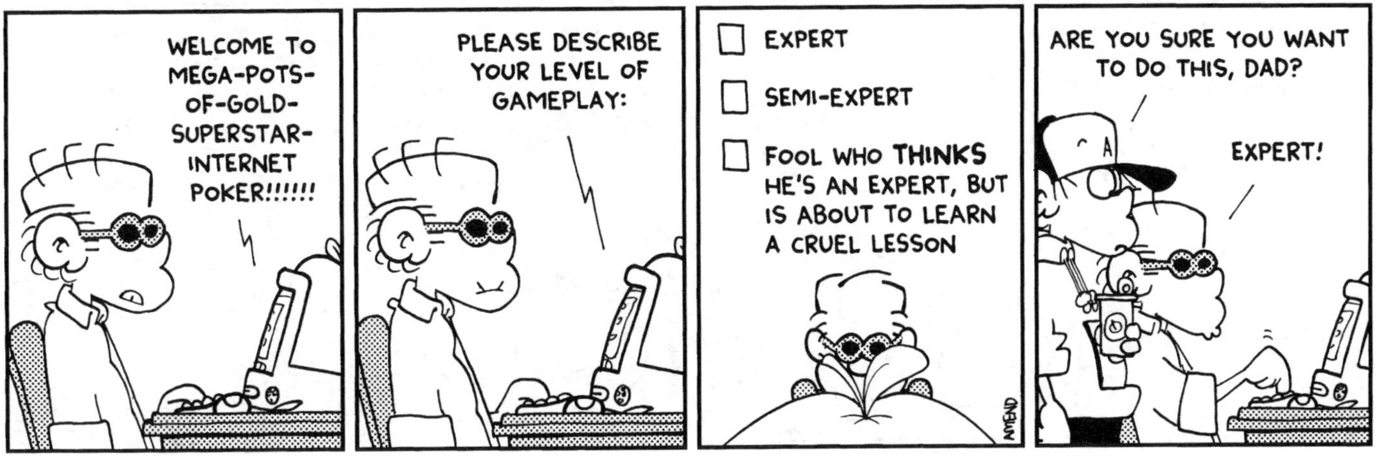
WELCOME TO MEGA-POTS-OF-GOLD-SUPERSTAR-INTERNET POKER!!!!!!
PLEASE DESCRIBE YOUR LEVEL OF GAMEPLAY:
EXPERT
SEMI-EXPERT
FOOL WHO THINKS HE'S AN EXPERT, BUT IS ABOUT TO LEARN A CRUEL LESSON
AMEND
ARE YOU SURE YOU WANT TO DO THIS, DAD?
EXPERT!

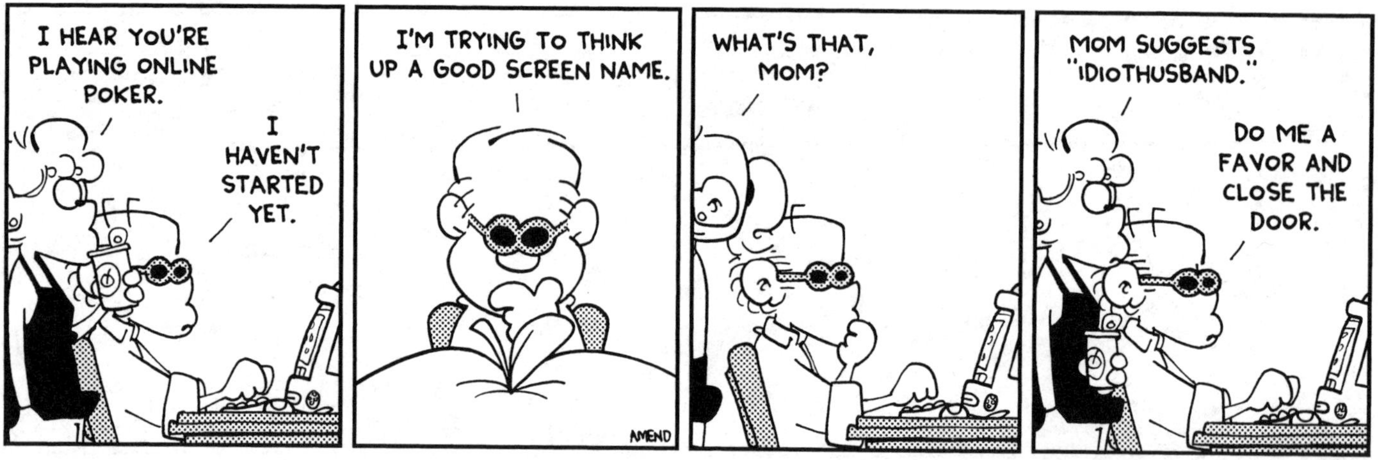
I HEAR YOU'RE PLAYING ONLINE POKER.
I HAVEN'T STARTED YET.
I'M TRYING TO THINK UP A GOOD SCREEN NAME.
AMEND
WHAT'S THAT, MOM?
MOM SUGGESTS "IDIOTHUSBAND."
DO ME A FAVOR AND CLOSE THE DOOR.

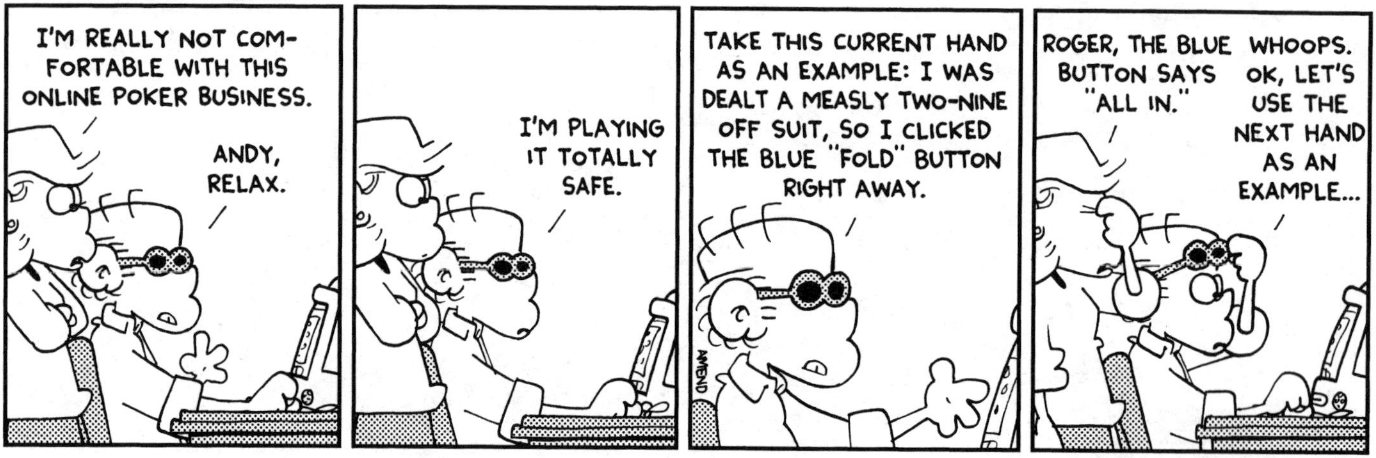
I'M REALLY NOT COM-FORTABLE WITH THIS ONLINE POKER BUSINESS.
ANDY, RELAX.
I'M PLAYING IT TOTALLY SAFE.
TAKE THIS CURRENT HAND AS AN EXAMPLE: I WAS DEALT A MEASLY TWO-NINE OFF SUIT, SO I CLICKED THE BLUE "FOLD" BUTTON RIGHT AWAY.
AMEND
ROGER, THE BLUE BUTTON SAYS "ALL IN."
WHOOPS. OK, LET'S USE THE NEXT HAND AS AN EXAMPLE...

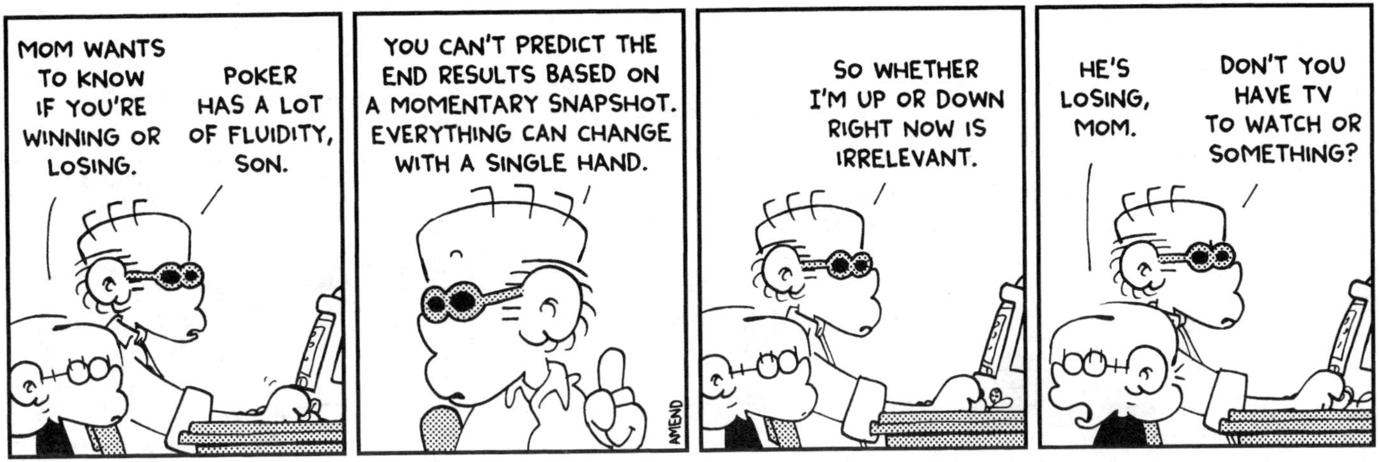
MOM WANTS TO KNOW IF YOU'RE WINNING OR LOSING.
POKER HAS A LOT OF FLUIDITY, SON.
YOU CAN'T PREDICT THE END RESULTS BASED ON A MOMENTARY SNAPSHOT. EVERYTHING CAN CHANGE WITH A SINGLE HAND.
AMEND
SO WHETHER I'M UP OR DOWN RIGHT NOW IS IRRELEVANT.
HE'S LOSING, MOM.
DON'T YOU HAVE TV TO WATCH OR SOMETHING?

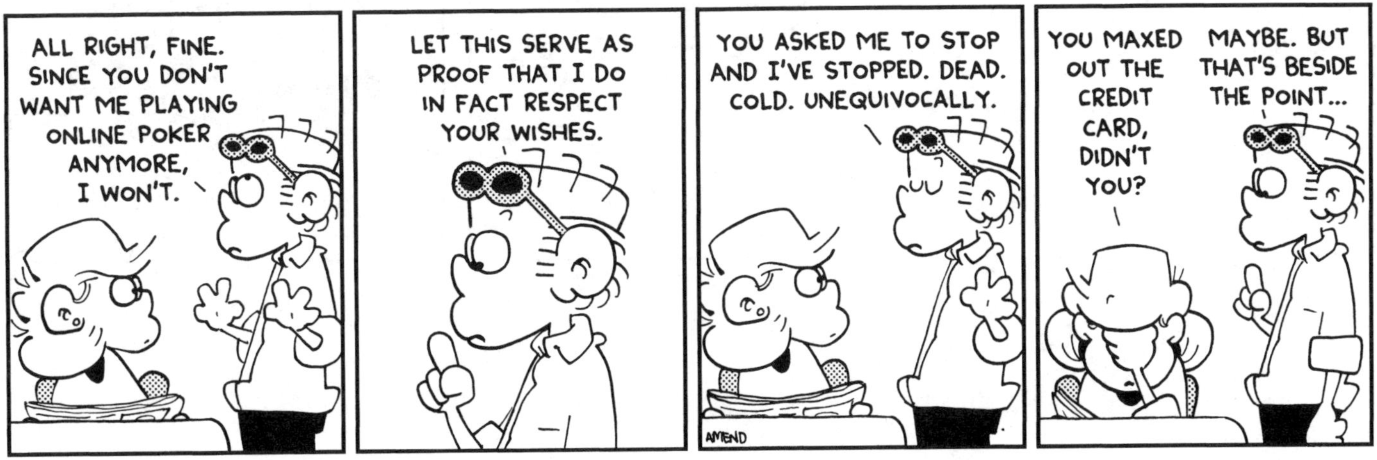
ALL RIGHT, FINE. SINCE YOU DON'T WANT ME PLAYING ONLINE POKER ANYMORE, I WON'T.
LET THIS SERVE AS PROOF THAT I DO IN FACT RESPECT YOUR WISHES.
YOU ASKED ME TO STOP AND I'VE STOPPED. DEAD. COLD. UNEQUIVOCALLY.
AMEND
YOU MAXED OUT THE CREDIT CARD, DIDN'T YOU?
MAYBE. BUT THAT'S BESIDE THE POINT...

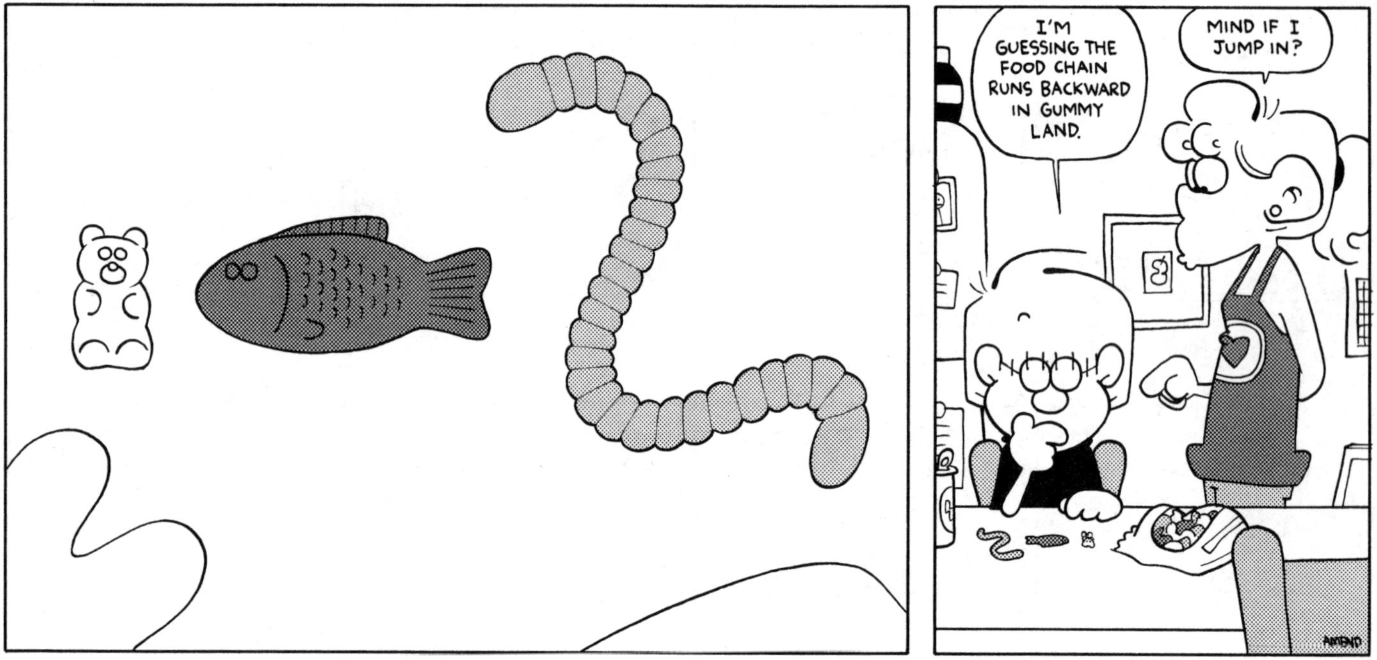
I'M GUESSING THE FOOD CHAIN RUNS BACKWARD IN GUMMY LAND.
MIND IF I JUMP IN?
AMEND

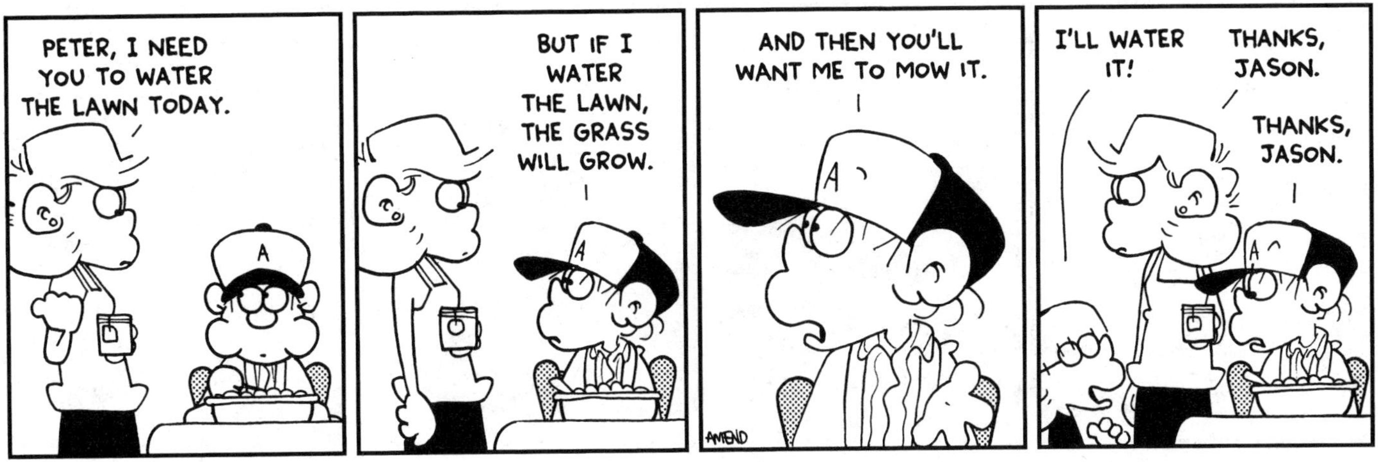
PETER, I NEED YOU TO WATER THE LAWN TODAY.
BUT IF I WATER THE LAWN, THE GRASS WILL GROW.
AND THEN YOU'LL WANT ME TO MOW IT.
AMEND
I'LL WATER IT!
THANKS, JASON.
THANKS, JASON.

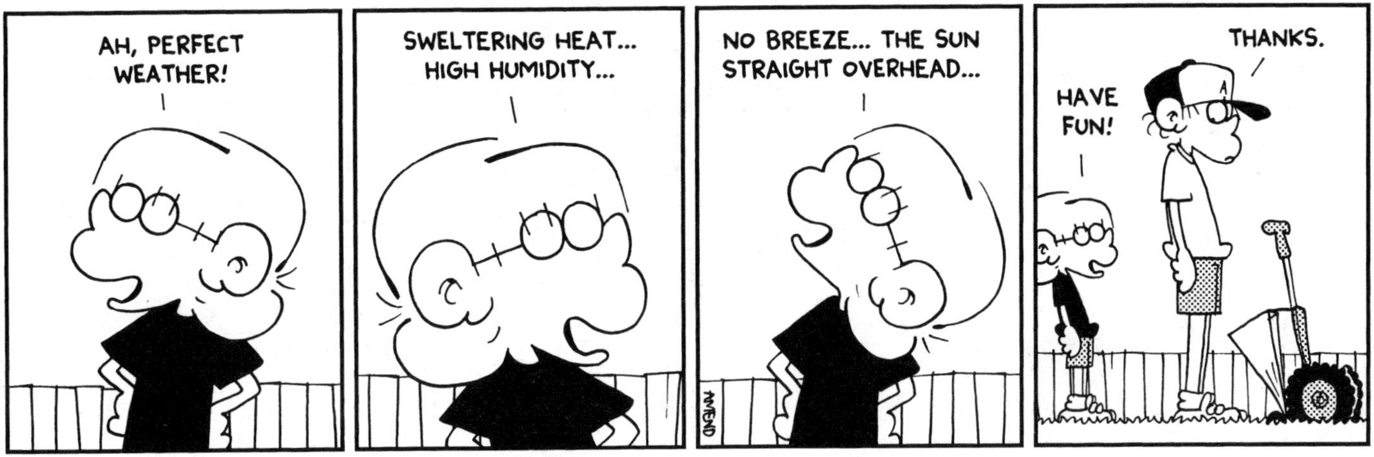
AH, PERFECT WEATHER!
SWELTERING HEAT... HIGH HUMIDITY...
NO BREEZE... THE SUN STRAIGHT OVERHEAD...
AMEND
HAVE FUN!
THANKS.

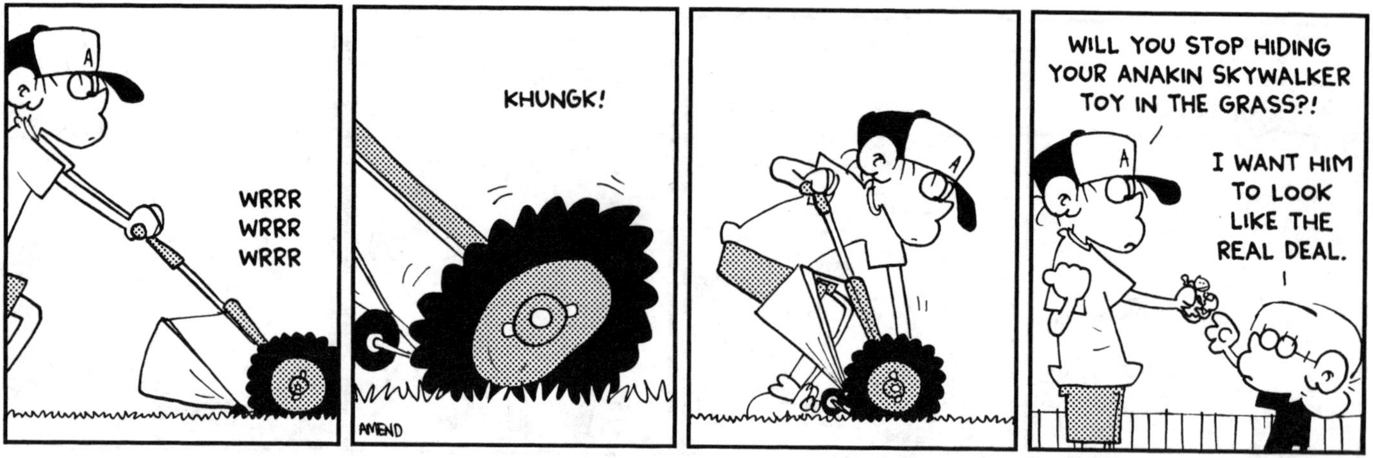
WRRR
WRRR
WRRR
AMEND
KHUNGK!
WILL YOU STOP HIDING YOUR ANAKIN SKYWALKER TOY IN THE GRASS?!
I WANT HIM TO LOOK LIKE THE REAL DEAL.

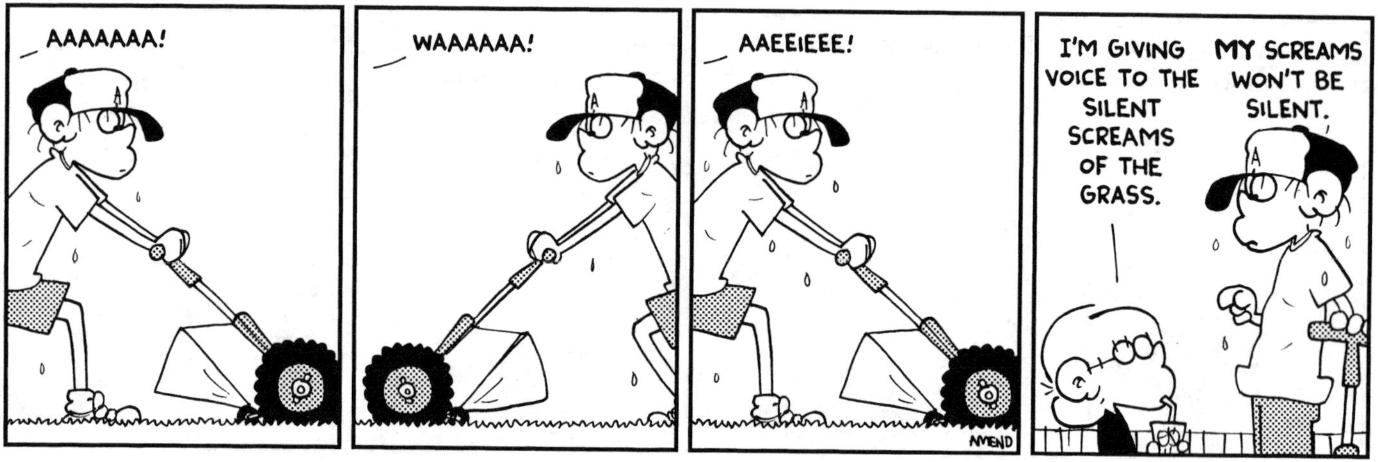
AAAAAAA!
WAAAAAA!
AAEEIEEE!
AMEND
I'M GIVING VOICE TO THE SILENT SCREAMS OF THE GRASS.
MY SCREAMS WON'T BE SILENT.

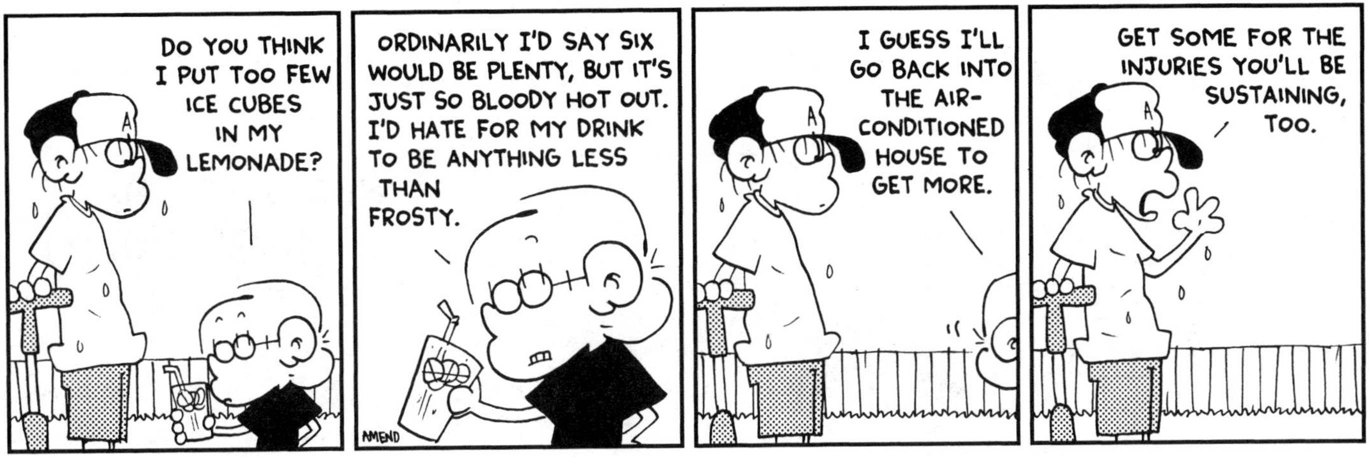
DO YOU THINK I PUT TOO FEW ICE CUBES IN MY LEMONADE?
ORDINARILY I'D SAY SIX WOULD BE PLENTY, BUT IT'S JUST SO BLOODY HOT OUT. I'D HATE FOR MY DRINK TO BE ANYTHING LESS THAN FROSTY.
AMEND
I GUESS I'LL GO BACK INTO THE AIR-CONDITIONED HOUSE TO GET MORE.
GET SOME FOR THE INJURIES YOU'LL BE SUSTAINING, TOO.

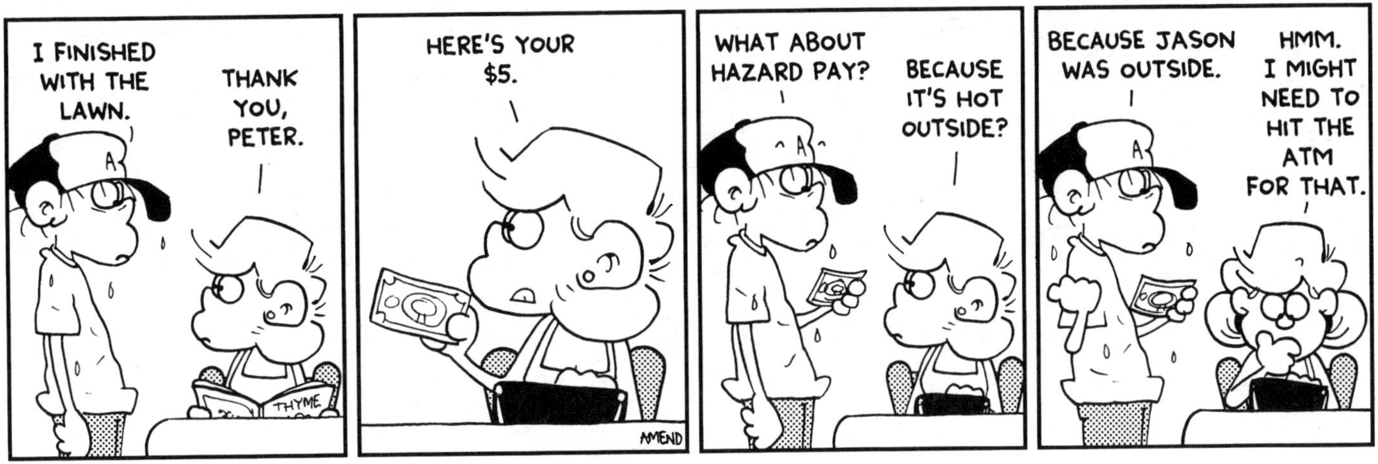
I FINISHED WITH THE LAWN.
THANK YOU, PETER.
THYME
HERE'S YOUR $5.
AMEND
WHAT ABOUT HAZARD PAY?
BECAUSE IT'S HOT OUTSIDE?
BECAUSE JASON WAS OUTSIDE.
HMM. I MIGHT NEED TO HIT THE ATM FOR THAT.

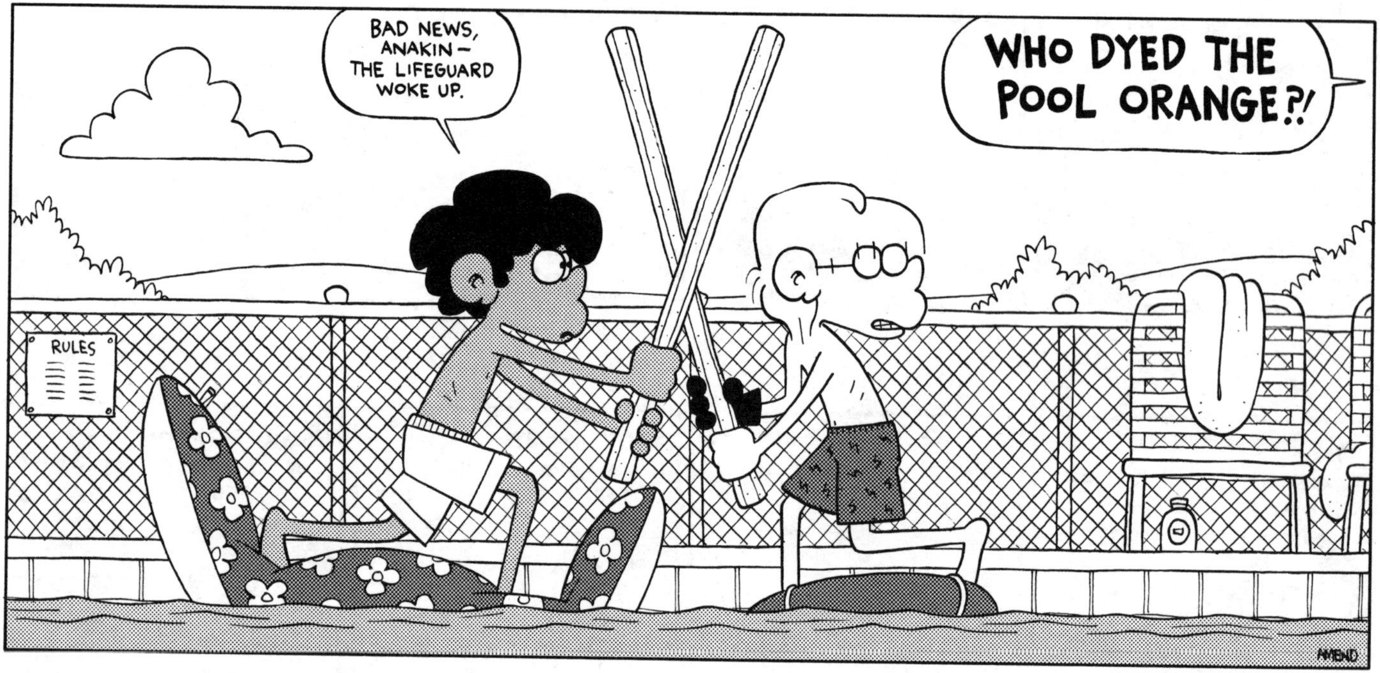
RULES
BAD NEWS, ANAKIN — THE LIFEGUARD WOKE UP.
WHO DYED THE POOL ORANGE?!
AMEND

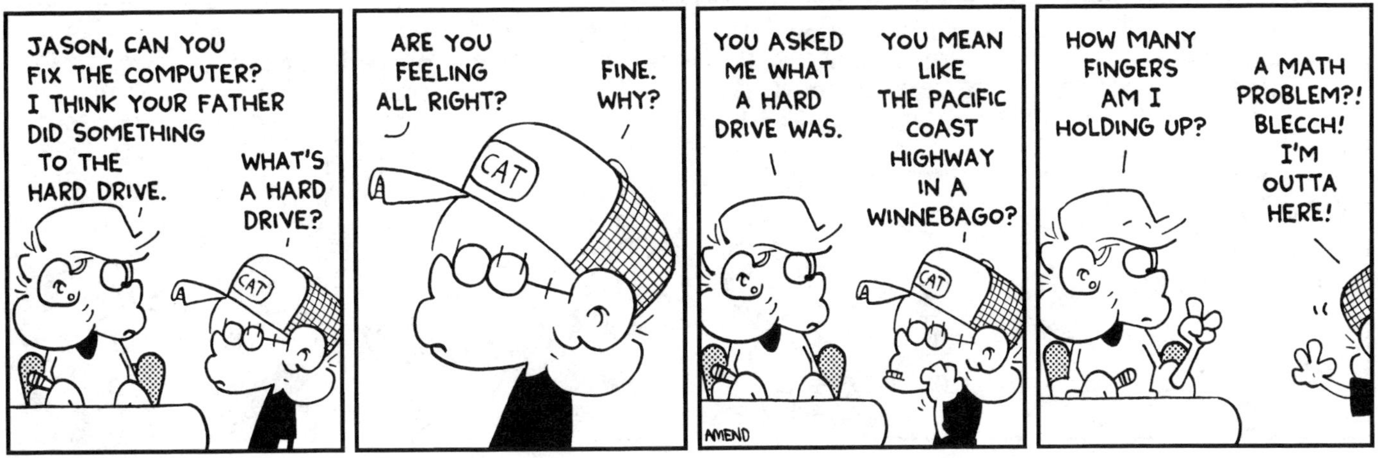
JASON, CAN YOU FIX THE COMPUTER? I THINK YOUR FATHER DID SOMETHING TO THE HARD DRIVE.
WHAT'S A HARD DRIVE?
ARE YOU FEELING ALL RIGHT?
FINE. WHY?
YOU ASKED ME WHAT A HARD DRIVE WAS.
YOU MEAN LIKE THE PACIFIC COAST HIGHWAY IN A WINNEBAGO?
AMEND
HOW MANY FINGERS AM I HOLDING UP?
A MATH PROBLEM?! BLECCH! I'M OUTTA HERE!

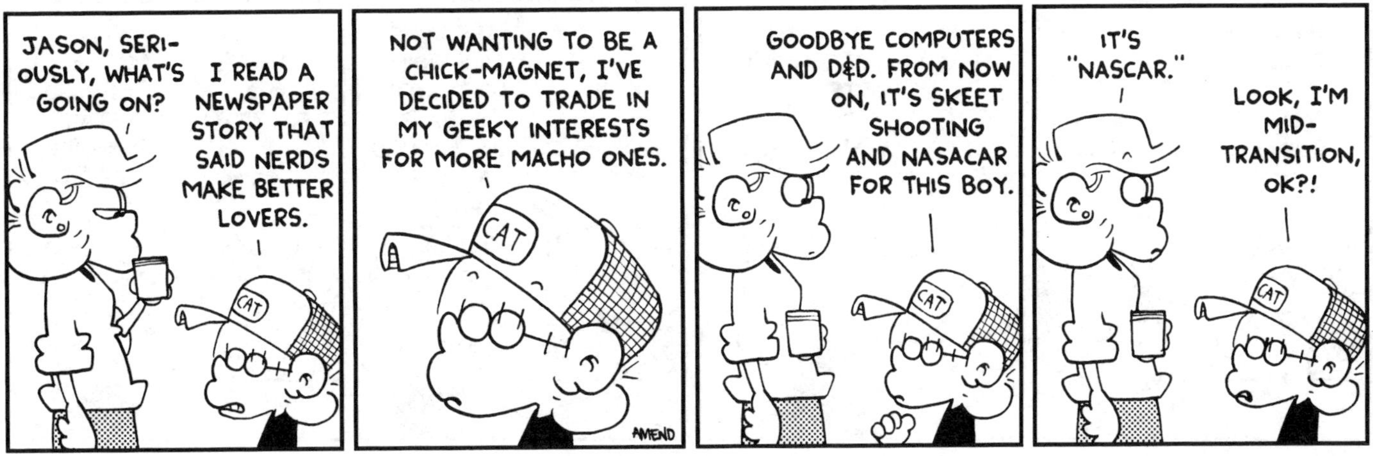
JASON, SERI-OUSLY, WHAT'S GOING ON?
I READ A NEWSPAPER STORY THAT SAID NERDS MAKE BETTER LOVERS.
NOT WANTING TO BE A CHICK-MAGNET, I'VE DECIDED TO TRADE IN MY GEEKY INTERESTS FOR MORE MACHO ONES.
AMEND
GOODBYE COMPUTERS AND D&D. FROM NOW ON, IT'S SKEET SHOOTING AND NASACAR FOR THIS BOY.
IT'S "NASCAR."
LOOK, I'M MID-TRANSITION, OK?!

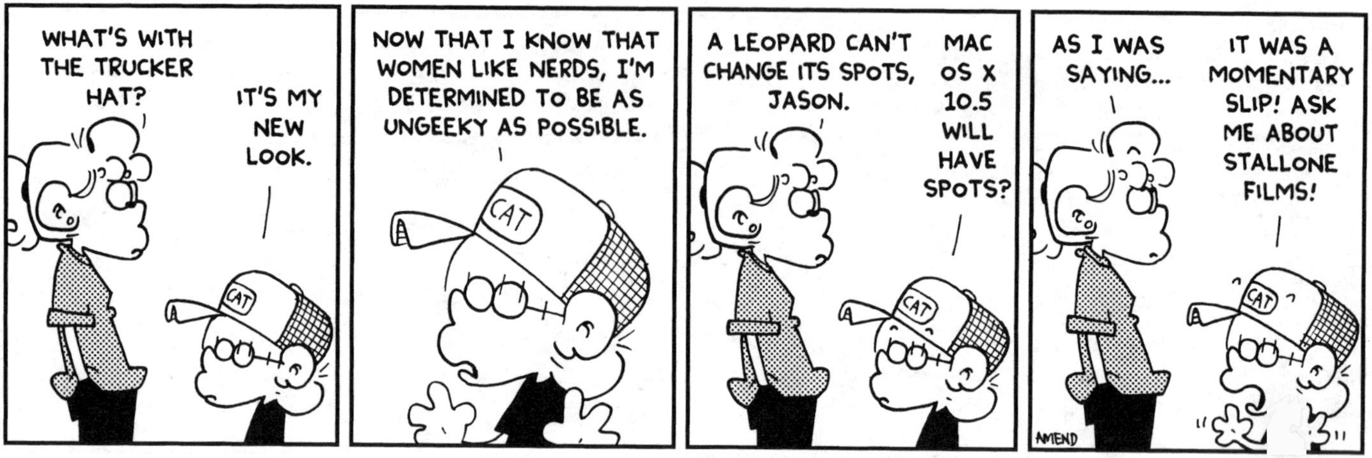
WHAT'S WITH THE TRUCKER HAT?
IT'S MY NEW LOOK.
NOW THAT I KNOW THAT WOMEN LIKE NERDS, I'M DETERMINED TO BE AS UNGEEKY AS POSSIBLE.
A LEOPARD CAN'T CHANGE ITS SPOTS, JASON.
MAC OS X 10.5 WILL HAVE SPOTS?
AS I WAS SAYING...
IT WAS A MOMENTARY SLIP! ASK ME ABOUT STALLONE FILMS!
AMEND

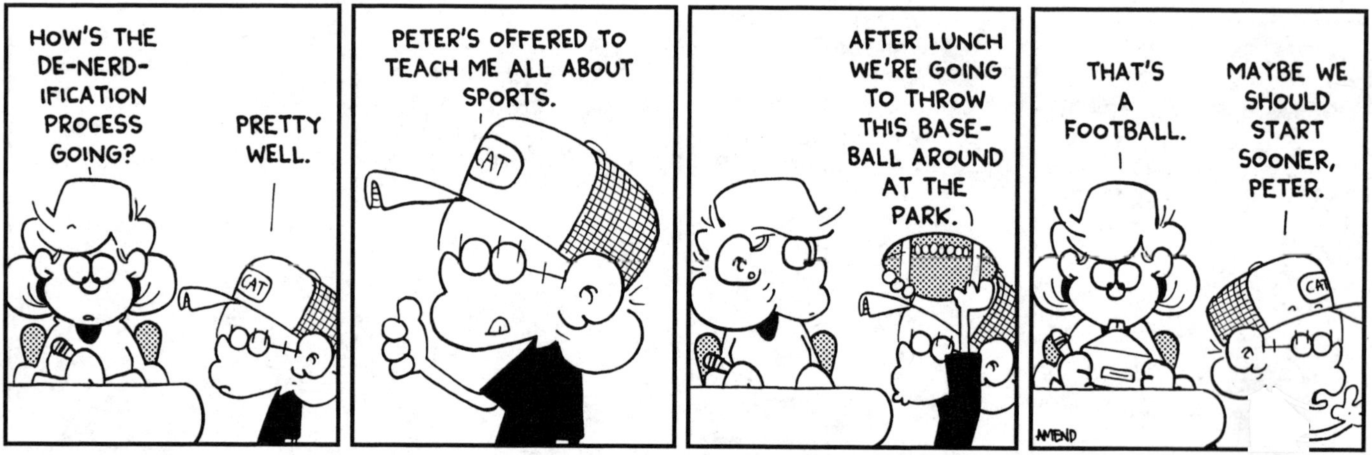
HOW'S THE DE-NERD-IFICATION PROCESS GOING?
PRETTY WELL.
PETER'S OFFERED TO TEACH ME ALL ABOUT SPORTS.
AFTER LUNCH WE'RE GOING TO THROW THIS BASE-BALL AROUND AT THE PARK.
THAT'S A FOOTBALL.
MAYBE WE SHOULD START SOONER, PETER.
AMEND

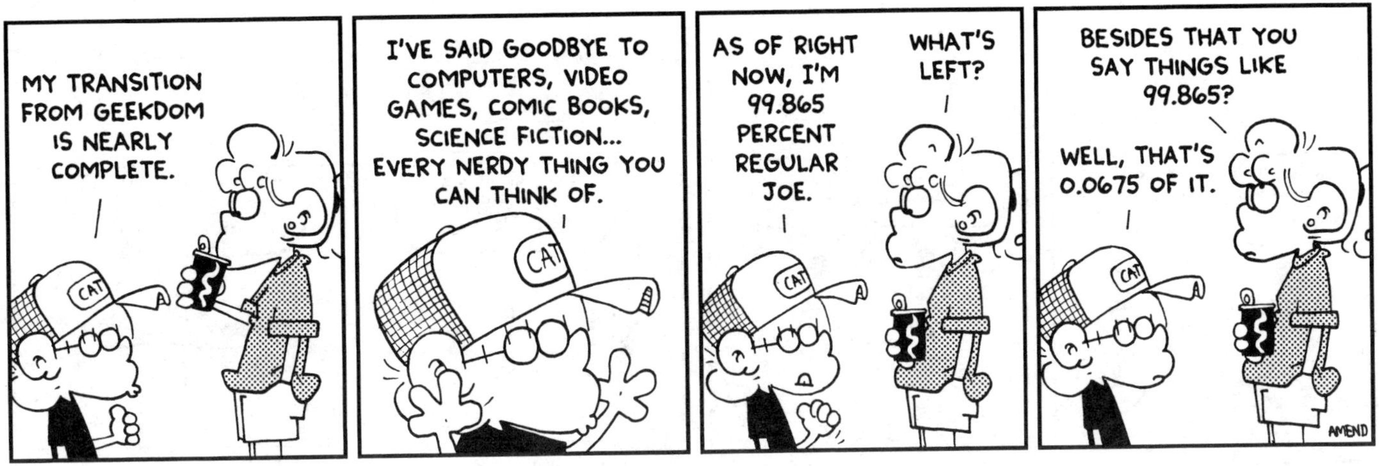

MY TRANSITION FROM GEEKDOM IS NEARLY COMPLETE.
CAT
I'VE SAID GOODBYE TO COMPUTERS, VIDEO GAMES, COMIC BOOKS, SCIENCE FICTION... EVERY NERDY THING YOU CAN THINK OF.
AS OF RIGHT NOW, I'M 99.865 PERCENT REGULAR JOE.
WHAT'S LEFT?
BESIDES THAT YOU SAY THINGS LIKE 99.865?
WELL, THAT'S 0.0675 OF IT.
AMEND

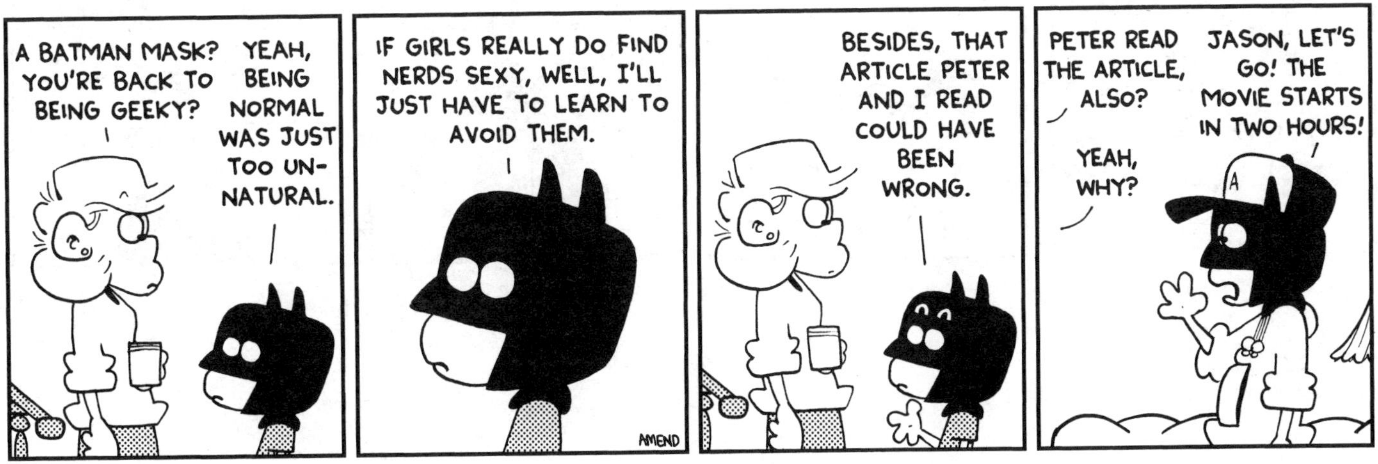

A BATMAN MASK? YOU'RE BACK TO BEING GEEKY?
YEAH, BEING NORMAL WAS JUST TOO UN-NATURAL.
IF GIRLS REALLY DO FIND NERDS SEXY, WELL, I'LL JUST HAVE TO LEARN TO AVOID THEM.
AMEND
BESIDES, THAT ARTICLE PETER AND I READ COULD HAVE BEEN WRONG.
PETER READ THE ARTICLE, ALSO?
YEAH, WHY?
JASON, LET'S GO! THE MOVIE STARTS IN TWO HOURS!

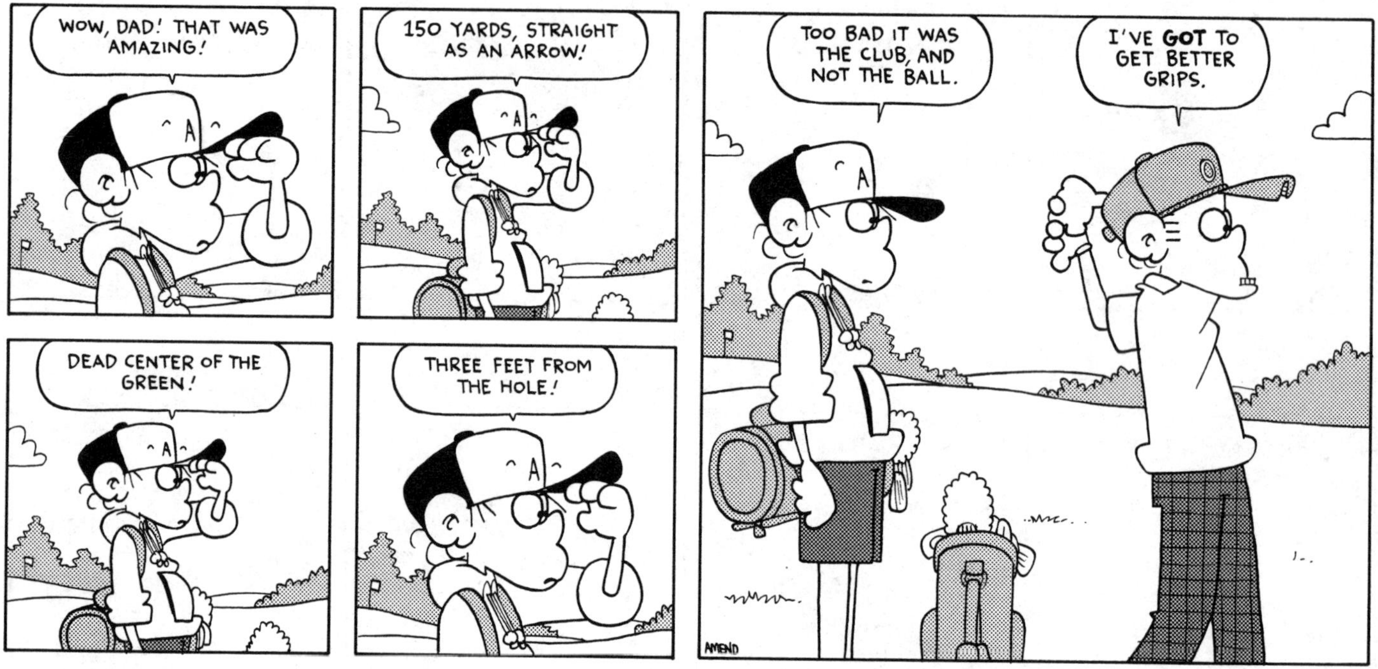
WOW, DAD! THAT WAS AMAZING!
150 YARDS, STRAIGHT AS AN ARROW!
DEAD CENTER OF THE GREEN!
THREE FEET FROM THE HOLE!
TOO BAD IT WAS THE CLUB, AND NOT THE BALL.
I'VE **GOT** TO GET BETTER GRIPS.
AMEND